THE ARTFUL BAKER

Extraordinary Desserts
From an Obsessive Home Baker

CENK SÖNMEZSOY

creator of **Café Fernando**

ABRAMS, NEW YORK

THE
ARTFUL
BAKER

Love! Nowhere like in İstanbul, 2005, by Mustafa Pilevneli,
which has welcomed my readers as the banner on my food blog for the past ten years.

for my mom and in loving memory of my dad

CONTENTS

From San Francisco to İstanbul, from Blog to Book

Fifteen years ago, had you told me I would someday write a cookbook, I would have laughed hysterically and gone right back to watching *The Golden Girls* while finishing a tub of chocolate ice cream. I probably also would have been annoyed that you'd wasted my precious energy by making me laugh so hard.

Even today, if you were to ask me my purpose in life or where I see myself in fifteen years, I would answer: I see myself in the living room of my falcon's nest of a house in Big Sur, on the couch, buried under a pile of blankets, watching *The Golden Girls*. There's a freezer in my kitchen so big a horse can roam freely inside. It is packed to the gills with ice cream. I've had a mechanism installed that, with the push of a button, delivers tubs of ice cream at 10°F (-12°C), slightly softened at the edges, from the freezer directly onto my lap. My life's ambition is to continue watching the girls without moving an inch, tubs of softened ice cream continually dropping onto my lap. Oh, and there's no one around asking questions.

Before you pass me off as lazy, I should remind you that you're holding a book that I've worked on for the last six years, laboring day and night to develop the recipes, write the narrative, style and photograph the images, and design the pages. It's not that I'm so burned out I need to rest for the remainder of my life. I was born like this.

According to my mom, I was an unusually calm and indolent child. I wasn't interested in playing with toys, protested only when she slowed down while feeding me, and would sit for hours in front of the TV watching *The Adventures of Tintin* without budging. She says that God showed her mercy after creating my curtain-climbing rug rat of a brother by following him with the meekest child he'd ever made.

This is why I have such a hard time believing that the kid with the giant head in the photo to the left is me. The photo was taken by my father during one of our summer holidays in Europe. I discovered the slide

after I lost my father, a few months before my Turkish cookbook was published, and I looked at it for a long while in disbelief. So, there were times when I was lively and ecstatic, even when there wasn't an ice cream cone in my hand. I look as if I am almost in a trance. Normally, I would have dropped everything to hug the dachshunds, but I don't think I even noticed them passing by. The reason: my toy basset hound, Foxy, which I dragged everywhere in a continuous, ear-splitting rattle.

I'm not sharing the photo to show off my toy, but rather because it reminds me of how I came to accomplish the improbable task of writing this book. How does someone who avoids lifting a finger for any task make croissants at home? I'll do anything for just-out-of-the-oven croissants, so the fact that I make them at home isn't extraordinary. What *is* extraordinary is that I find the drive to make them twenty times to perfect the recipe, to take thousands of photos to visually tell their story, then to write about them while pulling out my hair over every word. The fact that I like to eat more than I like to sit also doesn't explain how I eagerly juiced 130 pounds (60 kg) of pomegranates by hand while developing a jam recipe. The photo explains it all: With Foxy along, I'd climb Mount Everest.

I don't know, maybe I've been saving up my energy all these years just to write this book, but I couldn't have imagined a job that I'd love and obsess over this much.

When I was little I didn't have the slightest interest in cooking or baking. You know how most chefs and cookbook authors have childhood memories of rolling out dough with their mothers, or playing with pots and pans? I just watched TV. I started cooking at age eighteen, purely out of necessity, when I moved to a different city for college. That is, if you call tossing some overcooked pasta with a can of tuna *cooking*. During those first couple of years,

my kitchen adventures were confined to the dorm's kitchen, which I shared with dozens of people. It was equipped with just a single portable electric burner. There was a refrigerator, but you wouldn't dare use it, as anything you left behind evaporated the second you turned around. Thankfully, in my last year of school I moved to an apartment with two roommates and started cooking decent food. By the time I graduated, I could make most of the classic Turkish dishes, thanks to my mother, who spent endless hours on the phone coaching me through them.

Immediately after graduating from college, I moved to San Francisco for my MBA. I worked part-time as a research assistant for my graduate fellowship, which covered half of my tuition. To further unburden my family, I also worked as a teaching assistant and MBA advisor for as many hours as my student visa allowed, which left no time for cooking. I occasionally cooked for my roommates who missed their mothers' Turkish food, but if you had asked me, it was unnecessary given the amazing food choices all around us. Three blocks from our apartment was a place with wall-to-wall Kristi Yamaguchi posters that served juicy burgers and thick-cut fries. Two blocks farther was Ton Kiang, the dim sum heaven.

After graduating and landing a job, I moved to a studio the size of a small box on Chestnut Street. My bed and a love seat barely squeezed into the main living area, but the kitchen was big enough to fit a dining table and six chairs, and it came equipped with a brand-new oven. In the two-plus years I lived there, I never once used that oven, because in my new neighborhood there were great restaurants and bakeries at every step. On my way home from work, I would hop off the bus at the other end of the street and gather up whatever I felt like eating that night. Lunch at work was another joy. An Irish bar across from our offices served an Indian buffet at lunch, with unlimited curries, chicken tandoori, samosas, naan, and masala chai for $4.95. The Mediterranean restaurant two blocks down had the best falafel I had ever eaten. Once you started climbing Columbus Avenue, it got even harder to choose. Despite the fact that I was spending almost half of my paycheck on rent, I was able to feed myself (and an appetite big enough for two) very well without breaking the bank.

It seemed impossible to exhaust the options, so I never cooked or baked.

After I moved back to İstanbul, I found a good job and began working. I was reunited with family and friends, but I struggled with adapting to my new life. I soon discovered that the Exploratorium museum and learning center at the Palace of Fine Arts was broadcasting live images of my old neighborhood from its roof cameras. I could see glimpses of the Golden Gate Bridge and Alcatraz when the fog lifted, but mostly it offered images of people and cars passing by, seagulls perched on wooden pilings, and the sandwich shack on the Marina Green. It didn't matter what I was watching; I had a small window to my old neighborhood in the corner of my computer screen at all times. One of my favorite views was of the weeping maidens atop the columns of the Palace of Fine Arts— at the time, I didn't know that the reason for their sadness was separation grief, just like mine.

Right around that time, Google Maps launched its Street View feature, offering 360-degree panoramic views of streets, and I lost it. I would start from the mother-in-law studio I first rented in Outer Richmond and "walk" my way along the map, block by block, to my school, then to the Mel's Drive-In a few blocks away to reminisce about enjoying patty melts and Oreo milkshakes with my roommates, then all the way down to Ocean Beach, and finally back to where my San Francisco journey began: the Geary Parkway Motel. My body was in a dreary, fluorescent-lit cubicle in İstanbul, but my mind and soul were in San Francisco.

Watching my old neighborhood and "walking" the streets soothed me at first, but I started missing the food as much as I missed the city. It was impossible to find even a decent brownie in İstanbul back then, so I took matters into my own hands and started baking. One day my best friend, Özlem, who was still living in San Francisco, sent me a link to her food blog. I had no idea what a blog was. I started perusing her website and was surprised to see that she had transformed her house into a cupcake factory. She has become so popular that Flickr asked her to bake a cake for the site's second anniversary.

Then, one day I clicked on a link on Özlem's blog and up popped another blog.

Called *Nordljus* (nordljus.co.uk), it was written by a Japanese girl named Keiko who lived in Suffolk, in the UK. The first photo greeting me was of her rose-water, cardamom, and gum mastic ice cream sprinkled with dried rose petals. I clicked on a thumbnail of a photo that looked like a chocolate and pistachio cake but turned out to be a matcha opera cake, and it took my breath away. I had discovered many food blogs by then, but Keiko's photos were beyond compare. I went through all of her posts in a single day and was so inspired that I decided to start a blog of my own. I didn't know how I was going to do it, but it didn't matter; I wanted to bake cakes and take photos just like hers.

The first order of business was to find a name for my nascent blog. I didn't need to think twice about it; ever since I'd learned that my favorite character from *The Golden Girls*, Rose Nylund, had a one-eyed teddy bear called Fernando, I'd wanted to name my future dog after it. But I never got a dog, and my blog was the next best opportunity. After I discovered that fernando.com was taken, I decided on cafefernando. com and launched it on March 31, 2006. The first post I published was titled "San Francisco in Jello" and included a photo of the Painted Ladies made of Jell-O by the San Francisco–based artist Liz Hickok. Martha Stewart's chocolate ganache tart followed. A couple of months later, I discovered Dorie Greenspan, and then Pierre Hermé and Julia Child through Dorie's books, and I got more serious about baking. Initially, only a few friends and family members were following me, and my photos looked nowhere near as good as Keiko's, but I was having fun. Somehow the word spread and, with the encouragement of a handful of Turkish readers, after a few months I started the Turkish version of my blog.

About a year into my blogging adventure, I was gobsmacked when Dorie Greenspan left a comment on one of my posts. My baking heroine was reading my blog! Thanks to her, the great Nick Malgieri discovered my blog, too. He included one of my recipes and its photo in an article he wrote for the *Washington Post*. It was the first turning point of my blogging career (see page 90), increasing my readership a hundredfold overnight. My blog had previously been mentioned in an article Matt Gross wrote for the *New York Times* about culinary trends in İstanbul, but this was the

first time that a recipe and a photo of mine had been published internationally.

That same year, with the rising popularity of blogs, the most reputable web awards program in Turkey added a new category for blogs. I filled out the online form, and about a month later, my "Turkey's Best Blog" award arrived at the family advertising agency where I worked with my father and brother. My brother was so proud, he went out and bought me my first professional camera during his lunch break.

Another turning point came a couple of months later, when Janet Fletcher published an article about my San Francisco–inspired Turkish menu in the *San Francisco Chronicle*. Janet came to my apartment with her husband, Doug, after their vacation in Bozcaada (an island off the Aegean coast of Turkey), and I cooked them a Turkish dinner influenced by some of my favorite San Francisco food memories. I couldn't sleep the night my friend and fellow food writer Sean Timberlake sent me a photo of the printed article. My photos were on the cover of the *SF Chronicle* food section, the same paper on which I had left so many coffee rings way back when. A friend sent me five copies of the article, one of which my father kept in the inside pocket of his jacket for almost a year, proudly showing it off to everyone he knew.

As the years passed, many more proud moments followed. My blog was cited as one of the "World's 50 Best Food Blogs" by *The Times of London*, and it received awards at *Saveur* magazine's annual food blog awards three years in a row: Best Culinary Travel Blog in 2010, Best Original Baking and Desserts Recipe in 2011 for the brownies I designed for Dolce & Gabbana (see page 96), and Best Piece of Culinary Writing in 2012 for my blog post on dining at Chez Panisse.

By 2010, I had been working at our advertising agency for three years. I couldn't have imagined any-one better to work with than my father and brother, but the job was consuming me. It had become unbearable, and I decided to quit and become a full-time blogger. I didn't think I could make enough money to support myself, but I had some money saved and thought that, if worse came to worst, I'd go back to my job. Right after I quit, I got an offer from my Turkish publisher to write a book.

OD

Section 1

Franciso

ES SOAR,

▶ Push by Democrats for
▶ is blocked in Senate for

By Zachary Coile
Chronicle Washington Bureau

TURKISH
DELIGHTS

Living, eating in San Francisco infuses
Istanbul blogger's creations

"Bon Appetit, Y'all," Having
worked as a television producer,
food stylist, writer and kitchen
manager for Martha Stewart Vir-
ginia Willis

I'll never forget the first meeting I had at my publisher's office. Çağatay Kandaz, vice president and publisher back then, and Işıl Karahanoğlu, my editor, asked when I could have the book finished. I had already thought about that on my way to the meeting, estimating that it would take me at least five years to come up with a decent manuscript, but I knew that wasn't realistic. So I threw the ball in their court and asked when they would need it. When Çağatay told me that May would be perfect, I asked him, just to be sure, "Do you mean *this* May? As in three months from now?" Four and a half years after he said yes, I turned in my manuscript.

I also won't soon forget the dinner I had with the owner of the publishing house, a week before the book hit the shelves. I asked him if he thought it would be possible to sell out the first printing within a year. He explained the realities of the publishing world in Turkey and said that it would be wishful thinking. He told me we should consider ourselves lucky if the first printing *ever* sold out. My book was published on June 14, 2014, and the first printing sold out in three days. The second printing sold out by the end of the following week, and by the following June, we were into the sixth printing of the book. These were all firsts in the history of cookbook publishing in Turkey, where selling out the first printing in a year is considered a major success. Just when I thought it couldn't get any better, my book was selected "Best in the World—First Place" in the 2015 Gourmand World Cookbook Awards. A few months after that, competing among all past first-place winners, it was awarded first place in the blogger cookbooks category in Gourmand's "Best of the Best."

The past twelve years have been nothing short of a dream. And now, I wait impatiently to go into a San Francisco bookstore and see my own cookbook on the shelves. I'm sure I'll be glad I got off that couch.

Right around the time I started working on my Turkish cookbook, Özlem was taking her annual break from her cafe in Montezuma to spend some time in İstanbul. As we sipped our coffees, she reflected, "Isn't it extraordinary what life can bring to us? Do you remember the days you cooked me my favorite lentil stew? Could you have imagined back then that you'd one day be writing a cookbook? I wonder what else we're capable of that we can't even imagine right now."

I'm dying to find out.

Before We Begin

More than a decade of blogging has taught me a great deal about recipe writing and has honed my sensitivity to potential pitfalls. To help even the most inexperienced reader have a smooth baking experience with a reliable outcome, I've disclosed my every tip and trick for each recipe in its headnote and method. Here, before getting to the recipes, I share general advice that applies to all of the recipes. These are my golden rules, vital to achieving success, efficiency, and peace of mind in the kitchen.

STICK TO THE INGREDIENTS, MEASUREMENTS, AND EQUIPMENT.

Every recipe in this book has gone through a meticulous development process in which I've tested countless scenarios. I was conscious of the amounts of sugar and butter I used, not from a caloric or nutritional standpoint, but to achieve a balanced taste and optimal texture. After I was satisfied with the outcome, the recipes were tested by home bakers having varying levels of skill, equipment, and access to ingredients. Based on their feedback, I revised the recipes to ensure that they will work flawlessly in any kitchen. They were made at least once more to be photographed, and many times more than that just because these are the recipes I bake most frequently. After these many tests and revisions, I can confidently say that so long as you follow the ingredients, measurements, equipment, and instructions I've included, you'll have great results.

This doesn't mean that you shouldn't personalize the recipes to your taste. But if you do, be aware that every change you make will affect the outcome. Using orange zest instead of lemon, or substituting almond flour for hazelnut, are straightforward changes that most likely will not affect the texture or over-all success of a recipe. Other changes, no matter how seemingly minor, may greatly affect the outcome—using brown sugar instead of white, for example. The same holds true for equipment. A cake that rises up beautifully in a loaf pan may not behave the same way in a round cake pan.

In baking, most of the time you don't have the option to taste and adjust as you go along. You prepare a cake batter, pop it into the oven, and that's it; you are stuck with whatever comes out. If you don't like surprises, stick to the ingredients, measurements, and equipment in the recipes, at least the first time. This will help you to know the texture and taste I am aiming for. After that, should you wish to experiment, make the recipe again, changing only one or two factors to suit your own preference, keeping in mind that your experiment may have unexpected results, either happy or disappointing. When in doubt, check the Ingredients (page 350), Measurements and Conversions (page 353), and Equipment (page 354) sections for clarification and my suggested substitutions.

GET TO KNOW YOUR OVEN.

I inherited my electric oven from my brother and sister-in-law, who inherited it from the previous owner of their house. It is at least fifteen years old and has its quirks. The temperature displayed on its digital panel matches the actual temperature inside the oven only at 400°F (200°C) and it is off by at least 25°F (15°C) at other temperatures. It sometimes switches to another function midway through baking or to the default temperature that the function I'm using is set to. Despite these idiosyncrasies, we get along very well because I've gotten to know it. When it misbehaves, it warns me with a faint clicking sound that I can hear from anywhere in the house.

If you have an oven that works as expected, your job is much easier. Still, it's worth checking the accuracy of your oven's temperature once a year, as I do. I use my oven thermometer (see page 361) to conduct tests at the temperatures I use most frequently. I place the thermometer in the center of a rack set in the middle of the oven and run the oven at each temperature for at least 30 minutes. I make a note of the thermometer's reading at each setting and, when baking, set the oven temperature based on those findings.

If you notice your cookies and cakes getting too dark—or remaining too pale—when following the baking times in the recipes, your oven temperature may be the culprit. Testing it can help you to adjust the temperature accordingly.

READ THE WHOLE RECIPE AND GATHER ALL THE INGREDIENTS AND EQUIPMENT BEFORE YOU START BAKING.

There is nothing more annoying than discovering midway through a recipe that you lack an ingredient or neglected to bring the eggs to room temperature. This happened to me often before I discovered the importance of *mise en place*, a French culinary phrase meaning "put in place," referring to the preparation of all ingredients and equipment needed for a recipe before beginning to cook or bake.

Begin by reading the recipe, start to finish, to learn whether or when you'll need to preheat the oven, and to get a clear idea of how long each step and the full recipe will take to prepare. Some recipes, like Croissants (page 220) and Sourdough Simit (page 212), span multiple days; you'll want to plan accordingly. Set out the bowls, pans, and utensils you'll need, weigh or measure the ingredients, and carry out simple preparations included in the ingredient list, like chopping chocolate, juicing lemons, or bringing ingredients to room temperature.

TRUST YOUR SENSES.

I've done my best to make the recipe instructions as precise as possible. But as we're not baking in the same kitchen using the exact same ingredients and equipment, my suggested cooking, baking, and chilling times may vary from your experience when using your own oven, stovetop, refrigerator, and freezer. For this reason, I've provided visual clues along with time frames for baking, cooking, and chilling—knowing what you are looking for can help you to trust your own senses. My recipes have been tested in different homes under varying conditions, and I've adjusted baking, cooking, and chilling times to reflect these variations. Take the specified ranges as an estimate, always keeping an eye out toward the end, and judge readiness by watching, smelling, listening, touching, and tasting. If you sense that something is done before the alarm goes off, listen to your instincts.

BE FEARLESS, PATIENT, AND DILIGENT.

When I first started baking, I was scared of making mistakes but never of tackling recipes. I believed that as long as I used the same ingredients in the exact amounts, worked with the right equipment, and followed every step as instructed, I could make anything I put my mind to. A few recipes demanded more patience and diligence than I expected, but that only magnified the joy of finally getting them right. When a recipe included a complicated technique I had no experience with, I became even more motivated, as it meant learning something new. I've had a few kitchen disasters along the way and can tell you that these have been the greatest lessons.

Had I been scared off by assuming that croissants were beyond my skill level, I wouldn't now be enjoying fresh baked croissants at home. If I had been satisfied with an earlier version of my pomegranate jam, I might never have discovered the gelling power of pectin, which has completely changed my jam making. And most frightening of all, had I given up on making ice cream after finding that the ice cream–maker attachment I'd brought back from the States didn't fit my European stand mixer, I might still be settling for a chocolate ice cream that someone else makes. The thought of that alone makes me shudder.

COOKIES

CENK'S HOUSE COOKIES

One day in my early years of blogging, the food processor's pulse button got stuck while I was making a tart dough. I was supposed to pulse until the butter pieces were the size of fat peas, but instead the dough gathered around the blade. There was no question that I was going to start the dough from scratch, but I couldn't bear the thought of wasting the "ruined" dough. So I rolled it out, cut it into rounds, and jammed it into the freezer, ready to salvage it as cookies on a rainy day. I forgot all about it until one day when I was clearing out the freezer to make space for the ice cream I was churning.

The following day, I popped a tray of those cookies into the oven, still warm from a cake I'd baked for the blog. As I cleaned the kitchen, a familiar scent wafted from the oven—the aroma of the cookies I ate as a child while playing with my toy animals at the foot of my grandma's chair, where she knitted for hours on end. They were Danish butter cookies from a royal-blue tin, separated with ruffled papers into five sections, each holding a different shape. I would take a long whiff before choosing which one to eat. Would it be the swirly one that instantly melts in your mouth? Or the extra-sweet one shaped like a small pretzel, topped with sugar crystals?

I experienced that same childhood excitement while those tart-dough cookies baked, and when I took a bite of a warm cookie it tasted the same, too: buttery and sweet, with a hint of coconut. What an amazing feeling it had been, knowing that those cookies would always be there waiting when I visited my grandmother. I reached for my notebook and wrote this: *Everyone should have a house cookie. A dozen in a jar for last-minute guests, and stacks in the freezer, ready to be baked for those clever enough to call ahead. A cookie that will intoxicate guests with its aroma the moment you open the door. A cookie they will come to identify with you for life.*

Months later, as I was going through the stack of recipe notes on my desk, I read that note and decided to stow the recipe away for a future book.

That day has come. I commence this book with the revamped version of my house cookies, served on the most beautiful plate I own, sitting gracefully on the most beautiful tablecloth I have ever set my eyes on—the cloth my spiritual grandmother, Esin Giz (see page 283), embroidered seventy-nine years ago as a ten-year-old girl.

Makes 24 cookies

2 cups (280 grams) all-purpose flour

¾ cup plus 2 tablespoons (140 grams) confectioners' sugar

¾ cup (75 grams) blanched almond flour

¼ cup (20 grams) unsweetened shredded dried coconut

¼ teaspoon (2 grams) fine sea salt

14 tablespoons (7 ounces; 200 grams) cold unsalted butter, cut into small pieces

1 large egg, separated

⅔ cup (67 grams) sliced blanched almonds

In the bowl of a food processor fitted with a metal blade, process the flour, sugar, almond flour, coconut, and salt until the coconut pieces are as fine as the almond flour, 1 to 2 minutes. Add the butter and pulse until coarse crumbs form. Add the egg yolk and process until the dough gathers around the blade, about 3 minutes, scraping down the sides of the bowl as needed.

Scrape the dough onto a large sheet of parchment paper. Cover with another sheet of parchment and roll out the dough into a round about 10 inches (25.5 cm) in diameter and ⅜ inch (1 cm) thick, occasionally flipping the dough with the parchment, then lifting and smoothing the parchment to avoid creases.

Transfer the dough and parchment to a baking sheet and chill until firm, at least 2 hours in the refrigerator or about 25 minutes in the freezer.

Line a baking sheet with parchment paper. Place the chilled dough on a flat surface and peel off the top sheet of parchment. Using a 2-inch (5-cm) plain round cookie cutter, cut out as many cookies as you can and transfer them to the prepared baking sheet. Gather the scraps into a ball, roll the dough out again between the parchment sheets, and continue to cut out cookies until you run out of dough.

Spread out the almonds on one of the parchment sheets in a single layer. In a small bowl, whisk the egg white with a fork until frothy.

(continued on page 26)

Using a pastry brush, brush a layer of egg white over the cookies. Invert the cookies onto the almonds one by one, gently pressing them into the nuts to coat the cookie tops. Turn the cookies almond side up and place them back on the baking sheet, then freeze them, uncovered, until firm, 10 to 15 minutes. (Once they are firm, you can wrap them airtight and refrigerate for up to 3 days or freeze for up to 2 months. No need to thaw, though you may need to add a couple of minutes to the baking time.)

Meanwhile, set a rack in the middle of the oven and preheat the oven to 350°F (175°C). Line a baking sheet with parchment paper.

Arrange as many cookies as you can fit on the prepared baking sheet, leaving about 1¼ inches (3 cm) all around them. Keep the rest of the unbaked cookies in the refrigerator.

Bake until the edges of the cookies are golden and the almonds are golden brown, 22 to 24 minutes. Set the sheet on a wire rack to cool for 10 minutes, then transfer the cookies directly onto the rack to cool completely. Repeat with the remaining cookies.

Storage: The cookies will keep in an airtight container at room temperature for up to 3 days.

CHOCOLATE CHIP COOKIES

When I get my hands on a new baking book, I immediately turn to the chocolate chip cookie recipe. It is the ideal recipe to discover whether the author's tastes match mine. If I see chocolate chips among the ingredients, I keep flipping the pages in hopes of finding a different recipe through which I can connect with the author, but deep down I know there is very little chance for us to become close friends. I've never understood the point of using chocolate manufactured specifically *not* to melt; if it doesn't melt in the heat of the oven, how is it going to melt in my mouth?

If instead I see good-quality chocolate with an instruction to chop it into small pieces, the clouds open up, the angels start to sing, and we embark on a new road lined with melted chocolate and, hopefully, crispy edges and chewy centers, too.

To cement our newly formed friendship, I rush to the kitchen and give the recipe a try. Will it be cakey or crispy? If it turns out crispy on the edges and chewy in the center, we're friends for life.

Over the years, I've made many friends this way, eventually creating my ideal version based on what I've learned from them. I thought I had perfected the recipe until I read David Leite's article on chocolate chip cookies in the *New York Times*, where he revealed Maury Rubin's secret for City Bakery's chocolate chip cookies. Rubin's tip—refrigerating the dough for thirty-six hours to develop a stronger toffee flavor—was so inspirational, I spent the next day and a half in the kitchen baking small batches of cookies at two-hour intervals to monitor the flavor development. As *BakeWise* author Shirley O. Corriher explains in the article, the extended resting period allows the flour particles, safeguarded with butter, to fully soak up the wet ingredients. The resulting cookie has not only a stronger toffee flavor, but also a chewier center.

I consider melted chocolate such an integral part of the cookie that, in addition to the chopped chocolate in the dough, I top each dough mound with a chocolate fève (see page 80) before baking. The *fève*—an oval disk of couverture chocolate, slightly larger than a quarter and about ¼ inch (6 mm) thick—melts and spreads together with the dough, creating an enticing chocolate veil. To achieve this effect, the chocolate must be very high in cocoa butter; Valrhona Guanaja, which is 42.2 percent cocoa butter, is perfect for the job.

Now: cookies topped with a shiny chocolate veil, or lifeless chips stuck here and there? Are we friends or strangers?

Makes 26 cookies

2 ¼ cups (315 grams) all-purpose flour

1 teaspoon (4 grams) baking powder

¾ teaspoon (5 grams) baking soda

½ teaspoon (4 grams) fine sea salt

14 tablespoons (7 ounces; 200 grams) unsalted butter, softened

¾ cup plus 1 tablespoon (163 grams) packed light brown sugar

¾ cup (150 grams) granulated sugar

1 large egg

1 large egg yolk

In a medium bowl, whisk together the flour, baking powder, baking soda, and salt.

In the bowl of a stand mixer fitted with the paddle attachment, beat the butter at medium-high speed until creamy, about 2 minutes. Add the brown and granulated sugars and beat until light and fluffy, about 3 minutes. Add the egg, egg yolk, and vanilla and beat until well blended, about 2 minutes, scraping down the sides of the bowl as needed. Add half of the flour mixture and beat at the lowest speed just until incorporated. Add the remaining flour mixture together with the chopped chocolate and beat just until the flour is incorporated and the chocolate pieces are evenly distributed. Cover the bowl tightly with plastic wrap, pressing it directly onto the surface of the dough. Refrigerate for at least 4 hours, or preferably 36 hours for a stronger toffee flavor.

To bake, set a rack in the middle of the oven and preheat the oven to 350°F (175°C). Line a baking sheet with parchment paper.

(ingredients and method continued on page 31)

1 teaspoon (5 grams) pure vanilla extract

7 ounces (200 grams) bittersweet chocolate (70% cacao), chopped into small pieces

26 (2.7 ounces; 75 grams) bittersweet chocolate (70% cacao) fèves with about 42% cocoa butter (see headnote)

Let the bowl stand at room temperature until the dough is soft enough to be scooped, about 20 minutes. Using an ice cream scoop with a 2-tablespoon (30-ml) capacity and a release mechanism, drop as many scoops of the dough (1.4 ounces; 40 grams each) as you can fit onto the prepared baking sheet, leaving about 2 inches (5 cm) all around them. (At this point, you can shape all the cookies, arrange them close together on the baking sheet, wrap them airtight, and refrigerate for up to 3 days. Alternatively, you can freeze them until firm, place them in a resealable plastic freezer bag, and freeze for up to 2 months. No need to thaw, though you may need to add a couple of minutes to the baking time.) Press one chocolate fève—whole or broken into a few pieces—close to the center of each cookie, flattening the dough slightly.

Bake until the edges of the cookies are golden brown, 14 to 16 minutes. Set the sheet on a wire rack to cool until the cookies are firm enough to handle, 2 to 3 minutes, then transfer the cookies directly onto the rack to cool just until warm. Repeat with the remaining cookies.

Storage: The cookies are best eaten warm, with the chocolate lace layer on top still shiny, but they will keep in an airtight container at room temperature for up to 3 days. Before serving, briefly wave a hair dryer set to low over the cookies to make the chocolate layer glisten.

Vanilla

Vanilla is one of the world's most labor-intensive agricultural products. After the flowers of the vanilla orchid bloom in the spring, each must be pollinated to produce fruit, which happens naturally only by a certain genus of bee native to Mexico. In other parts of the world, including Madagascar—the world's principal supplier of vanilla—each flower must be hand pollinated within a short window after opening. Natural pollination has a very low success rate, so nearly all the vanilla grown today is artificially pollinated.

After pollination come numerous other labor-intensive stages of production. As each fruit ripens at a different time, the beans are harvested daily. Once harvested, the pods are exposed to high temperatures to stop their growth. They are cured at a specific temperature and humidity, dried in the shade with occasional exposure to sunlight, then stored in closed boxes to develop their characteristic aroma. The next step is grading the pods according to specific criteria. Factors that determine quality include length, appearance, moisture content, and whether or not the pod has split on the end during the curing process. Pods shorter than 6 inches (15 cm)—or that are matte, blemished, low in moisture, or split—are assigned lower grades. Because the flavor intensity isn't factored into these criteria, a higher grade doesn't necessarily mean a higher concentration of flavor. For this reason, when buying vanilla beans, don't judge them on their looks alone. The best judge is your nose.

The most common varieties of vanilla are Bourbon, Tahitian, and Mexican. Bourbon vanilla from Madagascar contains the highest ratio of *vanillin*—the main phenolic compound that contributes to vanilla flavor—making it the ideal variety for baking and making vanilla extract. Tahitian and Mexican varieties contain much less vanillin, and each has its own distinctive aroma. I prefer the floral Tahitian vanilla with tropical fruits, and I keep a small stock of the woody Mexican vanilla for milk-based desserts, which are usually mild enough to let the nuances in flavor shine through.

Making vanilla extract is a great way to preserve and extend the fruit. Using a whole bean would be overkill in most recipes, and as the bean quickly dries and loses its potency after cutting, it doesn't make sense to save a partial bean for future use. Considering that we can make about sixteen teaspoons of vanilla extract from a single bean, and that we use 1 to 2 teaspoons of extract in most recipes, we can extend a single or partial bean's life to many recipes. When you buy vanilla beans, wrap them tightly with plastic wrap, place them inside an airtight container, and store them in a cool, dark place.

HOW TO SPLIT AND SCRAPE THE SEEDS FROM A VANILLA BEAN

Place the vanilla bean on a cutting board with the curled tip facing away from you. If the pod has curled, hold down the curled tip and run the blunt side of a paring knife along the pod to straighten it.

Holding the knife parallel to the board, insert the blade right below the curled tip. Holding down both ends of the pod with the index finger and thumb of one hand, run the knife down the entire length to split the bean in half.

Working with one half at a time, hold down the tip of the pod and scrape the seeds by running the blunt side of the knife along the open pod. Use the seeds right away, as instructed in recipes.

Use the leftover pod halves to feed Homemade Vanilla Extract (page 323) or to make Vanilla Sugar (page 326).

VANILLA BEAN MELTAWAYS

This is my version of the beloved Turkish cookie, *un kurabiyesi* (literally, "flour cookie"). A dough that barely comes together is the key to its tender texture. The classic version is made by rolling the dough into a log, embossing the top with the tines of a fork, then cutting it into diamond shapes before baking. I prefer to cut fairly thick rounds so that they don't dry out before turning a nice golden color at the edges.

A close friend of mine who was visiting the day I tested this recipe ate half a dozen of them, then asked me to pack a few for a friend he was meeting later. A couple of hours later, my phone rang. His friend was ecstatic: "That smell, that crumb! Two teas later and I can still taste them." It's the vanilla bean.

Makes 30 cookies

17 tablespoons (8.5 ounces; 240 grams) unsalted butter, softened

⅔ cup plus 2 tablespoons (127 grams) confectioners' sugar

1 vanilla bean, split and seeds scraped (see page 32)

2½ cups (350 grams) all-purpose flour

¼ cup (30 grams) cornstarch

¼ teaspoon (2 grams) fine sea salt

In the bowl of a stand mixer fitted with the paddle attachment, beat the butter, ⅔ cup (107 grams) of the sugar, and the vanilla seeds at the lowest speed just until the sugar is incorporated. Raise the speed to medium-high and beat until creamy, about 3 minutes. Add the flour, cornstarch, and salt. Beat at the lowest speed until coarse crumbs form. Remove the bowl from the mixer and press the dough into a ball with your hands. You may use the leftover vanilla pod halves in Homemade Vanilla Extract (page 323) or Vanilla Sugar (page 326).

Roll out the dough between two large sheets of parchment paper into a round about 9 inches (23 cm) in diameter and ⅝ inch (1.6 cm) thick, occasionally flipping the dough with the parchment, then lifting and smoothing the parchment to avoid creases.

Transfer the dough and parchment to a baking sheet and chill until firm, at least 2 hours in the refrigerator or about 25 minutes in the freezer.

Line a baking sheet with parchment paper. Place the chilled dough on a flat surface and peel off the top parchment. Using a 1½-inch (4-cm) fluted round cookie cutter, cut out as many cookies as you can and transfer them to the prepared baking sheet. Gather the scraps into a ball, roll the dough out again between the parchment sheets, and continue to cut out cookies until you run out of dough. Freeze the cookies, uncovered, until firm, 10 to 15 minutes. (Once they are firm, you can wrap them airtight and refrigerate for up to 3 days or freeze for up to 2 months. No need to thaw, though you may need to add a couple of minutes to the baking time.)

Meanwhile, set a rack in the middle of the oven and preheat the oven to 325°F (160°C). Line a baking sheet with parchment paper.

Arrange as many cookies as you can fit on the prepared baking sheet, leaving about 1¼ inches (3 cm) all around them. Keep the rest of the unbaked cookies in the refrigerator.

Bake until the edges of the cookies are golden, 33 to 35 minutes. Set the sheet on a wire rack to cool for 10 minutes, then transfer the cookies directly onto the rack to cool completely. Repeat with the remaining cookies.

Put the remaining 2 tablespoons (20 grams) of sugar in a fine-mesh shaker and dust the tops and sides of the cookies.

Storage: The cookies will keep in an airtight container at room temperature for up to 5 days.

PISTACHIO & MATCHA SABLÉS

One look at the photo on the right and you'd think I'd baked intergalactic cookies to welcome guests from hundreds of light-years away and arranged them in a bowl straight from *The Jetsons*, just so that they'd feel right at home.

That was not my intention, but now that I think about it, if you had told me that aliens were sending representatives to all the countries of the world and asked me to come up with a cookie that represents Turkey, this is exactly what I would have baked. It is a cookie version of one of Turkey's delicacies, *fıstık ezmesi* ("pistachio paste"). That said, it has an ingredient that is alien to the world of Turkish desserts: matcha—powdered green tea made from leaves that have been shade grown, deveined, destemmed, and stone milled.

My first experiment with matcha was ten years ago, when I baked a matcha cheesecake for a friend's birthday (see page 140). I was unaware of its potency, so I kept adding matcha to the batter until it turned the color I envisioned—an emerald green, which required pretty much the whole container. It must have traumatized my friends deeply, because after all these years they still haven't stopped teasing me. I had sworn not to touch a container of matcha ever again until I visited Pâtisserie Sadaharu Aoki in Paris and discovered matcha's wonders when handled with subtlety and harmonized with other ingredients. The combinations that excited me the most were matcha with white chocolate and with pistachio. The latter was the inspiration for these cookies.

I haven't had the chance to offer these cookies to an extraterrestrial, but I've had the privilege of gifting a small box of them to an extra-special hero of mine, Nick Malgieri, the first time I met him in İstanbul. Since he asked for the recipe when he got back to New York, I believe the cookie did its job.

Makes 20 cookies

¼ cup plus 2 tablespoons (53 grams) all-purpose flour

1½ teaspoons (3 grams) matcha

½ teaspoon (2 grams) baking powder

5 tablespoons plus 1 teaspoon (2.7 ounces; 75 grams) unsalted butter, softened

⅓ cup plus 1 tablespoon (79 grams) granulated sugar

Pinch of fine sea salt

1 large egg yolk

¾ cup (68 grams) blanched pistachio flour

60 (3 tablespoons; 25 grams) whole blanched pistachios

Sift together the flour, matcha, and baking powder into a small bowl.

In the bowl of a stand mixer fitted with the paddle attachment, beat the butter, sugar, and salt at medium-high speed until light and fluffy, about 2 minutes. Add the egg yolk and beat until well blended, about 1 minute. Add the pistachio flour and beat at medium speed until incorporated, about 30 seconds, scraping down the sides of the bowl as needed. Add the flour mixture and beat at the lowest speed just until incorporated.

Scrape the soft, sticky dough onto a large sheet of parchment paper. Cover with another sheet of parchment and use a flat-bottomed pan to gently press and flatten the dough into an even round, about 6¼ inches (16 cm) in diameter and ⅝ inch (1.6 cm) thick.

Transfer the dough and parchment to a baking sheet and chill until firm, at least 2 hours in the refrigerator or about 30 minutes in the freezer.

Line a baking sheet with parchment paper. Place the chilled dough on a flat surface and peel off the top sheet of parchment. Using a 1⅜-inch (3.5-cm) plain round cookie cutter, cut out as many cookies as you can and transfer them to the prepared baking sheet. Gather the scraps into a ball, flatten the dough again between the parchment sheets, and continue to cut out cookies until you run out of dough.

Gently press three pistachios in the form of a three-pointed star on each cookie. Freeze the cookies, uncovered, until firm, about 15 minutes. (Once they are firm, you can wrap them airtight and refrigerate for up to 3 days or freeze for up to 2 months. No need to thaw, though you may need to add a couple of minutes to the baking time.)

(continued on page 38)

Meanwhile, set a rack in the middle of the oven and preheat the oven to 325°F (160°C). Line a baking sheet with parchment paper.

Arrange as many cookies as you can fit on the prepared baking sheet, leaving about 1¼ inches (3 cm) all around them. Keep the rest of the unbaked cookies in the refrigerator.

Bake until the edges of the cookies are lightly golden and the bottoms are light brown, about 20 minutes. Set the sheet on a wire rack to cool for 10 minutes, then transfer the cookies directly onto the rack to cool completely. Repeat with the remaining cookies.

Storage: The cookies are best the day they are made, but they will keep in an airtight container at room temperature for up to 3 days. When you serve them later, you can crisp them in a preheated 325°F (160°C) oven until they are warmed through, 3 to 5 minutes.

LIME & GINGER COOKIES

This is the first recipe in the book using citrus zest, so it is most fitting that I share here an invaluable tip for fully capturing the essence of citrus fruits, and explain why I always call for the fruit itself, even in recipes where you only need the finely grated zest.

You know how when you peel an orange, the room fills with its intense aroma? What you're smelling is the fruit's essential oil, contained in the oil glands beneath the outer layer of the peel. As you peel the fruit, those glands burst, sending the aromatic oils wafting into the air. The same thing happens when you zest a citrus fruit. I'll bet you tend to grate the zest onto a cutting board or plate before measuring out what you'll need for a recipe. If so, you've been wasting much of that precious aromatic oil, because most of it lands on the cutting board and stays there. The same is true when you use a box grater: the oil is trapped in the grater instead of being released into your recipe. The only way to fully incorporate the fruit's aromatic oil into a dough or batter is to grate its zest directly into the mixing bowl, preferably with a fine-tooth rasp grater.

Makes 25 cookies

1½ cups (210 grams) all-purpose flour

1½ teaspoons (6 grams) baking powder

4 limes

¼ cup (50 grams) granulated sugar

7 tablespoons (3.5 ounces; 100 grams) unsalted butter, softened

½ cup (80 grams) confectioners' sugar

¼ teaspoon (2 grams) fine sea salt

1 tablespoon (18 grams) finely grated, peeled fresh ginger

2 large egg yolks

These cookies retain both their citrusy perfume and their crispness for a very long time. As I'm writing this, the cookies I made three months ago are as crisp and fragrant as the day I baked them. Sound too good to be true? There's only one way to find out.
Sift together the flour and baking powder into a medium bowl.

Using a fine-tooth rasp grater, grate the zest of the limes (avoiding the bitter white pith) directly into the bowl of a stand mixer until you have about 1 loosely packed tablespoon of zest. Add the granulated sugar and use your fingertips to rub the zest into the sugar. Add the butter, confectioners' sugar, and salt. Attach the bowl and fit the paddle attachment onto the mixer and beat at the lowest speed just until the sugar is incorporated. Raise the speed to medium-high and beat until light and fluffy, about 3 minutes. Add the ginger and egg yolks and beat until well blended, about 1 minute, scraping down the sides of the bowl as needed. Add the flour mixture and beat at the lowest speed until large clumps form. Remove the bowl from the mixer and press the dough into a ball with your hands.

Roll out the dough between two large sheets of parchment paper into a round about 10 inches (25.5 cm) in diameter and 5⁄16 inch (8 mm) thick, occasionally flipping the dough with the parchment, then lifting and smoothing the parchment to avoid creases.

Transfer the dough and parchment to a baking sheet and chill until firm, at least 2 hours in the refrigerator or about 25 minutes in the freezer.

Line a baking sheet with parchment paper. Place the chilled dough on a flat surface and peel off the top sheet of parchment. Using a 2-inch (5-cm) plain round cookie cutter, cut out as many cookies as you can and transfer them to the prepared baking sheet. Gather the scraps into a ball, roll the dough out again between the parchment

(continued on page 41)

sheets, and continue to cut out cookies until you run out of dough. Freeze the cookies, uncovered, until firm, about 15 minutes. (Once they are firm, you can wrap them airtight and refrigerate for up to 3 days or freeze for up to 2 months. No need to thaw, though you may need to add a couple of minutes to the baking time.)

Meanwhile, set a rack in the middle of the oven and preheat the oven to 325°F (160°C). Line a baking sheet with parchment paper.

Arrange as many cookies as you can fit on the prepared baking sheet, leaving about 1¼ inches (3 cm) all around them. Keep the rest of the unbaked cookies in the refrigerator.

Bake until the edges of the cookies are golden, about 24 minutes. Set the sheet on a wire rack to cool for 10 minutes, then transfer the cookies directly onto the rack to cool completely. Repeat with the remaining cookies.

Storage: The cookies will keep in an airtight container at room temperature for as long as you dare.

HAZELNUT & CARAMEL COOKIES

These cookies couldn't be more different than the way they started out. First they were the hazelnut thumbprint cookies I made as an excuse to use the sun-dried, saffron-yellow apricot jam a friend gifted me. When the time came to update the recipe for my Turkish cookbook, I decided to make a plain thumbprint, coating it with finely chopped hazelnuts for crunch. Then I learned that Banu Bingör, a dear friend and recipe tester extraordinaire, had turned the original thumbprint into a simple ball cookie studded with a single whole hazelnut. When she brought a jarful of them to one of my book signings and I found myself eating cookie after cookie to get to that perfectly toasted hazelnut, I wished for a chance to revise the recipe. Its beauty was in the restraint, and I was determined to get it right the next time.

I got that chance with this translation of my book into English, and I had every intention of staying true to Banu's version. However, restraint is not a virtue of mine. I embrace that gladly, because otherwise I would not have come up with a cookie that deserves the description "melt in your mouth" more than any other I have ever baked.

My plan was to maximize the hazelnuts on top, so I pressed the dough into a square pan, brushed the top with a thick layer of lightly beaten egg white, and covered the entire surface with coarsely chopped hazelnuts. I was ecstatic to have octupled the quantity of hazelnuts, but my excitement wasn't long lived—no matter how thickly I brushed on the egg white glaze, the hazelnuts would not stick. I needed a stronger glue. A thin layer of chocolate ganache was the easy way out, but I didn't want anything to steal the hazelnuts' thunder. I was about to give up until I remembered a tart I'd baked many years ago from David Lebovitz's blog. It was Lindsey Shere's Almond Tart, the most famous dessert at Chez Panisse for decades until it was taken off the menu—despite David lobbying against the change. Imagine a mixture of cream, sugar, and loads of sliced almonds, slowly transforming into an almond-layered caramel inside a baked tart shell. That was it! I would spread a layer of sweetened cream beneath the hazelnuts. It would caramelize in the oven, forming the most delectable glue known to humankind.

The revelation came with a challenge: prebaking the dough made it impossible to cut it into squares without shattering it into a million pieces, while skipping the prebake resulted in an underbaked crust. I tried scoring the dough before baking and experimented with various prebake times, but nothing helped. As a last resort, I stole a corner piece from the latest batch of unbaked dough and popped it into the oven to see what might happen. I expected the cream to run off the sides, but it didn't. In fact, it made the dough spread out, allowing it to crisp at the exact time the cream layer turned into caramel. Victory at last!

Makes 25 cookies

2½ cups (325 grams) whole blanched hazelnuts

1 cup (140 grams) all-purpose flour

¾ cup (150 grams) granulated sugar

1 stick (4 ounces; 115 grams) cold unsalted butter, cut into small pieces

⅓ cup (80 grams) heavy cream

¼ teaspoon fleur de sel or flaky sea salt, such as Maldon

Cut a sheet of parchment paper long and wide enough to cover the bottom and sides of an 8-inch (20.5-cm) square pan with 2 inches (5 cm) of overhang on all sides. Crumple up the parchment and straighten it out half a dozen times to soften it, so that it will fit into the corners without sharp edges. Line the pan with the parchment paper across the bottom and up the sides, pressing creases at the bottom and top edges.

In the bowl of a food processor fitted with a metal blade, process 1 cup (130 grams) of the hazelnuts, the flour, and 6 tablespoons (75 grams) of the sugar until the nuts are finely ground, about 2 minutes. Add the butter and process until the dough gathers around the blade, about 1 minute.

Scrape the dough into the prepared pan, press it with your hands into an even layer, and smooth the top with a small offset spatula.

Coarsely chop the remaining 1½ cups (195 grams) of hazelnuts with a knife, aiming for mostly halves and leaving some whole.

(continued on page 44)

In a medium saucepan over medium-high heat, bring the cream and the remaining 6 tablespoons (75 grams) of sugar to a boil, stirring frequently. Cook until it is thick enough to coat a spoon (running a finger down the back should leave a clear track), 3 to 5 minutes. Take the pan off the heat, immediately add the chopped nuts, and stir to coat them evenly. Use a spoon to distribute the nut mixture evenly over the dough, pressing lightly on the nuts with the back of the spoon to level them. Sprinkle the fleur de sel evenly over the surface. Freeze the dough, uncovered, until firm, 30 to 40 minutes.

Meanwhile, set a rack in the middle of the oven and preheat the oven to 350°F (175°C). Line a baking sheet with parchment paper.

Using the parchment overhang as handles, lift the dough out of the pan and transfer it to a cutting board. Using a large heavy knife, cut the dough into 5 equal strips in each direction to make 25 squares. Arrange as many cookies as you can fit on the prepared baking sheet, leaving about 1½ inches (4 cm) all around them. Keep the rest of the unbaked cookies in the refrigerator.

Bake until the tops are caramelized and the hazelnuts are golden brown, 26 to 28 minutes. Set the sheet on a wire rack to cool for 10 minutes, then transfer the cookies directly onto the rack to cool completely. Repeat with the remaining cookies.

Storage: The cookies will keep in an airtight container at room temperature for up to 5 days.

WALNUT PRALINE BISCOTTI

I'd intended to include my previous favorite biscotti in this book—a classic version with anise seeds and orange zest. That was until a friend tasted one and commented, "I wish you made these with walnuts. Oh, and caramel. Actually, walnuts covered in caramel. The caramel they dip the dough balls in to make that profiterole mountain; the kind that shatters like glass."

First off, let me clarify that the "profiterole mountain" my friend referred to is the French dessert *croquembouche*, in which cream puffs (not profiteroles) are dipped into hot caramel, stacked into a pyramid, and wrapped with a web of spun sugar.

At first, I prepared the caramel-covered walnuts just like he described, but I couldn't imagine them whole in the dough, so I whizzed them in the food processor and mixed the powdered walnut praline into the dough. Neither the walnut nor the caramel was detectable in the biscotti, so I decided to give his original idea a go—admittedly without expectations.

Sure enough, when I cut the dough log into slices I found a tasty surprise hiding inside: the caramel surrounding the walnuts had melted into sweet, sticky pockets. I am so glad I listened to my friend. He may not know a croquembouche from a mountain or a cream puff from a profiterole, but he sure knows his biscotti.

By the way, if you're curious about my previous favorite, omit the walnut praline and add 4 teaspoons (10 grams) of anise seeds and the finely grated zest of an orange to the dough when you add the sugar.

Makes 24 biscotti

WALNUT PRALINE

1 cup (90 grams) walnut halves

⅓ cup plus 1 tablespoon (79 grams) granulated sugar

1 tablespoon (15 grams) water

DOUGH

2 cups (280 grams) all-purpose flour

1 teaspoon (4 grams) baking powder

6 tablespoons (3 ounces; 85 grams) unsalted butter, softened

¾ cup (150 grams) granulated sugar

2 large eggs

½ teaspoon (3 grams) pure vanilla extract

Set a rack in the middle of the oven and preheat the oven to 350°F (175°C).

To make the walnut praline, spread out the walnut halves on an unlined baking sheet in a single layer and bake until fragrant and the skins are golden brown, 10 to 13 minutes. Immediately transfer the toasted nuts to a plate to cool. Turn the oven off. Line the baking sheet with parchment paper.

Put the sugar in a medium heavy-bottomed saucepan and shake the pan to level the sugar. Pour the water around the inside edge of the pan. Set the pan over medium-high heat and cook without stirring until the caramel turns a dark amber color, about 8 minutes (it should register 383°F [195°C] on an instant-read thermometer). Take the pan off the heat and stir in the walnuts with a silicone spatula. Immediately scrape the mixture onto the prepared baking sheet, spreading it in an even layer. Let cool completely, about 20 minutes.

Preheat the oven to 350°F (175°C). Line a baking sheet with parchment paper.

To make the dough, sift together the flour and baking powder into a medium bowl.

In the bowl of a stand mixer fitted with the paddle attachment, beat the butter and sugar at medium-high speed until light and fluffy, about 3 minutes. Add the eggs and vanilla and beat until well blended, about 2 minutes, scraping down the sides of the bowl as needed. Add the flour mixture and beat at the lowest speed just until incorporated.

Remove the bowl from the mixer, measure out ½ cup (130 grams) of the dough, and set it aside to cover the praline pieces that will stick out after shaping the dough.

(continued on page 47)

Chop the cooled walnut praline into bite-size pieces and stir them evenly into the remaining dough in the bowl. Scrape the dough onto the prepared baking sheet. With moistened hands, shape the dough into a rough log about 3¼ inches (8.5 cm) wide and 10¼ inches (26 cm) long, taking care when handling the sharp praline pieces. With moistened hands, cover the entire surface of the dough with the reserved dough so that no praline pieces are visible. Smooth the top and reshape the dough into a log about 3½ inches (9 cm) wide and 11 inches (28 cm) long.

Bake until the top and sides of the log are golden, about 35 minutes. Set the sheet on a wire rack to cool for 30 minutes. Reduce the oven temperature to 300°F (150°C).

Transfer the log to a cutting board and, using a large heavy serrated knife, cut it crosswise into ½-inch-thick (1.3-cm) slices. Arrange the slices cut side up in a single layer directly on the oven rack and bake until golden brown on the edges, 25 to 30 minutes. Set the oven rack over a baking sheet to cool the biscotti.

Storage: The biscotti will keep in an airtight container at room temperature for up to 10 days.

CRISPY-CHEWY OATMEAL WALNUT COOKIES

When developing recipes, if I have a clear idea of the result I want and my starting point isn't too far from it, I tweak the recipe by making subtle adjustments, just one at a time, so that I may clearly observe the effect of each change. But when I realize my idea wasn't great to begin with, no matter how crystal clear I had been, I stop caring about rules and ratios and go wild. And that is when I have the most fun.

Such was the case with this recipe. What I had in hand was a wonderfully chewy and moist but boring oatmeal cookie. I contemplated adding toasted walnuts for extra flavor and textural contrast but decided not to throw good money after bad. Instead of gradually adjusting this and that, I cut two-thirds of the flour and half of the oatmeal while keeping the other ingredient quantities the same. The drastic change in the ratio of wet to dry ingredients gave the cookies a texture I wasn't at all going for, but I suppose it's what I was subconsciously yearning for—crispy on the edges and chewy in the center, one of my favorite textures in baking.

It's hard to tell from the photo, but these cookies are packed with toasted walnuts. It's an extra step that requires you to heat the oven twice, but it's totally worth it. Don't assume that the walnuts would toast anyway while the cookies bake; the dough envelopes them, preventing them from toasting. I like my walnuts toasted dark, as I love the bitterness it brings out in their skins. If you don't, stick with the lower end of the toasting time.

Makes 28 cookies

3 cups (270 grams) walnut halves

2½ cups (200 grams) old-fashioned rolled oats

¾ cup (105 grams) all-purpose flour

1 teaspoon (4 grams) baking powder

¾ teaspoon (5 grams) baking soda

¼ teaspoon (2 grams) fine sea salt

14 tablespoons (7 ounces; 200 grams) unsalted butter, softened

1¼ cups (250 grams) granulated sugar

2 large eggs

1 teaspoon (5 grams) pure vanilla extract

Set a rack in the middle of the oven and preheat the oven to 350°F (175°C).

Spread out the walnuts on an unlined baking sheet in a single layer and bake until fragrant and the skins are golden brown, 10 to 13 minutes. Immediately transfer the toasted nuts to a plate to cool. Turn the oven off.

In a medium bowl, stir together the oats, flour, baking powder, baking soda, and salt.

In the bowl of a stand mixer fitted with the paddle attachment, beat the butter at medium-high speed until creamy, about 2 minutes. Add the sugar and beat until light and fluffy, about 3 minutes. Add the eggs and vanilla and beat until well blended, about 2 minutes, scraping down the sides of the bowl as needed. Add the oat mixture and beat at the lowest speed just until incorporated.

Remove the bowl from the mixer. Break the walnuts into large pieces by hand and stir them evenly into the dough. Cover the bowl tightly with plastic wrap and refrigerate until the dough is firm enough to scoop, about 1 hour. Line the baking sheet with parchment paper.

Using an ice cream scoop with a 2-tablespoon (30-ml) capacity and a release mechanism, drop scoops of the dough (1.4 ounces; 40 grams each) onto the prepared baking sheet. Freeze the cookies, uncovered, until firm, about 20 minutes. (Once they are firm, you can wrap them airtight and refrigerate for up to 3 days or place them in a resealable plastic freezer bag and freeze for up to 2 months. No need to thaw, though you may need to add a couple of minutes to the baking time.)

Meanwhile, preheat the oven to 350°F (175°C). Line a baking sheet with parchment paper.

(continued on page 51)

Arrange as many cookies as you can fit on the prepared baking sheet, leaving about 2 inches (5 cm) all around them. Keep the rest of the unbaked cookies in the refrigerator.

Bake until the edges of the cookies are golden brown, about 16 minutes. Set the sheet on a wire rack to cool until the cookies are firm enough to handle, 2 to 3 minutes, then transfer the cookies directly onto the rack to cool completely. Repeat with the remaining cookies.

Storage: The cookies will keep in an airtight container at room temperature for up to 3 days.

Macaron Madness

Who would have thought that a sandwich cookie would take the world by a storm?

Certainly not I. Before I inhaled a box of them at Pierre Hermé in Paris, a macaron was, to me, an overly sweet filling between two sickeningly sweet shells. I had no idea why they existed. They weren't on my ambitious list of things to eat in Paris, but back when I started blogging, a food blogger visiting Paris and *not* trying Pierre Hermé's macarons was unfathomable. So I bought a box of eight, perched on a sunny bench in the Luxembourg Gardens, took a bite of the Mogador—bumblebee-yellow shells with a passion fruit and milk chocolate ganache filling—and began to daydream . . .

How I wished I were twenty-one again—fresh out of college, full of passion, and ready to devote all my energy to a new career. If I were twenty-one today, without a doubt I'd sleep on Pierre Hermé's doorstep and beg until he accepted me as an apprentice. I'd gladly wash the dishes and scrape tart dough from his work station for years before he decided I was ready to pipe macaron shells. I'd hand him my soul and watch him mold it, too. Alas, I am about twenty-one years late for that, so the best I can do now is to devour as many of his creations as possible and draw inspiration from them.

If what I ate at Pierre Hermé were macarons, what had I been eating before? I had to know, so when I returned home I started reading everything I could find about macarons and searching for a reliable recipe with which to replicate the real deal. I was quickly overwhelmed. I had never before seen the food blogosphere this intimidated by a recipe, each ingredient down to the quarter teaspoon of food coloring questioned to death. Some advised aging the egg whites for a week in the refrigerator, while others favored aging them three days at room temperature. Some concluded that the main reason for most mishaps was the miniscule amount of cornstarch

in ordinary confectioners' sugar—the cornstarch-free kind professional bakers used was the solution. Some preferred store-bought almond flour, keeping it uncovered in the refrigerator until it dried out, while others stressed the importance of preparing the almond flour at home. There was disagreement on the type of food coloring, too: some were sure the only reason their macarons lacked the characteristic feet (the delicate frill around the edge) was their use of gel rather than powdered food coloring.

And then there was the meringue. Even if you had determined the optimal number of days to properly age the egg whites, had voted for or against cornstarch-free confectioners' sugar, had decided between homemade and store-bought almond flour, and had identified the ideal type of food coloring, you were still left to choose between three different approaches to making the meringue: French, Italian, or Swiss. Using the same amount of egg whites and sugar, each technique differs as to when and how the sugar is added to the egg whites. Judging from what I had read up until that point, it was apparent that the Swiss meringue was the least desirable and that most bakers preferred the French approach. But soon after, a handful of bloggers attended Pierre Hermé's macaron workshop and reported that God was making his macarons with Italian meringue.

Some left the whole ordeal to destiny, suggesting that we should accept unpredictable results—take joy in the process rather than fixating on perfect macaron feet. But isn't it better to enjoy the process and produce perfect macarons, too? What will you say to your guests—"They don't look like much, but I had a blast making them"?

Right around the time I was exploring these pithy questions, I came across an episode of *MasterChef Australia* in which four contestants who had performed poorly on the previous test were up against each other in what the judges deemed the most technically

difficult pressure test ever. After a terror-inducing intro-duction, in came Adriano Zumbo carrying a macaron tower. You could see the fear in the contestants' eyes and watch as it translated into endless mistakes. It was a perfect demonstration that fear ought not be an ingredient if your goal is to make the best macarons.

As much as I appreciated my fellow bloggers' efforts to dissect every step of the process, I never found a recipe that produced consistent results. The ratio of ingredients was more or less the same in every recipe, but the methods differed immensely. When I read the posts back to back, I saw many contradicting statements, but one thing was constant: home bakers left comments that they hadn't a clue what went wrong despite having followed the recipe's every detail.

You may have been discouraged by failed attempts to make macarons in the past. You may have read horror stories and decided not to even try. But let's not forget that Pierre Hermé is human. If he can do it, sooner or later we can, too.

That said, don't think I take the macaron recipe that follows lightly. As with every recipe involving meringue, conditions a home baker may not be able to control—ambient temperature, humidity—can affect the outcome. I've developed this recipe to be minimally affected by changes in those conditions, and even to tolerate minor mistakes. As long as you stick to the recipe, shiny shells with perfect feet will no longer be a pipe dream. Keep trying and, sooner or later, you will bake the perfect macaron. I promise.

MACARON SHELLS

After making macarons with recipes I found in print and online, I noticed that even after following the techniques religiously, much was left to chance. During the *macaronnage* stage—the critical step where you fold the dry ingredients into the meringue—just a few extra folds could make the difference between a perfect consistency and a ruined batter.

The day I set those recipes aside and examined the ingredients instead was the day my foolproof macaron shells began to emerge. First, you don't need to track down cornstarch-free confectioners' sugar; the amount of cornstarch in the regular kind is negligible, at about 3 percent. The type of food coloring is also unimportant. I prefer the gels, but I've had great results with the powdered ones, too. I prefer store-bought almond flour, but feel free to make it at home, processing the almonds with the confectioners' sugar to prevent them from releasing their oils. You also don't need to age your egg whites. In fact, you shouldn't: While aged egg whites whip to a greater volume, fresher whites will create a more stable meringue.

The stability of the meringue is paramount to this recipe. A stable meringue makes a stable batter, less likely to be ruined by a few extra folds. The rate and timing used in adding the sugar to the whites also contribute to the meringue's stability, which brings me to the most vital part of this recipe: Building a stable meringue begins with creating plentiful small air bubbles rather than fewer large ones. This is accomplished by whisking the egg whites slowly at first, then gradually increasing the speed. Sugar is added only after the foam is thick enough that the whisk leaves a trail as it mixes, and it is added gradually after that, allowing the crystals time to dissolve, a key to maintaining volume. Following these steps creates a meringue so stable that cream of tartar—the most common stabilizer used in meringue—isn't needed. A stand mixer is ideal for the job, as it can be started at a slower speed than a handheld mixer. If you don't own a stand mixer, whip the egg whites by hand with a wire whisk, continuing with the handheld mixer only after the sugar has been whisked in.

For any meringue, make certain that your whites are completely free of yolk, and thoroughly wash, rinse, and dry your mixing bowl and whisk before you begin. Even a trace of egg yolk, oil, or washing liquid will reduce stability.

By the way, Italian meringue—made by slowly adding hot sugar syrup to whipped egg whites—is more stable than French meringue, but I find that the French method yields a superior macaron texture.

You will need at least two matching rimmed baking sheets, preferably four: three will hold the macaron shells and the fourth will remain in the oven, ready to cushion the sheets of macarons while baking. If you have only two identical sheets, put one in the oven and use the other for the first batch of macarons, leaving the remaining two parchment sheets of piped macarons on a flat surface until you are ready to bake them. After removing the first batch from the oven and letting the shells cool briefly on the sheet, transfer the shells on their parchment to a rack to cool and repeat to bake the remaining two batches.

The macarons are made so similarly that I have included the instructions for all three flavors in a single recipe. Each flavor option makes shells for 30 macarons.

*Makes 60 macaron shells
in one flavor (for 30 macarons)*

Draw twenty 1⅜-inch (3.5-cm) circles on each of three sheets of parchment paper, leaving about 1¼ inches (3 cm) all around them. Line three rimmed baking sheets with the parchment, writing side down. Fit a large pastry bag with a ⅜-inch (1-cm) plain round tip (Ateco #804), twist the tip of the bag, place it in a tall glass, and fold the top of the bag down over the edge of the glass.

(continued on page 58)

PISTACHIO MACARON SHELLS

¾ cup plus 3 tablespoons (150 grams) confectioners' sugar, plus more if needed

¾ cup plus 4 teaspoons (75 grams) blanched pistachio flour

¾ cup (75 grams) blanched almond flour

¼ teaspoon (2 grams) fine sea salt

3.5 ounces (100 grams; about 3 large) egg whites, at room temperature

⅓ cup plus 1 tablespoon (79 grams) granulated sugar

Green gel food coloring, optional

COCOA MACARON SHELLS

1¼ cups (125 grams) blanched almond flour

¾ cup plus 3 tablespoons (150 grams) confectioners' sugar, plus more if needed

¼ cup (25 grams) Dutch-processed unsweetened cocoa powder

¼ teaspoon (2 grams) fine sea salt

3.5 ounces (100 grams; about 3 large) egg whites, at room temperature

⅓ cup plus 1 tablespoon (79 grams) granulated sugar

2 tablespoons (11 grams) blanched pistachio flour, optional

HAZELNUT MACARON SHELLS

1½ cups (150 grams) blanched hazelnut flour

¾ cup plus 3 tablespoons (150 grams) confectioners' sugar, plus more if needed

¼ teaspoon (2 grams) fine sea salt

3.5 ounces (100 grams; about 3 large) egg whites, at room temperature

⅓ cup plus 1 tablespoon (79 grams) granulated sugar

Pink or red gel food coloring, optional

In the bowl of a food processor fitted with a metal blade, *for pistachio macaron shells,* combine the confectioners' sugar, pistachio flour, almond flour, and salt; *for cocoa macaron shells,* combine the almond flour, confectioners' sugar, cocoa powder, and salt; and *for hazelnut macaron shells,* combine the hazelnut flour, confectioners' sugar, and salt. Pulse until the nut flour is almost as fine as confectioners' sugar, about 3 minutes.

Using a fine-mesh strainer, sift the mixture into a large bowl in several batches (this may take several minutes). If there are only a few small lumps remaining in the strainer, discard any bits too large to pass through with a gentle push. However, if more than a tablespoon or two remains in the sifter, pulse the lumps in the food processor with a few teaspoons of confectioners' sugar and sift again.

In the bowl of a stand mixer fitted with the whisk attachment, beat the egg whites at medium-low speed until foamy (photo 1), about 2 minutes. Raise the speed to medium and beat until the whisk begins to leave a trail as it mixes, about 2 minutes. Gradually beat in the granulated sugar over the next minute (photo 2). Raise the speed to medium-high and beat until medium-stiff peaks form, about 2 minutes, scraping down the sides of the bowl as needed. When you invert the whisk, the peak should hold its shape firmly with the tip curling over on itself (photo 3).

If you are using food coloring, dip two toothpicks into the gel and add the coloring by swirling the toothpicks in the meringue (photo 4). Beat at medium-high speed until the food coloring is evenly blended, about 10 seconds. Keeping in mind that the shells will lighten in the oven, gradually whisk in more coloring until the meringue is slightly darker than ultimately desired.

Remove the bowl from the mixer and add half of the dry ingredients to the meringue (photo 5). Using a large silicone spatula, fold the dry ingredients into the meringue by cutting through the meringue and folding up and over, scraping the bottom and sides of the bowl and giving the bowl a quarter turn with each fold (photos 6 to 8). Aim to blend in half of the dry ingredients in about 15 folds. Add the rest of the dry ingredients, folding them in with about 30 firm strokes to knock out some of the air bubbles (photos 9 to 12).

As soon as the dry ingredients are evenly blended, begin testing the consistency of the batter, keeping in mind that each fold will thin the batter considerably. Since there is no reliable way to save an overmixed batter, it is safer to start testing the consistency early on. Lift a portion of the batter with the spatula and let it cascade into the pan. If the batter doesn't cascade but rather drops in pieces, or if the ribbon of batter doesn't disappear (photo 13), the batter needs more mixing. Fold the batter a few more times and check again. When it is ready, the batter should thickly coat the spatula and cascade from it in a thick, solid ribbon that disappears into the batter within 10 to 15 seconds (photos 14 and 15). The number of folds needed to achieve the optimal consistency will depend on the strength of your strokes. For me, it is between 40 and 50 folds after adding the second half of the dry ingredients. If the batter coats the spatula thinly and the ribbon disappears instantly (photo 16), the batter is overmixed and you will want to start again.

(continued on page 61)

Scrape the batter into the prepared pastry bag, unfold the cuff, and twist to enclose the batter (photo 17). Dab small amounts of batter under the four corners of each parchment to secure it to the baking sheet. Holding the pastry bag at a 90-degree angle to the parchment with the tip ⅜ inch (1 cm) above the surface, pipe the batter onto the parchment following the templates you drew on the back, finishing each by quickly lifting the tip upward (photos 18 and 19). If your consistency is right, the pointed peaks on the first batch will flatten almost completely by the time you complete the second batch (photo 20).

Tap the sheets against a flat surface a few times to release any air bubbles and further flatten the peaks (photo 21 and 22). If the peaks do not flatten completely, smooth them gently with a moistened fingertip (photo 23).

For Cocoa and Chestnut Macarons (page 65), sprinkle the optional pistachio flour evenly over the tops of the cocoa shells before baking.

Let the macaron shells rest in a cool, dry place until they develop a crust, 45 to 75 minutes, depending on the temperature and humidity. Do not let them rest too much longer than needed, as the crusts may thicken and crack when baked. After 30 minutes, set a rack in the middle of the oven, center an empty baking sheet on the rack, and preheat the oven to 285°F (140°C).

With your fingertip, touch the top and sides of a shell to see if a crust has formed. If the shell doesn't stick to your finger, they are ready to bake right away (photo 24).

Nest the sheet of macarons on the empty baking sheet in the oven and bake for 24 minutes. Transfer the sheet to a wire rack (leaving the bottom sheet in the oven) and let cool completely.

The shells will develop their characteristic feet and will lighten in color as they bake, but you can check for doneness only after the shells are completely cooled. Carefully peel away a shell and press the top and bottom lightly with your fingertip. If the shell peels away easily and the top and bottom crusts are firm and crisp, it is ready (photo 25). If the shell sticks to the parchment, or if the top and bottom crusts are soft, bake the second batch 3 minutes longer (27 minutes). After removing the second batch from the oven, bake the first batch 3 minutes more. Continue checking for doneness, adjusting the baking time accordingly.

Repeat to bake the remaining shells.

Peel the cooled shells from the parchment paper and place them upside down on a tray. The macaron shells are now ready to be filled using the recipes that follow.

Storage: The macaron shells are best used the day they are made, but they will keep in an airtight container in the refrigerator for up to 3 days.

PISTACHIO, QUINCE & KAYMAK MACARONS

For the macarons in this book, I wanted to shy away from the classic flavor combinations. My most inspired idea was to transform traditional Turkish desserts into macarons. I made a list of my favorite Turkish desserts, but I wasn't ready to tackle the macaron challenge just yet. Too many fruits were disappearing from the market stalls, and I had only a short time to finalize a dozen or so recipes.

When it was time to work on the macarons, two of the recipes I'd developed in the meantime excited me more than most of the desserts on my list. The chestnut puree from the Monte Bianco recipe (page 158) reminded me of my favorite childhood treat, which inspired me to create the Cocoa and Chestnut Macarons (page 65). When I first tasted Esin Giz's Sour Cherry Liqueur (page 288), I knew those soaked sour cherries had to be enrobed in white chocolate ganache and sandwiched between pink macaron shells. And then I had to try one from my earlier list of Turkish desserts. I eliminated those I feared might get lost in translation and started with the one that intrigued me most among the remaining candidates: *Kaymaklı Ayva Tatlısı*. Picture half a quince braised in sugar syrup until it turns a deep orange-red, served with a dollop of cold *kaymak*—Turkey's version of clotted cream—sprinkled with pistachios.

Kaymak is made by skimming the cream that rises to the top after simmering water buffalo milk and rolling it into logs. There are shops in Turkey that specialize in kaymak, and it is the breakfast of champions when combined with honey and fresh-from-the-oven Turkish bread. It is served alongside many Turkish desserts to cut through their sweetness, and it provides a rich, milky contrast to bold flavors. It has a fat content of around 65 percent. You might find it in a Middle Eastern grocery shop or online, but if you can't, mascarpone would work well. For the braised quince, I'm offering two methods: one from scratch using fresh quinces, and the other using membrillo, either store-bought or homemade (see page 312).

After I took the photo on the right I took two steps back, opened my arms, and, nearly swooning with excitement, blurted out, *"Look at that beauty!"* (Please understand that this is quite unlike me. But ever since my friend told me about his dentist who, after seeing that the filling she'd just made perfectly matched the rest of my friend's teeth, stepped back and, seeking applause, exclaimed, *"Look at that beauty! Please just look at it. Be proud of me,"* I never miss a chance to repeat it.)

Be proud of me.

Makes 30 macarons

FILLING (FROM SCRATCH)

1.1 pounds (500 grams; 1 large or 2 medium) fresh quinces

1 cup (200 grams) granulated sugar

¾ cup (180 grams) water

2 tablespoons (30 grams) freshly squeezed lemon juice

6 whole cloves

⅓ cup (70 grams) kaymak (Turkish clotted cream) or mascarpone

To make the filling from scratch, remove the stems from the quinces and peel them. Cut each quince lengthwise into quarters and remove the cores with a paring knife. Cut each quarter lengthwise into ½-inch-thick (1.3-cm) slices. Put the slices together with the peels, cores, and seeds in a 6-quart (6-liter) saucepot. Add the sugar, water, lemon juice, and cloves. Set the pot over medium-high heat, cover, and bring to a boil. Reduce the heat to medium and cook, partially covered, until the slices turn coral and the juices thicken, about 50 minutes, stirring occasionally and watching it closely toward the end to prevent scorching. Take the pot off the heat and use a fork to transfer the quince slices to a medium heatproof bowl, letting the excess syrup drip back into the pot. Let the quince slices cool for 30 minutes. You will have about 8.8 ounces (250 grams) of cooked quince. (Strain the syrup remaining in the pot and enjoy it later as jelly; discard the solids.) Add the kaymak to the quince and puree with an immersion blender (or in a food processor fitted with a metal blade) until smooth.

(ingredients and method continued on page 64)

FILLING (WITH MEMBRILLO)

7 ounces (200 grams) Membrillo (page 312), cut into small pieces

3 tablespoons (45 grams) water

½ cup (105 grams) kaymak (Turkish clotted cream) or mascarpone

MACARON SHELLS

60 Pistachio Macaron Shells (page 56)

To make the filling with membrillo, combine the membrillo and water in a small saucepan. Set the pan over medium heat and cook, pressing the pieces against the bottom of the pan with a silicone spatula and stirring constantly, until the membrillo melts and the water evaporates, about 8 minutes. Take the pan off the heat and scrape the membrillo into a medium heatproof bowl. Add the kaymak and puree with an immersion blender (or in a food processor fitted with a metal blade) until smooth.

Cover the filling tightly with plastic wrap, pressing it directly onto the surface. Refrigerate until firm enough to hold its shape when piped, 2 to 3 hours. (The filling will keep, wrapped airtight, in the refrigerator for up to 2 days.)

To assemble the macarons, fit a large pastry bag with a ⅜-inch (1-cm) plain round tip (Ateco #804), twist the tip of the bag, place it in a tall glass, and fold the top of the bag down over the edge of the glass. Scrape the filling into the bag, unfold the cuff, and twist to enclose the filling.

Pipe about 2 teaspoons (0.3 ounces; 9 grams) of filling onto the flat sides of half (30) of the macaron shells. Top with the other half of the shells, flat sides down, pressing lightly to spread the filling to the edges. Put the macarons on a baking sheet, cover the sheet tightly with plastic wrap, and refrigerate for at least 4 hours, or preferably 24 hours. Before serving, let them stand at room temperature for 30 minutes.

Storage: The macarons will keep in an airtight container in the refrigerator for up to 24 hours.

COCOA & CHESTNUT MACARONS

My father never cooked in his life, but he loved shopping for food. He was obsessed with the quality of everything he bought. He had his favorites and didn't mind driving long distances to find them. He would cover the European side of İstanbul, where his office was, during the weekdays, and spent most of his time on Saturdays searching out his favorites on the Anatolian side, where we lived.

Come chestnut season, I would jump up and down by the door on Friday nights, waiting for my father to arrive with a box of my favorite treat. He spent his Friday afternoons shopping around Taksim Square and would add a stop at Divan Hotel's patisserie to buy me a box of *marrons déguisés*, "chestnuts in disguise"—tablespoon size portions of chestnut puree shaped into chestnuts and coated with chocolate, with the flat ends dipped in pistachio flour. These macarons are inspired by that favorite treat.

In loving memory of my father, on the next page are pistachio-flecked cocoa and chestnut macarons, somewhat disguised in the grooves of the wall plaque below which I once jumped up and down.

Makes 30 macarons

FILLING

8.8 ounces (250 grams) fresh chestnuts

¾ cup (180 grams) whole milk, plus more if needed

¼ cup (50 grams) granulated sugar

3 tablespoons (1.5 ounces; 40 grams) cold unsalted butter, cut into small pieces

MACARON SHELLS

60 Cocoa Macaron Shells (page 56), sprinkled with 2 tablespoons (11 grams) blanched pistachio flour before baking

To make the filling, bring a medium saucepan of water to a boil. With a chestnut (or bird's beak) knife, make a horizontal slit on the fat side of each chestnut, cutting through the tough outer shell and the thin skin underneath, but avoiding the meat.

Boil the chestnuts for 10 minutes. With a slotted spoon, transfer the boiled chestnuts to a colander. While they are still hot, peel away their outer shells and skins and transfer the meats to a cutting board. (It's helpful to place a bowl of ice water nearby to cool your fingers as you peel.) You will have about 6.5 ounces (185 grams) of chestnut meat. If they yield less, adjust the other ingredients accordingly.

Finely chop the chestnut meats, transfer them to a medium saucepan, and add the milk and sugar. Bring the mixture to a boil over medium-high heat, then reduce the heat to medium and cook until the chestnuts soak up most of the milk, 8 to 10 minutes, stirring frequently and scraping the bottom of the pan with a silicone spatula to prevent scorching. Do not let the milk evaporate completely; the mixture should look like oatmeal.

Take the pan off the heat and puree the mixture with an immersion blender (or in a food processor fitted with a metal blade) until smooth. Add the butter and puree until blended. You will have about 1¼ cups (325 grams) of filling. Check the consistency; the puree should be thick enough to firmly hold its shape when piped but soft enough to be piped without too much pressure. If it appears too thick or stiff— and keeping in mind that it will thicken further as it cools—blend in more milk, 1 tablespoon (15 grams) at a time, to reach the desired consistency. Let the puree cool for 15 minutes.

To assemble the macarons, fit a large pastry bag with a ⅜-inch (1-cm) plain round tip (Ateco #804), twist the tip of the bag, place it in a tall glass, and fold the top of the bag down over the edge of the glass. Scrape the filling into the bag, unfold the cuff, and twist to enclose the filling.

(continued on page 67)

Pipe about 2 teaspoons (0.4 ounces; 11 grams) of filling onto the flat sides of half (30) of the macaron shells. Top with the other half of the shells, flat sides down, pressing lightly to spread the filling to the edges. Put the macarons on a baking sheet, cover the sheet tightly with plastic wrap, and refrigerate for at least 4 hours, or preferably 24 hours. Before serving, let them stand at room temperature for 30 minutes.

Storage: The macarons will keep in an airtight container in the refrigerator for up to 24 hours.

SOUR CHERRY & WHITE CHOCOLATE MACARONS

Drunk on Cognac and perfumed with spices, the sour cherries from Esin Giz's Sour Cherry Liqueur recipe (page 288) play the starring role in this macaron recipe. The white chocolate is in the supporting role, balancing the cherries' tartness and the warm flavors of winter spices in the liqueur.

Since sour cherry season is relatively short and it takes at least three months for the cherries to get properly drunk, I offer two alternatives, in case you are too impatient to wait. Option one is to buy a jar of sour cherries soaked in liqueur, such as Griottines, made with Morello cherries, brandy, and kirsch. The second option, if sour cherries are in season and you are open to forgoing the alcohol, is to squeeze and press a heaping cup of pitted fresh sour cherries through a strainer set over a medium bowl to extract one-third cup (80 grams) of juice. Use the juice in place of the liqueur, and the cherries left in the strainer in place of the drunken cherries. The ganache won't have the same depth of flavor, but it will be delicious nonetheless.

Makes 30 macarons

FILLING

7 ounces (200 grams) white chocolate, coarsely chopped

⅓ cup (80 grams) strained Esin Giz's Sour Cherry Liqueur (page 288) or freshly squeezed sour cherry juice (see headnote)

⅓ cup (60 grams) drained drunken sour cherries from Esin Giz's Sour Cherry Liqueur (page 288) or fresh sour cherries left from juicing (see headnote)

MACARON SHELLS

60 Hazelnut Macaron Shells (page 56)

To make the filling, in a medium heatproof bowl set over a medium saucepan filled with 2 inches (5 cm) of barely simmering water, melt the chocolate, stirring occasionally with a silicone spatula. Stir in the liqueur. The chocolate may seize at first; keep stirring until a smooth ganache forms. Remove the bowl from the pan and let cool to room temperature, stirring occasionally.

Press the drained sour cherries between paper towels to remove excess moisture. Cut them into ¼ inch (6 mm) pieces and stir them into the white chocolate ganache.

Scrape the filling into a shallow bowl and cover tightly with plastic wrap, pressing it directly onto the surface. Refrigerate until the filling is firm enough to hold its shape when piped, 2 to 3 hours. (The filling will keep, wrapped airtight, in the refrigerator for up to 2 days. If the filling has chilled longer than 3 hours, let it stand at room temperature until soft enough to pipe.)

To assemble the macarons, fit a large pastry bag with a ⅜-inch (1-cm) plain round tip (Ateco #804), twist the tip of the bag, place it in a tall glass, and fold the top of the bag down over the edge of the glass. Scrape the filling into the bag, unfold the cuff, and twist to enclose the filling.

Pipe about 2 teaspoons (0.3 ounces; 9 grams) of filling onto the flat sides of half (30) of the macaron shells. Top with the other half of the shells, flat sides down, pressing lightly to spread the filling to the edges. Put the macarons on a baking sheet, cover the sheet tightly with plastic wrap, and refrigerate for at least 4 hours, or preferably 24 hours. Before serving, let them stand at room temperature for 30 minutes.

Storage: The macarons will keep in an airtight container in the refrigerator for up to 24 hours.

CHOCOLATE & LAVENDER MACARONS

When I sat down to write the descriptions for the macaron recipes, I realized that the previous three all call for a seasonal ingredient. I couldn't bear the thought of your waiting for the right season to make macarons. I'm sure you would have thought of matching a basic filling with any of the shells, but I had been aching for an opportunity to couple chocolate with lavender for the longest time.

Makes 30 macarons

FILLING

⅔ cup (160 grams) heavy cream, plus more if needed

1 tablespoon plus 1 teaspoon (2 grams) dried culinary lavender flowers

4.2 ounces (120 grams) bittersweet chocolate (70% cacao), finely chopped

2 tablespoons (25 grams) granulated sugar

2 tablespoons (1 ounce; 30 grams) unsalted butter, softened

MACARON SHELLS

60 Cocoa Macaron Shells (page 56)

To make the filling, in a medium saucepan over medium-high heat, bring the cream and lavender flowers to a simmer, stirring occasionally. Take the pan off the heat, cover, and let steep for 20 minutes. Pour the cream through a fine-mesh strainer set over a glass measuring cup, pressing hard on the flowers with a silicone spatula to extract as much of the infused cream as possible. Discard the flowers. Add additional cream if needed to make ½ cup (120 grams) of infused cream.

Put the chocolate in a medium heatproof bowl.

Pour the infused cream into a medium saucepan and add the sugar. Set the pan over medium heat and bring to just below a boil, stirring frequently. Take the pan off the heat and pour about half of the hot cream over the chocolate. Stir gently with a silicone spatula until blended. Add the rest of the cream, stirring gently until the chocolate melts completely. Gently stir in the butter.

Cover the bowl tightly with plastic wrap, pressing it directly onto the surface of the filling. Refrigerate until the filling is firm enough to hold its shape when piped, about 1 hour. (The filling will keep in the refrigerator for up to 3 days. If the filling has chilled longer than 1 hour, let it stand at room temperature until soft enough to pipe.)

To assemble the macarons, fit a large pastry bag with a ⅜-inch (1-cm) plain round tip (Ateco #804), twist the tip of the bag, place it in a tall glass, and fold the top of the bag down over the edge of the glass. Scrape the filling into the bag, unfold the cuff, and twist to enclose the filling.

Pipe about 2 teaspoons (0.3 ounces; 9 grams) of filling onto the flat sides of half (30) of the macaron shells. Top with the other half of the shells, flat sides down, pressing lightly to spread the filling to the edges. Put the macarons on a baking sheet, cover the sheet tightly with plastic wrap, and refrigerate for at least 4 hours, or preferably 24 hours. Before serving, let them stand at room temperature for 30 minutes.

Storage: The macarons will keep in an airtight container in the refrigerator for up to 24 hours.

CHEESE & SESAME STRAWS

Give me a *simit*—a ring-shaped Turkish bread beaded with sesame seeds—cut crosswise, overstuffed with slices of aged *Trakya kaşar* cheese, and a strong Turkish tea alongside, and I'll ask for nothing more. I can eat that sandwich for days on end and never tire of it. But I have one condition: the simit must be fresh from the oven. For that to happen, you would have to either make it at home (see page 212)—at least a three-hour process—or camp outside a simit bakery. To satisfy my craving for a just-out-of-the-oven version of this sandwich almost instantly, I came up with these straws that round out my cookie collection, to which I've allocated a permanent parking space in my ever packed-to-the-brim freezer. With sharp cheese and butter comprising more than half of the dough, the only thing missing is a glass of strong Turkish tea.

At home, I make these straws with aged kaşar cheese from the Trakya region (the European side of Turkey). The semi-hard, salty, sharp cheese is made with a mixture of sheep's and goat's milk. A good-quality aged Trakya kaşar cheese is difficult if not impossible to find outside of Turkey, so I recommend Pecorino Romano here, the closest cheese I know.

Brown sesame seeds are my favorite coating, but I receive just as many compliments when I coat these with poppy seeds, flax seeds, anise seeds, nettle seeds, or a combination of them. If you're feeling adventurous, feel free to add spices to the dough—black or cayenne pepper for heat, turmeric for a woody aroma and vibrant color, or thyme for an herbaceous accent.

Makes 28 straws

6.3 ounces (180 grams) aged Trakya kaşar cheese or Pecorino Romano, finely grated

1 cup (140 grams) all-purpose flour

1 teaspoon (4 grams) baking powder

5 tablespoons plus 2 teaspoons (2.8 ounces; 80 grams) cold unsalted butter, cut into small pieces

1 tablespoon (15 grams) water

1 large egg white, lightly beaten

¼ cup plus 1 tablespoon (50 grams) brown sesame seeds

In the bowl of a food processor fitted with a metal blade, process the cheese, flour, and baking powder until well blended, about 2 minutes. Add the butter and pulse until coarse crumbs form. Add the water and process until the dough gathers around the blade, about 30 seconds.

Cut a 28-inch-long (71-cm) sheet of parchment paper. Following the photos on page 74, fold the parchment in half lengthwise, then fold over the three open sides to create an 8-by-11-inch (20.5-by-28-cm) envelope. Unfold the envelope and scrape the dough into the center of the 8-by-11-inch rectangle. Leaving about a ⅜-inch (1-cm) border all around, spread out the dough with your fingertips as evenly as possible. Fold the envelope, creasing it firmly, and flip it so that the open sides are secured. Roll out the dough from the center to the edges to create an 8-by-11-inch slab of even height. Flip the dough and unfold the envelope.

Using a pastry brush, brush a layer of egg white over the surface. Sprinkle the sesame seeds evenly on top. Fold the parchment paper over the sesame seeds and gently press it all over with your palm to adhere the seeds to the dough. Fold over the other two sides, transfer the envelope to a baking sheet, and chill until firm, at least 2 hours in the refrigerator or about 25 minutes in the freezer.

Meanwhile, set a rack in the middle of the oven and preheat the oven to 350°F (175°C). Line a baking sheet with parchment paper.

Place the chilled dough on a flat surface and unfold the envelope. Cut the dough crosswise into ⅜-inch-thick (1-cm) slices to make 28 straws, each ⅜ inch by 8 inches (1 cm by 20.5 cm). (At this point, you can wrap them airtight and refrigerate for up to 3 days or freeze for up to 2 months. No need to thaw, though you may need to add a couple of minutes to the baking time.)

(continued on page 75)

Arrange as many straws as you can fit on the prepared baking sheet, leaving 1 inch (2.5 cm) between them. Keep the rest of the unbaked straws in the refrigerator.

Bake until the edges of the straws are golden, about 24 minutes. Set the sheet on a wire rack to cool for 10 minutes, then transfer the straws directly onto the rack to cool completely. Repeat with the remaining straws.

Storage: The straws will keep in an airtight container at room temperature for up to 5 days.

BROWNIES

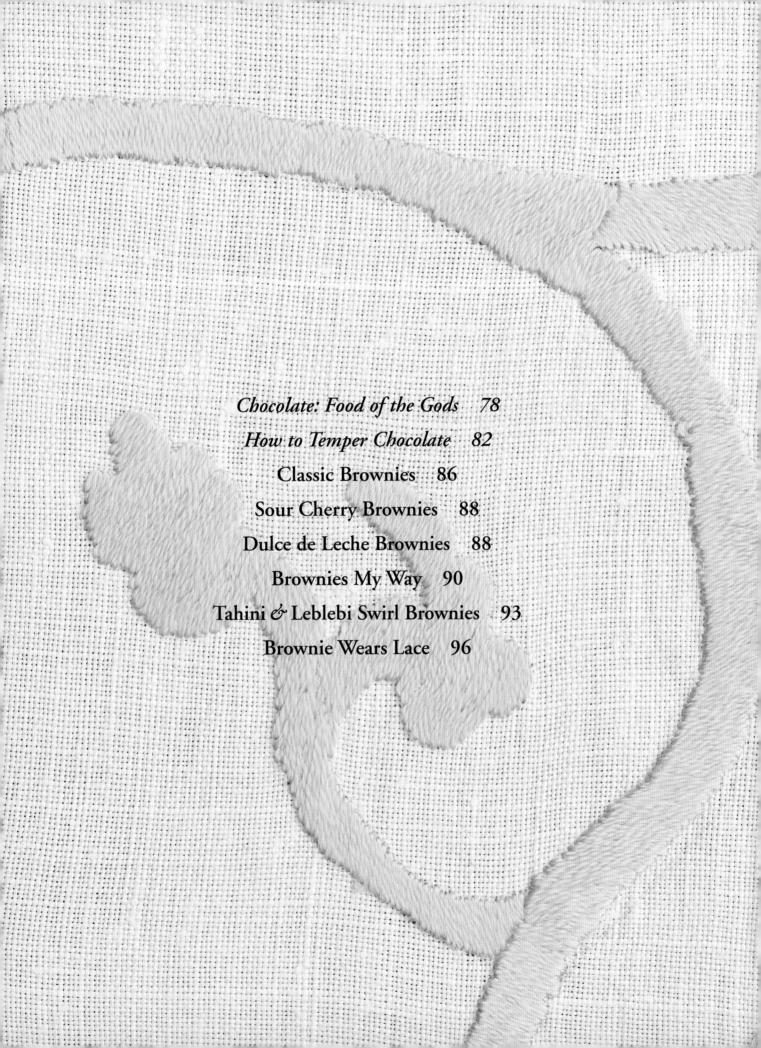

Chocolate: Food of the Gods

Life is too short to eat average brownies, and time spent in the kitchen is gone forever. I'm a big believer in spending not only the time and effort necessary to find the best ingredients but also the money to buy them. The best isn't always the most expensive, but at those times when it is I remind myself of something my father used to say: "Always buy the best ingredient money can buy. If it's out of your budget buy half as much, but buy the best."

Generally, I'd rather explain the defining characteristics of my preferred ingredients than identify name brands so that you won't feel pressured to seek out a certain product. Here, I'm making an exception to share greater detail about my choices. Let's start with a few terms that will help you to identify the best chocolate for a given recipe.

CACAO CONTENT

As you'll see throughout the book, I generally call for bittersweet chocolate with 70 percent cacao, a reference to the percentage of cacao solids (dry [nonfat] cacao solids plus cocoa butter) in the chocolate. For all types of sweetened dark chocolate, you can assume that the rest (30 percent in this case) is sugar. (I'll ignore the minute amounts of lecithin and vanilla, which together make up less than 1 percent.) Knowing this, you can easily calculate the sugar in chocolate: with 55 percent cacao content, a typical semisweet chocolate has 45 percent sugar, for example. For a typical 4-ounce (115-gram) chocolate bar, the difference in sugar between a chocolate with 70 percent and 55 percent cacao is 0.6 ounces (17 grams). That may not seem like a lot, but bear in mind that the higher percentage chocolate has not only less sugar but also more (bitter) dry cacao solids, making the difference in sweetness more significant than it might seem. You may not notice the difference in recipes using small amounts of chocolate, but it will be pronounced in those with larger amounts, such as brownies. Varying cacao content also affects the baked good's texture, as those with higher percentages add more solids.

The cacao percentage on a chocolate label accounts for both the dry cacao solids and the cocoa butter, the latter having no effect on bitterness. The proportions of each, along with the type(s) of cacao beans and production methods used, will affect the intensity of chocolate flavor, so a chocolate with a higher cacao percentage won't *always* taste more bitter.

Manufacturers don't usually break down the percentages of dry cacao solids and cocoa butter, but it is useful to know, as the amount of cocoa butter is a good indicator of melting quality: chocolate with more cocoa butter has lower viscosity when melted, making it perfect for forming thin coatings when dipping and molding.

BITTERSWEET CHOCOLATE

The U.S. Food and Drug Administration (FDA) defines semisweet chocolate and bittersweet chocolate as "sweet chocolate that contains not less than 35 percent by weight of chocolate liquor." That definition allows for a large range and doesn't make a clear distinction between semisweet and bittersweet, so it's best to rely on the cacao content rather than the description.

The recipes in this book were tested using chocolate with a cacao content of 62 percent to 70 percent from a variety of brands, including Callebaut, Guittard, Lindt, Michel Cluizel, Scharffen Berger, and Valrhona.

My top choice for bittersweet chocolate is Valrhona Guanaja. It has an intense and earthy flavor with coffee and molasses notes, and most important of all, the creamiest mouthfeel I've ever experienced in a bittersweet chocolate. It has a 70 percent cacao content, of which 42.2 percent comes from cocoa butter. Another favorite is Valrhona Manjari, which is acidic and sharp with red fruit notes. It has a 64 percent cacao content, including 39.4 percent cocoa butter.

(continued on page 81)

MILK CHOCOLATE

In addition to the FDA-required minimum of 10 percent cacao solids (dry cacao solids plus cocoa butter) and sugar, milk chocolate contains milk solids and milk fat, usually in the form of whole milk powder. None of the recipes in this book calls for milk chocolate, but if you use it for baking, I'd recommend a chocolate with a much higher cacao percentage than the FDA minimum, such as Scharffen Berger Extra Rich Milk (41 percent cacao) or Valrhona Jivara Lactée (40 percent cacao).

WHITE CHOCOLATE

White chocolate is made up of cocoa butter, sugar, milk solids, milk fat, vanilla, and lecithin. With no dry cacao solids, the cacao percentage on the label refers to cocoa butter only. Avoid white chocolate that contains other fats. My favorite white chocolates are Lindt (29 percent cacao) and Valrhona Ivoire (35 percent cacao).

Because it contains no dry cacao solids, I refused to call it chocolate for the longest time. Finally, I accepted it for what it is and now I can't stop baking with it. Make the Three-Bean Vanilla Bundt Cake (page 106) and you'll be amazed at the velvety crumb, thanks to white chocolate.

BLOND CHOCOLATE

There have been many crazes in the food blogosphere over the last decade, and I am surprised that blond chocolate wasn't one of them. Technically, blond chocolate is not a designated category. It is essentially caramelized white chocolate, which is nothing new, but Valrhona was the first to produce a stable couverture version.

Frédéric Bau, the founder of L'Ecole du Grand Chocolat Valrhona, is the mastermind behind Valrhona Dulcey, the first couverture blond chocolate. It has a toasty, buttery, biscuit-like flavor, with a final hint of salt, akin to a freshly baked croissant dipped in dulce de leche.

With a cacao content of 32 percent, Dulcey is made from cocoa butter, sugar, whole milk powder, dried skimmed milk, whey, butter, lecithin, and vanilla. I use it for the ganache layer of Brownie Wears Lace (page 96), pair it with cream cheese

and ground cinnamon to make the frosting for my carrot cake (see page 122), and turn it into a glaze for Mocha Éclairs (page 234). If you can't find it, substitute a good-quality white chocolate.

CACAO NIBS

Cacao nibs are cacao beans that have been fermented, dried, roasted, separated from their husks, and cracked into smaller pieces. They don't taste as bitter as you might expect, and they have a delicate crunch, thanks to their 55 percent cocoa butter content. You'll need them only for the Mocha Éclairs (page 234) in this book, but you can use them in other recipes when you'd like to introduce a crunchy texture and a mild bitterness. When I make Granola (page 236) with hazelnuts and milk chocolate, I sometimes add a small handful to balance the sweetness of the chocolate. They also make an interesting addition to Chocolate Chip Cookies (page 27).

UNSWEETENED CHOCOLATE & COCOA POWDER

In the chocolate-making process, cacao nibs are ground into a paste, which becomes chocolate liquor. Unsweetened chocolate is made with this paste and contains no sugar.

To make cocoa powder, most of the cocoa butter is removed from the chocolate liquor and the remaining solids are processed into a fine powder. There are two kinds of unsweetened cocoa powder: natural and Dutch-processed. Natural cocoa powder is acidic and has a pronounced bitterness and light brown color. Dutch-processed cocoa powder is made from cacao beans that have been treated with an alkalizing agent, which neutralizes the acidity, raising the pH level from an acidic 5 to a neutral 7. In the process, it becomes darker in color and milder in flavor.

Whether or not the two may be used interchangeably depends on the recipe. In cake and cookie recipes that include chemical leaveners like baking powder and baking soda, my answer would be a definite no—do not substitute one for the other. For the most reliable result, I recommend that you always use the type of cocoa called for in recipes.

I am a big fan of Valrhona cocoa powder (Dutch-processed) for its deep, intense flavor and dark, reddish-brown color.

How to Temper Chocolate

We have cocoa butter to thank for chocolate's ability to melt in our mouths. Solid at room temperature, cocoa butter has a melting point just below our body temperature. And whom shall we credit for chocolate's glorious sheen and fascinating snap? Again, cocoa butter (and the kind people who temper it).

When you buy chocolate, assuming that it has been stored properly, it comes in tempered form—meaning that it is glossy, has a firm snap, and melts smoothly. When you melt it to use for dipping, enrobing, molding, shaping, or other applications, chocolate loses its temper. If you use it without tempering it first, the chocolate will look dull and become soft when solidified. In order for the chocolate to regain its gloss and snap, and melt smoothly in your mouth after it has set, you must temper it.

Tempering is the process of melting chocolate, cooling it to a specific temperature range while agitating (stirring) it, and finally rewarming it to a specific temperature range and maintaining it in that range for as long as you work with it.

Before I get into more detail about tempering, you should know that there's just one recipe in the book that requires it (Fernando Rocher, page 279), and a few others that benefit from tempering. If you're not ready to tackle this challenge just yet, or simply are not interested in the subject, feel free to skip ahead to the brownie recipes.

In my opinion, there are only two reliable methods of tempering chocolate suitable for the home baker: seeding and tabling.

In the seeding method, you melt three-quarters of the chocolate and use the remaining unmelted chocolate (still in temper) to seed the melted (now untempered) chocolate. In the tabling method, you melt all of the chocolate, work three-quarters of it on a marble slab, and then stir it back into the remaining melted chocolate in the bowl.

I'll explain each method in detail, including the temperature ranges required for the brand of sweetened dark chocolate I prefer. (Those ranges may differ slightly for other brands; if the manufacturer has provided temperature ranges on the label, use

those.) For milk, white, and blond chocolates, follow the same steps, but refer to the temperature ranges provided in the chart opposite.

For both methods, you'll need a heatproof bowl (preferably stainless steel), a saucepan, a silicone spatula, and an instant-read thermometer. For the tabling method, you'll also need a 16-by-24-inch (40.5-by-61-cm) marble slab and a large offset spatula. Before starting, make sure that the bowl, utensils, and marble slab are all thoroughly washed, rinsed, and dried. Even a drop of water may cause the chocolate to seize and become a dull, grainy paste.

TEMPERING BY SEEDING

Finely chop one-quarter of the chocolate you will temper and reserve. Coarsely chop the remaining three-quarters of chocolate and place it in a medium heatproof bowl. Set the bowl over a medium saucepan filled with 2 inches (5 cm) of barely simmering water and melt the chocolate, stirring occasionally with a spatula. Maintain the water in the pan at a bare simmer, and keep the bottom of the bowl above (not touching) the water throughout the process. When completely melted, the chocolate will be around 122°F (50°C). Remove the bowl from the pan, add the reserved chocolate in small batches, and stir until an instant-read thermometer registers between 82°F and 84°F (28°C and 29°C). Place the bowl back over the simmering water and stir until it registers between 88°F and 90°F (31°C and 32°C).

Pros and cons: In this method, you're adding tempered (unmelted) chocolate to untempered (melted) chocolate, which brings the temperature down to the desired range and introduces stable fat crystals that will seed the untempered chocolate, bringing the entire mass into temper. It is an easy, clean, and efficient method, but it has a few disadvantages. First, stirring in the reserved pieces to cool the melted chocolate takes a lot of time. The tabling method is much faster, as the chocolate is agitated on a naturally cold surface. Also, the chocolate may reach the desired temperature range before the added pieces melt completely, in which case you may need to remove the unmelted pieces.

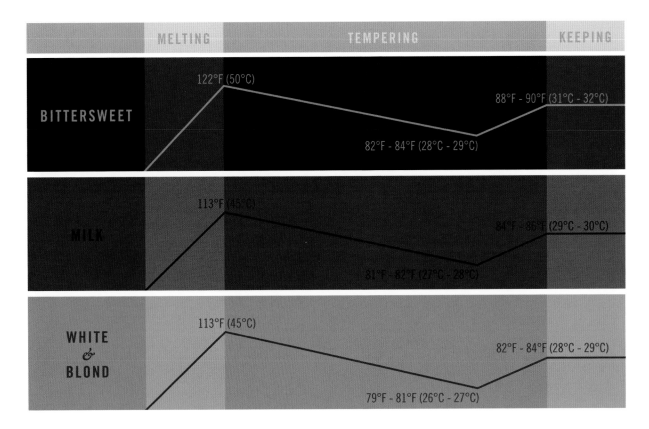

	MELTING	TEMPERING	KEEPING
BITTERSWEET	122°F (50°C)	82°F - 84°F (28°C - 29°C)	88°F - 90°F (31°C - 32°C)
MILK	113°F (45°C)	81°F - 82°F (27°C - 28°C)	84°F - 86°F (29°C - 30°C)
WHITE & BLOND	113°F (45°C)	79°F - 81°F (26°C - 27°C)	82°F - 84°F (28°C - 29°C)

TEMPERING BY TABLING

Coarsely chop all of the chocolate you will temper and place it in a medium heatproof bowl. Set the bowl over a medium saucepan filled with 2 inches (5 cm) of barely simmering water and melt the chocolate, stirring occasionally with a spatula. Maintain the water in the pan at a bare simmer, and keep the bottom of the bowl above (not touching) the water throughout the process. When completely melted, the chocolate will be around 122°F (50°C). Remove the bowl from the pan, wipe the bottom of the bowl with a clean cloth, and pour three-quarters of the chocolate onto a 16-by-24-inch (40.5-by-61-cm) or larger marble slab. Using a large metal offset spatula, cool and agitate the chocolate by spreading it back and forth, occasionally dragging the outer edges to the center, until the chocolate begins to thicken and registers between 82°F and 84°F (28°C and 29°C) on an instant-read thermometer (see photos on page 84). Immediately scrape the

chocolate back into the bowl of melted chocolate, stirring until smooth. The chocolate should be between 88°F and 90°F (31°C and 32°C). If it is lower, briefly place the bowl back over the simmering water and stir until it is in that range.

Pros and cons: This is the method I use at home. It requires more skill and is messier than the seeding method, but it is faster and more reliable when working with small amounts of chocolate. Run the marble slab under hot water and the chocolate will quickly melt away.

TESTING

To determine whether the chocolate is properly tempered, smear a small amount on a naturally cool surface, such as marble or stainless steel, and allow it to set. If the chocolate sets within 2 minutes and is smooth and glossy, you've done it. If it doesn't set at all, or is dull and streaky when set, you'll have to start the process over again (using the same chocolate).

MAINTAINING TEMPER

If you're planning to work with tempered chocolate for an extended period of time (such as to make the Fernando Rocher on page 279) you will need to hold the tempered chocolate within the desired temperature range. Keep the thermometer in the bowl at all times and your eye on the display. If it goes below range, briefly place the bowl back over the simmering water and stir until it is back in range.

TEMPERING SMALL AMOUNTS OF CHOCOLATE

When you work with very small amounts of chocolate—5 ounces (140 grams) or less—your chances of success are slim with the seeding and tabling methods. A small amount of chocolate responds to changes very quickly, making it hard to control its temperature and to agitate it sufficiently to form stable crystals. I've come up with a method similar to seeding for tempering small amounts of chocolate, with which I've had an 80 percent success rate. I use this method only when tempering is optional, such as in the case of Brownie Wears Lace (page 96), which may be refrigerated and served cold.

First, the water in the saucepan should be at the barest simmer and the bottom of the bowl should never touch the water. It is important that the chocolate warm up slowly, so be sure to chop the chocolate into large pieces. If you're using fèves (oval disks of couverture chocolate, slightly larger than a quarter), use them whole.

Put the chocolate in a medium heatproof bowl, set it over a medium saucepan filled with 2 inches (5 cm) of water at the barest simmer, and wait without stirring until approximately two-thirds of the chocolate pieces melt. Remove the bowl from the pan, wipe the bottom with a cloth, and scrape the chocolate into a separate bowl. Place the bowl on a naturally cool surface, such as marble or stainless steel. Using a silicone spatula, stir the chocolate until the unmelted pieces melt completely. If there are any remaining unmelted pieces, place the bowl briefly over the hot water, then remove the bowl from the pan and stir until the chocolate melts completely.

CLASSIC BROWNIES

After buying my first dozen cookbooks and baking the things I was familiar with, I noticed something odd: brownies were always included in the cookie chapter. I knew exactly why they weren't included with cakes, but classifying them as cookies seemed even less appropriate. Although I eventually learned that the word "cookie" has a broader meaning in the United States than in Turkey, I still have trouble classifying them as cookies. To me, they are neither cookies nor cakes, so I've given them their own chapter.

This is my classic brownie—fudgy, intensely chocolaty, and crisp around the edges, with a tissue-thin crinkly crust and a chewy-creamy center. I use the best chocolate I can find (see page 78) and never add whole nuts to the batter (a nuisance, in my opinion). What I do add in two of my favorite variations are drunken sour cherries from Esin Giz's Sour Cherry Liqueur (page 288), or puddles of Dulce de Leche (page 315).

Makes 9 large or 16 small brownies

10 tablespoons plus 2 teaspoons (5.3 ounces; 150 grams) unsalted butter, cut into large pieces, plus more for pan

10.6 ounces (300 grams) bittersweet chocolate (70% cacao), coarsely chopped

⅔ cup (93 grams) all-purpose flour

2 tablespoons (13 grams) Dutch-processed unsweetened cocoa powder

½ teaspoon (4 grams) fine sea salt

3 large eggs

1 cup plus 2 tablespoons (225 grams) granulated sugar

Set a rack in the middle of the oven and preheat the oven to 350°F (175°C).

Butter the bottom and sides of an 8-inch (20.5-cm) square baking pan. Line the pan with two overlapping strips of parchment paper that are the width of the pan bottom and long enough to cover the bottom and sides with 2 inches (5 cm) of overhang on each side. Butter the lower parchment to secure the top sheet.

In a medium heatproof bowl set over a medium saucepan filled with 2 inches (5 cm) of barely simmering water, melt the butter and chocolate, stirring occasionally with a silicone spatula. Remove the bowl from the pan and let cool completely, stirring occasionally.

Sift together the flour, cocoa powder, and salt into a medium bowl.

In the bowl of a stand mixer fitted with the whisk attachment, beat the eggs and sugar at medium-high speed until the sugar dissolves and the mixture is pale and thick, about 4 minutes. Add the cooled chocolate mixture and beat at medium speed until blended, about 30 seconds. Add the flour mixture and beat at the lowest speed just until incorporated.

Remove the bowl from the mixer and scrape down the sides with a silicone spatula, reaching down to the bottom to incorporate any unmixed dry ingredients. Scrape the batter into the prepared pan and spread it evenly with a small offset spatula.

Bake until a paper-thin crinkly crust forms on the surface of the brownie, about 25 minutes. A wooden toothpick inserted into the center should come out with thick, gooey batter clinging to it. Set the pan on a wire rack to cool completely. As the brownie cools, the center will sink slightly.

Using the parchment overhang as handles, lift the brownie out of the pan and transfer it to a cutting board. Cut the brownie into 3 or 4 equal strips in each direction to make 9 or 16 squares. Serve at room temperature or chilled.

Storage: The brownies will keep, wrapped airtight, at room temperature for up to 2 days or in the refrigerator for up to 5 days.

(variations on page 88)

SOUR CHERRY BROWNIES

Prepare the classic brownie batter as directed on page 86. Scrape the batter into the prepared pan and spread it evenly with a small offset spatula. Use a slotted spoon to retrieve ½ cup (90 grams) of drunken sour cherries from Esin Giz's Sour Cherry Liqueur (page 288) or from a jar of store-bought sour cherries soaked in liqueur, such as Griottines. Press the cherries between paper towels to remove excess moisture. Scatter the cherries evenly over the brownie and use a fingertip to push them into the batter. Smooth the batter with an offset spatula to completely bury the cherries. Bake the brownie as directed in the recipe.

DULCE DE LECHE BROWNIES

Prepare the classic brownie batter as directed on page 00. Scrape the batter into the prepared pan and spread it evenly with a small offset spatula. Drop ⅓ cup (110 grams) chilled Dulce de Leche or Cajeta (page 315) in teaspoon-size dollops evenly over the batter. Bury the dulce de leche by using a fingertip to repeatedly poke each dollop into the batter. The dulce de leche will stick to your fingertip at first but will release eventually. Bake the brownie as directed in the recipe.

BROWNIES MY WAY

In 2007, about a year into my blogging journey, I'd baked enough brownies to identify my ideal version, and I wanted the world to know, too. It was a fudgy brownie topped with melted milk chocolate and sprinkled with sliced pistachios. The angels must have been on my side the day I took its photo, because when I cut a slice, the chocolate layer snapped at just the right place, with the perfect piece of sliced pistachio staring you right in the face. I didn't know anyone who wouldn't want to grab it right off the screen.

My readers loved the photo, and many of them tried the recipe with great success. When I say "my readers," I mean a few dozen people. But little did I know that one of them was the inimitable baker Nick Malgieri. I learned this when he sent me an e-mail asking for a recipe for an article about baking blogs he was writing for the *Washington Post*. A couple of weeks later, Brownies My Way was published in the paper along with my photo of it. The icing on the cake was a chart about baking blogs that ran with the online version of the article. I was listed alongside legends like Dorie Greenspan, Peter Reinhart, and Rose Levy Beranbaum. It was just a list of blogs mentioned in the article and in no way equated me with the others, but the mere fact that my name was a few pixels below theirs put me over the moon. I melted like the chocolate on my brownie.

My readership increased a hundredfold overnight and several other interviews and media mentions followed. It was the first turning point in my blogging career, and it led to many proud moments I couldn't have dreamed of.

Ten years have passed and I've learned a lot about brownies and baking in general, so the recipe has changed a bit. Sliced pistachios are whole now (chopped into coarse pieces), because there's no such thing as too much pistachio. There is such a thing as too much chocolate, however, even for a brownie. Back then, my priority was to increase the chocolate as much as I could, by any means possible. Now, it is all about balance, with a less sweet, less chocolaty brownie topped with intense bittersweet chocolate. I still like to serve these cold, but I've reduced their size by cutting the brownie into twenty-five pieces rather than nine.

Makes 25 tiny brownies

BROWNIE

12 tablespoons (6 ounces; 170 grams) unsalted butter, cut into large pieces, plus more for pan

8.8 ounces (250 grams) bittersweet chocolate (70% cacao), coarsely chopped

⅔ cup (93 grams) all-purpose flour

¼ cup (25 grams) Dutch-processed unsweetened cocoa powder

¼ teaspoon (2 grams) fine sea salt

3 large eggs

1 cup (200 grams) granulated sugar

Set a rack in the middle of the oven and preheat the oven to 350°F (175°C).

Butter the bottom and sides of an 8-inch (20.5-cm) square baking pan. Line the pan with two overlapping strips of parchment paper that are the width of the pan bottom and long enough to cover the bottom and sides with 2 inches (5 cm) of overhang on each side. Butter the lower parchment to secure the top sheet.

To make the brownie, in a medium heatproof bowl set over a medium saucepan filled with 2 inches (5 cm) of barely simmering water, melt the butter and chocolate, stirring occasionally with a silicone spatula. Remove the bowl from the pan and let cool completely, stirring occasionally.

Sift together the flour, cocoa powder, and salt into a medium bowl.

In the bowl of a stand mixer fitted with the whisk attachment, beat the eggs and sugar at medium-high speed until the sugar dissolves and the mixture is pale and thick, about 4 minutes. Add the cooled chocolate mixture and beat at medium speed until blended, about 30 seconds. Add the flour mixture and beat at the lowest speed just until incorporated.

Remove the bowl from the mixer and scrape down the sides with a silicone spatula, reaching down to the bottom to incorporate any unmixed dry ingredients. Scrape the batter into the prepared pan and spread it evenly with a small offset spatula.

(ingredients and method continued on page 92)

5 ounces (140 grams) bittersweet
chocolate (70% cacao), coarsely
chopped

⅓ cup (45 grams) whole blanched
pistachios, coarsely chopped (and
toasted, if desired)

Bake until a paper-thin crinkly crust forms on the surface of the brownie, about 25 minutes. A wooden toothpick inserted into the center should come out with thick, gooey batter clinging to it. Set the pan on a wire rack to cool completely. As the brownie cools, the center will sink slightly.

Using the parchment overhang as handles, lift the brownie out of the pan, peel away the parchment, and transfer it to a wire rack set over a baking sheet.

To make the topping, in a medium heatproof bowl set over a medium saucepan filled with 2 inches (5 cm) of barely simmering water, melt the chocolate, stirring occasionally with a silicone spatula. Remove the bowl from the pan and let cool for 10 minutes, stirring occasionally.

Scrape the melted chocolate onto the center of the brownie and, using an offset spatula, spread it evenly over the top, allowing it to cascade over the sides. Scatter the pistachios evenly over the top. Refrigerate, uncovered, until the topping is firm, about 1 hour.

Using a cake lifter, transfer the brownie to a cutting board. Warm the blade of a large knife with a kitchen torch or under hot running water (wipe dry before using) and cut the brownie into 5 equal strips in each direction to make 25 squares, wiping the blade clean with a damp paper towel between cuts and rewarming it as needed. Serve cold.

Storage: The brownies will keep, wrapped airtight, in the refrigerator for up to 5 days.

TAHINI & LEBLEBİ SWIRL BROWNIES

Brownie recipes are among the easiest to make gluten-free. As the flour plays no essential role (many recipes have none at all), you can freely substitute it with an array of gluten-free alternatives. I'm sure you've seen several versions, but have you tried brownies made with *sarı leblebi* flour?

Sarı leblebi refers to double-roasted hulled chickpeas (leblebi) that are yellow (sarı). It is a beloved Turkish snack, available at every *kuruyemişçi* (specialty shop selling dried nuts, seeds, and fruits), sometimes roasted right by the entrance to entice customers with its toasty smell. Roasting the chickpeas twice chars them in spots, giving them an intensely toasty flavor. There is also *beyaz* (white) leblebi, made from unhulled chickpeas; these go through a different process and aren't as toasty. Sarı leblebi may be found ground into a flour, but as I always have the snack on hand, I grind the flour at home using a mortar and pestle.

Used in place of all-purpose flour in a brownie recipe, sarı leblebi would be nearly impossible to detect—it does not change the brownies' taste, texture, or color. And that is what we call a successful gluten-free conversion, right? Exactly, but I can't claim that as an achievement because the same would be true using almost any gluten-free flour. Instead, my objective was to highlight the stand-in's toasty flavor, not only making it gluten-free but also adding a new nuance. Since adding additional sarı leblebi flour to the batter would upset the recipe's balance, I tried reducing the chocolate and replacing almost half of the butter with another toasty ingredient: tahini. The brownies had an earthy flavor, but neither the toasty flour nor the tahini was pronounced. To bring that toasty flavor forward, I came up with a tahini swirl thickened with sarı leblebi flour. Yes, I found a way to sneak more in!

Look for sarı leblebi in Middle Eastern grocery stores or online, or substitute roasted chickpea flour (also called roasted gram flour or *besan*), found in Indian or Burmese food shops. Alternatively, roast regular chickpea flour in a cast-iron skillet over medium-low heat until it is lightly browned and smells nutty.

Makes 9 large or 16 small brownies

BROWNIE

6 tablespoons (3 ounces; 85 grams) unsalted butter, cut into large pieces, plus more for pan

8.8 ounces (250 grams) bittersweet chocolate (70% cacao), coarsely chopped

½ cup (124 grams) tahini, at room temperature

¾ cup (78 grams) sarı leblebi (double-roasted chickpea) flour or roasted chickpea flour (see headnote)

2 tablespoons (13 grams) Dutch-processed unsweetened cocoa powder

¼ teaspoon (2 grams) fine sea salt

3 large eggs

1 cup plus 2 tablespoons (225 grams) granulated sugar

Set a rack in the middle of the oven and preheat the oven to 350°F (175°C).

Butter the bottom and sides of an 8-inch (20.5-cm) square baking pan. Line the pan with two overlapping strips of parchment paper that are the width of the pan bottom and long enough to cover the bottom and sides with 2 inches (5 cm) of overhang on each side. Butter the lower parchment to secure the top sheet.

To make the brownie, in a medium heatproof bowl set over a medium saucepan filled with 2 inches (5 cm) of barely simmering water, melt the butter and chocolate, stirring occasionally with a silicone spatula. Remove the bowl from the pan, stir in the tahini, and let cool completely.

Sift together the chickpea flour, cocoa powder, and salt into a medium bowl.

In the bowl of a stand mixer fitted with the whisk attachment, beat the eggs and sugar at medium-high speed until the sugar dissolves and the mixture is pale and thick, about 4 minutes. Add the cooled chocolate mixture and beat at medium speed until blended, about 30 seconds. Add the chickpea flour mixture and beat until incorporated.

Remove the bowl from the mixer and scrape down the sides with a silicone spatula, reaching down to the bottom to incorporate any unmixed dry ingredients. Scrape the batter into the prepared pan and spread it evenly with a small offset spatula.

(ingredients and method continued on page 95)

¼ cup (62 grams) tahini, at room
temperature, plus more if needed

3 tablespoons (20 grams) sarı
leblebi (double-roasted chickpea)
flour or roasted chickpea flour
(see headnote)

Pinch of fine sea salt

To make the topping, in a small bowl, whisk the tahini, chickpea flour, and salt until blended. Check the consistency; when you lift a portion of the topping, it should cascade from the whisk in a thick, solid ribbon that disappears into the topping within 5 seconds. If it appears too thick or stiff, whisk in more tahini, 1 teaspoon (5 grams) at a time, to reach the desired consistency.

Drop the topping in teaspoon-size dollops over the brownie batter, spacing them evenly apart. Gently drag the tip of a dull knife through the dollops of topping to create a swirl pattern.

Bake until a paper-thin crinkly crust forms on the naked parts of the brownie, about 25 minutes. A wooden toothpick inserted into the center should come out with moist crumbs clinging to it. Set the pan on a wire rack to cool completely. As the brownie cools, the center will sink slightly.

Using the parchment overhang as handles, lift the brownie out of the pan and transfer it to a cutting board. Cut the brownie into 3 or 4 equal strips in each direction to make 9 or 16 squares. Serve at room temperature or chilled.

Storage: The brownies will keep, wrapped airtight, at room temperature for up to 2 days or in the refrigerator for up to 5 days.

BROWNIE WEARS LACE

When Dolce & Gabbana asked me to create a dessert in honor of the launch of their digital magazine, *Swide*, I have to admit, I was completely lost. First of all, my fashion knowledge was—and still is—limited to a few seasons of *Project Runway*, and the closest I'd ever gotten to anything by D&G was when I once happened to shop side by side with Domenico Dolce and Stefano Gabbana at Fouquet in Paris. The only thing I knew about them was that they liked chocolate almost as much as I do, but beyond that I had no idea where to start. How I wished I was Pierre Hermé; he would know exactly what to do. I decided to take a look at their website, and after a cheerful welcome from Madonna, I watched a video of their fall/winter runway show.

What I saw on the runway was seduction, wisely (and tastefully, of course) camouflaged with transparent fabric. I already had my heart set on a brownie and thought of a thin layer of hazelnut butter as the seductive element, but I still needed another element to illustrate camouflage. Then the show ended and the team of tailors behind the collection appeared on screen, looking proud and gracious. It was the most inspiring part of the show, reminding me of the appreciation and celebration of craftsmanship. There was only one way to translate craftsmanship into my recipe: chocolate lace. This time, how I wished I were Jacques Torres. He would have piped what I had in mind in the blink of an eye.

It took me many attempts to achieve my vision, but my efforts paid off well: about a year later, Brownie Wears Lace was awarded Best Original Baking and Desserts Recipe in *Saveur* magazine's Best Food Blog Awards in 2011.

But that's the past. I now have an even better brownie recipe and a much more fashionable ingredient to dress it with: blond chocolate, also known as caramelized white chocolate (see page 81).

I can only hope that Mr. Dolce and Mr. Gabbana would be proud.

Makes 9 large brownies

BROWNIE
Classic Brownies (page 86), baked and cooled

GANACHE
5 ounces (140 grams) blond chocolate (preferably Valrhona Dulcey) or white chocolate, finely chopped

⅓ cup (80 grams) heavy cream

CHOCOLATE LACE
2.8 ounces (80 grams) bittersweet chocolate (70% cacao), coarsely chopped

Using the parchment overhang as handles, lift the cooled brownie out of the pan and transfer it to a wire rack. Level the top of the brownie with a large serrated knife and return it to the pan.

To make the ganache, put the chocolate in a medium heatproof bowl.

In a small saucepan over medium heat, bring the heavy cream to just below a boil, stirring frequently. Take the pan off the heat and pour about half of the hot cream over the chocolate. Stir gently with a silicone spatula until blended. Add the rest of the hot cream, stirring gently until the chocolate melts completely.

Scrape the ganache over the brownie and spread it evenly with a small offset spatula. Refrigerate the brownie, uncovered, until the ganache is firm, about 2 hours.

Lift the brownie out of the pan, carefully peel away the parchment, and transfer it to a serving plate.

Press lightly on the ganache with a large knife to mark the brownie in 3 equal strips in each direction. These will provide your border guides for the chocolate lace decoration.

To make the chocolate lace, fit a small pastry bag with an extra-small (1-mm) plain round tip (Ateco #261), twist the tip of the bag, place it in a small glass, and fold the top of the bag down over the edge of the glass.

(continued on page 99)

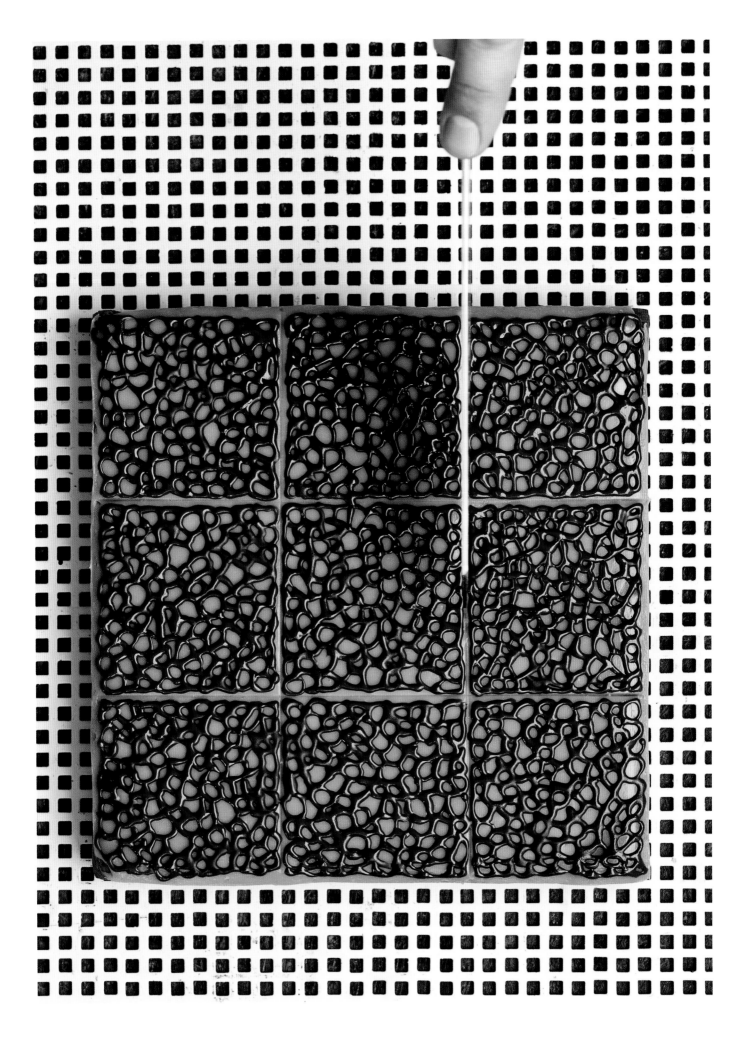

Put the chocolate in a medium heatproof bowl, set it over a medium saucepan filled with 2 inches (5 cm) of water at the barest simmer, and wait, without stirring, until approximately two-thirds of the chocolate pieces melt. Remove the bowl from the pan, wipe the bottom of the bowl with a cloth, and scrape the chocolate into a separate bowl. Place the bowl on a naturally cool surface, such as marble or stainless steel. Using a silicone spatula, stir the chocolate until it melts completely. If any unmelted pieces remain, briefly return the bowl to the pan of hot water, then remove the bowl from the pan and stir to completely melt the chocolate.

Scrape the chocolate into the prepared pastry bag, unfold the cuff, and twist to enclose the chocolate. Pipe the chocolate onto the chilled and marked squares in a lace pattern. If you have succeeded in tempering the chocolate using the method I have described (I have about an 80 percent success rate), the lace layer will set quickly. If it does not set within a few minutes, refrigerate the brownie, uncovered, until the lace is firm, about 20 minutes.

Cut the brownie into 9 equal squares along your guidelines and serve, either at room temperature or chilled.

Storage: The brownies will keep, wrapped airtight, at room temperature for up to 2 days or in the refrigerator for up to 5 days.

CAKES, MUFFINS, CHEESECAKES & MERINGUES

DOUBLE CHOCOLATE BUNDT CAKE

More than half of the six years I spent writing my Turkish cookbook, then creating this English-language version, were devoted to perfecting the recipes. Give me another three years, and I can assure you that some of the recipes would change.

It's not that the recipes are lacking in any way. It's just my nature to continually retest until I've explored every nook and cranny, which sometimes results in my preferring a new version. I have yet to decide whether this compulsion is a blessing or a curse, but knowing that I've done everything I can to perfect a recipe is the only way I find comfort and peace.

Here's something else I can guarantee: If I'm lucky enough to one day publish a book of my greatest hits, drawn from my long list of works published through the years, *this* is the chocolate Bundt cake recipe I will include, exactly as you see it here.

To me, this cake is perfection: strong enough to stand upright, yet fragile enough to yield to the slightest prick of a fork. The intense punch from strong brewed coffee and cocoa powder is softened by the sweet, sticky ganache glaze. Achieving this balance was no easy feat, but I was relentless—I baked one cake after another, tasted them all with and without the glaze, took all kinds of notes, ate more cake while comparing my notes, and finally reached a conclusion. The things I do for you!

Serves 10 to 12

CAKE

14 tablespoons (7 ounces; 200 grams) unsalted butter, softened, plus more for pan

5 ounces (140 grams) bittersweet chocolate (70% cacao), coarsely chopped

½ cup (50 grams) Dutch-processed unsweetened cocoa powder

2 teaspoons (10 grams) pure vanilla extract

½ cup (120 grams) very strong brewed coffee or espresso

½ cup (120 grams) heavy cream

2 cups (280 grams) all-purpose flour

1½ teaspoons (6 grams) baking powder

½ teaspoon (3 grams) baking soda

½ teaspoon (4 grams) fine sea salt

1¾ cups (350 grams) granulated sugar

4 large eggs, at room temperature

Set a rack in the lower third of the oven and preheat the oven to 325°F (160°C).

Generously butter a 10-cup (2.4-liter) Bundt pan. If your pan has an intricate design, use a pastry brush to reach all the nooks and crannies.

To make the cake, in a medium heatproof bowl, combine the chocolate, cocoa powder, and vanilla.

In a small saucepan over medium-high heat, bring the coffee and cream to a boil, stirring occasionally. Take the pan off the heat, pour the coffee mixture over the chocolate mixture, and whisk until the chocolate melts and the cocoa powder dissolves. Let cool completely.

In a medium bowl, whisk together the flour, baking powder, baking soda, and salt.

In the bowl of a stand mixer fitted with the paddle attachment, beat the butter at medium-high speed until creamy, about 2 minutes. Add the sugar and beat until light and fluffy, about 3 minutes. Add the eggs, one at a time, and beat for 1 minute after each addition, scraping down the sides of the bowl as needed. Reduce the speed to low and beat in one-third of the flour mixture, followed by half of the chocolate mixture. Repeat with another third of the flour mixture and the remaining chocolate mixture. Finally, add the remaining flour mixture and beat just until incorporated.

Remove the bowl from the mixer and scrape down the sides of the bowl with a silicone spatula, reaching down to the bottom to incorporate any unmixed dry ingredients. Scrape the batter into the prepared pan and smooth the top.

Bake until a wooden toothpick inserted into the cake comes out clean, 50 to 55 minutes. Set the pan on a wire rack to cool for 10 minutes. Invert the cake onto the rack, set the rack over a baking sheet lined with parchment paper, and let cool completely.

(ingredients and method continued on page 104)

5 ounces (140 grams) bittersweet chocolate (70% cacao), coarsely chopped

¾ cup (180 grams) heavy cream

2 tablespoons (25 grams) granulated sugar

1 teaspoon (5 grams) pure vanilla extract

To make the glaze, put the chocolate in a medium heatproof bowl.

In a medium saucepan over medium-high heat, bring the cream, sugar, and vanilla to just below a boil, stirring frequently. Take the pan off the heat and pour about half of the hot cream mixture over the chocolate. Stir gently with a silicone spatula until blended. Add the rest of the hot cream mixture, stirring gently until the chocolate melts completely. Immediately scrape the glaze into a small heatproof pitcher and pour it over the cake, allowing it to drip down the sides.

Using a cake lifter, transfer the cake onto a serving plate, and serve. (You can scrape the excess glaze on the parchment into a bowl and enjoy it later as an ice cream topping.)

Storage: The cake will keep under a cake dome at room temperature for up to 3 days.

THREE-BEAN VANILLA BUNDT CAKE

The day I accepted white chocolate for what it is—an ingredient made up of fat, sugar, and dry milk solids—rather than air-quoting the word *chocolate* and deeming it unworthy because it contains no dry cacao solids, I opened up a whole new world of possibilities. What if I substituted white chocolate for butter and sugar in a cake?

Darn it, Cenk! You can't beat white chocolate with sugar. How are you going to integrate air into the batter? was my first reaction. *Well, how about a portion of it? Just imagine the added aroma of the cocoa butter. You know you'll like it. You know it is the only reason "real" chocolate melts in your mouth. Think of what it will do to your cakes. Think of the possibilities,* urged the adventurous glutton in me.

I couldn't resist, and the vanilla cake I was working on at the time was the perfect candidate. The cake's starting point was another mini revelation: Sherry Yard's Seven-Bean Vanilla Ice Cream from her book *Desserts by the Yard*. It was one of many components of a dessert she created for the seventy-fifth anniversary of the Oscars: Chocolate Truffle Tart with Chocolate Crème Brûlée Diamonds and Seven-Bean Vanilla Ice Cream. Wouldn't you have fallen off your chair if you had seen it on the menu? I made it and devoured every spoonful. People don't become pastry goddesses for no reason.

This recipe is a humbler version of that ice cream, made as a cake. Three vanilla beans, a couple teaspoons of vanilla extract to amplify their flavor, and white chocolate for that heavenly aroma of cocoa butter.

And just wait until the cake is two days old. When it is tough enough to stand in a toaster without risk of crumbling, cut a thin slice and toast it. The heat revives the vanilla seeds, which become tiny flavor bombs as you nibble on the crusty crumbs. You know you'll like it.

Serves 10 to 12

13 tablespoons (6.5 ounces; 185 grams) unsalted butter, softened, plus more for pan

2¼ cups (315 grams) all-purpose flour, plus more for pan

6.3 ounces (180 grams) white chocolate, coarsely chopped

1¾ teaspoons (7 grams) baking powder

½ teaspoon (4 grams) fine sea salt

3 vanilla beans, split and seeds scraped (see page 32)

1 cup plus 2 tablespoons (225 grams) granulated sugar

4 large eggs, at room temperature

2 teaspoons (10 grams) pure vanilla extract

½ cup (120 grams) whole milk, at room temperature

⅓ cup plus 1 tablespoon (95 grams) heavy cream, at room temperature

Set a rack in the lower third of the oven and preheat the oven to 325°F (160°C).

Generously butter a 10-cup (2.4-liter) Bundt pan. If your pan has an intricate design, use a pastry brush to reach all the nooks and crannies. Dust the pan with flour and tap out the excess.

In a medium heatproof bowl set over a medium saucepan filled with 2 inches (5 cm) of barely simmering water, melt the chocolate, stirring occasionally with a silicone spatula. Remove the bowl from the pan and set aside to cool, stirring occasionally.

Sift together the flour, baking powder, and salt into a large bowl.

In the bowl of a stand mixer fitted with the paddle attachment, beat the butter and vanilla seeds at medium-high speed until creamy, about 2 minutes. Add the sugar and beat until light and fluffy, about 5 minutes. Add the eggs, one at a time, and beat for 1 minute after each addition, scraping down the sides of the bowl as needed. Add the vanilla. Stir the melted chocolate to make sure it is still fluid (if not, warm it just slightly), then beat it in at medium speed until blended, about 30 seconds. Reduce the speed to low and beat in one-third the flour mixture, followed by the milk. Beat in another third of the flour mixture, followed by the cream. Finally, add the remaining flour mixture and beat just until incorporated. You may use the leftover vanilla pod halves in Homemade Vanilla Extract (page 323) or Vanilla Sugar (page 326).

Remove the bowl from the mixer and scrape down the sides of the bowl with a silicone spatula, reaching down to the bottom to incorporate any unmixed dry ingredients. Scrape the batter into the prepared pan and smooth the top.

(continued on page 109)

Bake until a wooden toothpick inserted into the cake comes out clean, 60 to 65 minutes. Set the pan on a wire rack to cool for 10 minutes, then invert the cake directly onto the rack to cool completely.

Using a cake lifter, transfer the cake to a serving plate, and serve.

Storage: The cake will keep, wrapped airtight, at room temperature for up to 3 days. Alternatively, individually wrap slices in plastic wrap and freeze for up to 2 weeks. Before serving, toast the slices in a toaster—no need to thaw.

DEEPLY APPLEY APPLE CAKE

How many pounds of apples can you fit into a Bundt cake that weighs around two-and-a-half pounds straight from the oven? One pound? Two?

I'm proud to report that I've managed to stuff more than four pounds of apples into this cake. More importantly, I've managed to do so without sacrificing texture. This is by far the lightest cake that has come out of my oven.

How I wish *applest* were a word. There really is no better way to describe this cake. After considering several titles, some bordering on the outrageous—The Applest Apple Cake, Ridiculously Appley Apple Cake, Appleooza Cake, and the humble Sweet and Sour Apple Bundt Cake—I've named it Deeply Appley Apple Cake after Nigel Slater's Deeply Appley Apple Crumble from his beautiful book *Ripe.*

The recipe starts by preparing a mildly sour and intensely apple-y apple puree, then continues like a classic butter cake recipe. There are three important notes. First, do not let the apple puree dry out too much. It should be soft enough to dissolve completely in the batter. Second, avoid using a very sweet apple variety; you're already adding plenty of natural sugar with the apples. Decreasing the granulated sugar to balance out a sweeter apple won't work, as the sugar is needed to beat air into the batter for the cake's incredibly soft, spongy texture. Lastly, please don't try to prepare the puree on a stovetop; baking it retains the apples' aroma and yields that "deeply appley" flavor.

A friend who took a bite exclaimed, "Wow! Did I just bite into an apple?" Exactly what I was after!

Serves 10 to 12

4.4 pounds (2 kilograms; 8 to 10 medium) tart, tangy, and firm apples, such as Winesap

14 tablespoons (7 ounces; 200 grams) unsalted butter, softened, plus more for pan

2 cups (280 grams) all-purpose flour, plus more for pan

2 teaspoons (8 grams) baking powder

½ teaspoon (3 grams) baking soda

¼ teaspoon (2 grams) fine sea salt

1½ cups (300 grams) granulated sugar

1¼ teaspoons (4 grams) ground cinnamon

½ teaspoon (2 grams) ground allspice

4 large eggs, at room temperature

1 tablespoon (10 grams) confectioners' sugar, for dusting

½ teaspoon (2 grams) ground cinnamon, for dusting

Set a rack in the middle of the oven and preheat the oven to 350°F (175°C).

Peel, core, and cut the apples into 1¼-inch (3-cm) pieces. Arrange the apple pieces in an even layer on a large rimmed baking sheet lined with parchment paper. Bake for 1 hour, stirring once halfway through the baking time. Remove the baking sheet from the oven and reduce the oven temperature to 300°F (150°C).

Transfer the baked apples to a medium heatproof bowl and puree with an immersion blender (or in a food processor fitted with a metal blade) until smooth. Scrape the apple puree into an unlined 15-by-10-inch (38-by-25.5-cm) jelly-roll pan, spreading it evenly with a small offset spatula to cover the surface of the pan.

Bake until the puree is thick enough to firmly hold its shape when stirred, 30 to 60 minutes, stirring and smoothing it every 15 minutes to prevent a crust from forming. (The baking time may vary greatly based on the apples' moisture content, which also will affect yield.) Remove the pan from the oven and scrape the puree into a medium heatproof bowl. To ease cleanup, fill the pan with hot water and let stand for 30 minutes before washing. You will have about 1⅔ cups (435 grams) of apple puree. (The apple puree will keep, wrapped airtight, in the refrigerator for up to 3 days or in the freezer for up to 1 month. Bring to room temperature before using.)

Raise the oven temperature to 350°F (175°C) and carefully move the rack to the lower third of the oven.

Generously butter a 10-cup (2.4-liter) Bundt pan. If your pan has an intricate design, use a pastry brush to reach all the nooks and crannies. Dust the pan with flour and tap out the excess.

(continued on page 112)

Check the consistency of the puree; if it is very thick and stiff, use the immersion blender to add water, 1 tablespoon (15 grams) at a time, until you have a thick paste that is soft enough to dissolve completely in the cake batter.

Sift together the flour, baking powder, baking soda, and salt into a medium bowl.

In the bowl of a stand mixer fitted with the paddle attachment, beat the butter at medium-high speed until creamy, about 2 minutes. Add the sugar, cinnamon, and allspice and beat until light and fluffy, about 3 minutes. Add the eggs, one at a time, and beat for 1 minute after each addition, scraping down the sides of the bowl as needed.

Measure out 1½ cups (390 grams) of the apple puree (you may wish to sweeten the remaining puree to enjoy later as apple butter), add it to the batter, and beat at medium speed until blended, about 1 minute. Add the flour mixture and beat at the lowest speed just until incorporated, about 30 seconds. The batter will be very thick.

Remove the bowl from the mixer and scrape down the sides of the bowl with a silicone spatula, reaching down to the bottom to incorporate any unmixed dry ingredients. Scrape the batter into the prepared pan and smooth the top.

Bake until a wooden toothpick inserted into the cake comes out clean, 45 to 50 minutes. Set the pan on a wire rack to cool for 10 minutes, then invert the cake directly onto the rack to cool completely.

Stir together the confectioners' sugar and cinnamon in a fine-mesh shaker and dust it evenly over the cake. Using a cake lifter, transfer the cake to a serving plate, and serve.

Storage: The cake will keep, wrapped airtight, at room temperature for up to 3 days.

SOUR CHERRY & ALMOND UPSIDE-DOWN CAKE

I'll say without hesitation that this cake is my favorite recipe in the book. Considering that there is a chocolate cake using more than a pound of chocolate (see page 144), passion fruit caramels that make me weak in the knees (see page 274), and several ice creams that I can't live without, this is a big statement. I'm not sure whether it's the sticky-sweet sour cherries against that buttery, almond-y crumb, or the fact that the fruit layer gets sweeter and stickier each time I apply the sour cherry glaze to refresh it, but this cake is what I crave most.

It is also one of the easiest recipes in the book. For the cake, you put the ingredients into the bowl of a food processor one after another and press a button. For the fruit layer, you'll cook the cherries before arranging them on the bottom, enabling you to fit in more and preventing the bubbling juices from leeching into the cake. Since the fruit won't shrink further in the oven, there will be no gaps between cherries when you invert the cake onto a serving plate.

The cake is so flavorful it doesn't really need the fruit layer, but if sour cherries aren't in season or are hard to find where you live and you still want that sticky-sweet layer, try using another tart fruit with a low moisture content—one that will retain its shape after an hour in the oven. Without a doubt, Raspberry Jewel pluots (see page 192) would be my second choice.

Not that you need yet another reason to run immediately into the kitchen, but the cake gets better with time, too.

Serves 8

FRUIT LAYER & GLAZE

5¼ cups (1.62 pounds; 735 grams) pitted fresh sour cherries (from about 1.9 pounds; 860 grams sour cherries with pits and stems)

⅔ cup (133 grams) granulated sugar

CAKE

10 tablespoons plus 2 teaspoons (5.3 ounces; 150 grams) unsalted butter, cut into large pieces and softened, plus more for pan

3 large eggs, at room temperature

1 teaspoon (5 grams) pure vanilla extract

1½ cups (150 grams) blanched almond flour

¾ cup (105 grams) all-purpose flour

¾ cup (150 grams) granulated sugar

1½ teaspoons (6 grams) baking powder

¼ teaspoon (2 grams) fine sea salt

To make the fruit layer and glaze, in a large, high-sided skillet over medium heat, cook the cherries and sugar until the juices released from the cherries begin to simmer and the sugar dissolves, about 10 minutes, stirring gently so as not to break up the cherries. Raise the heat to medium-high and cook until the juices thicken but are still fluid, 15 to 20 minutes, stirring occasionally. Scrape the cherries with their juices into a mesh strainer set over a medium heatproof bowl and let drain completely, shaking the strainer gently to help drain the juices. Reserve the juices for glazing the cake.

To make the cake, set a rack in the middle of the oven and preheat the oven to 325°F (160°C).

Butter the bottom of an 8-inch (20.5-cm) round cake pan, line the bottom with a parchment round, and wrap a dampened cake strip around the pan. (I highly recommend using a cake strip [see page 356] to prevent a domed top, which can cause the fruit layer to crack after the cake is inverted onto the serving plate.)

In a small bowl, whisk the eggs and vanilla with a fork until blended.

In the bowl of a food processor fitted with a metal blade, process the almond flour, flour, sugar, baking powder, and salt until well blended, about 1 minute. Add the butter pieces and pulse until the dough gathers around the blade, about 1 minute. Add the egg mixture and process until blended, about 20 seconds, scraping down the sides of the bowl as needed. The batter will be very thick.

Arrange the drained sour cherries in a tightly packed single layer on the bottom of the prepared pan. Scrape the batter over the cherries and spread it evenly with a small offset spatula.

(continued on page 115)

Bake until a wooden toothpick inserted into the cake comes out clean, 55 to 60 minutes. Set the pan on a wire rack to cool completely. Pressing firmly against the pan, run a small knife around the edge to loosen the cake, invert onto a serving plate, and remove the parchment round.

Skim off the foamy layer on the sour cherry glaze with a spoon and discard. Use a pastry brush to apply a generous amount of glaze to the cherries, and serve.

Transfer the remaining glaze to a small bowl, cover tightly with plastic wrap, and store in the refrigerator.

Storage: The cake will keep, wrapped airtight, at room temperature for up to 4 days. Before serving, refresh the fruit layer with leftover glaze warmed in a small saucepan over low heat. You can substitute leftover glaze for the raspberry syrup in Raspberry Lemonade (page 292) to make sour cherry lemonade.

RASPBERRY & PISTACHIO CRUMB CAKE

Many years ago, while I was slaving away in the corporate world and dragging myself out of bed every morning, unable to open my eyes before two cups of coffee, I came up with something I called Monday morning syndrome cake. I would bake a cake every Sunday night so that I would have something comforting to look forward to in the office for breakfast every working day of the week—something to remind me of my home sweet home. Well, either that or I'm hardwired to create excuses to eat more cake.

Nowadays, I have all the time in the world to prepare myself breakfast and enjoy a leisurely cup of coffee, but I have never given up on that tradition. The very first Monday morning syndrome cake I baked was a raspberry crumb cake. The cake's short lifespan doesn't make it ideal, and there are many other cakes more suitable for the job, but none of them offer that playful interaction between a crispy topping, a tender cake below, and tangy surprises entangled between the two.

Serves 9

TOPPING

1 cup plus 2 tablespoons (101 grams) blanched pistachio flour

½ cup (80 grams) confectioners' sugar

½ cup (70 grams) all-purpose flour

Pinch of fine sea salt

7 tablespoons (3.5 ounces; 100 grams) unsalted butter, melted and cooled

CAKE

9 tablespoons (4.5 ounces; 125 grams) unsalted butter, softened, plus more for pan

1½ cups (210 grams) all-purpose flour

½ teaspoon (2 grams) baking powder

½ teaspoon (3 grams) baking soda

¼ teaspoon (2 grams) fine sea salt

⅓ cup (80 grams) heavy cream, at room temperature

¼ cup (58 grams) plain full-fat strained (Greek-style) yogurt, at room temperature

1 teaspoon (5 grams) pure vanilla extract

¾ cup plus 1 tablespoon (163 grams) granulated sugar

2 large eggs, at room temperature

1⅔ cups (7 ounces; 200 grams) fresh raspberries

To make the topping, in a medium bowl, stir together the pistachio flour, sugar, flour, and salt. Pour the melted butter over the mixture and stir with a fork until large crumbs form.

To make the cake, set a rack in the middle of the oven and preheat the oven to 350°F (175°C).

Butter the bottom and sides of an 8-inch (20.5-cm) square baking pan. Line the pan with two overlapping strips of parchment paper that are the width of the pan bottom and long enough to cover the bottom and sides with 2 inches (5 cm) of overhang on each side. Butter the lower parchment to secure the top sheet.

Sift together the flour, baking powder, baking soda, and salt into a large bowl.

In a medium bowl, whisk the cream, yogurt, and vanilla until blended.

In the bowl of a stand mixer fitted with the paddle attachment, beat the butter and sugar at medium-high speed until light and fluffy, about 3 minutes. Add the eggs, one at a time, and beat for 1 minute after each addition, scraping down the sides of the bowl as needed. Add the cream mixture and beat until blended, about 2 minutes. Reduce the speed to low and beat in the flour mixture just until incorporated, about 1 minute. The batter will be very thick.

Remove the bowl from the mixer and scrape down the sides of the bowl with a silicone spatula, reaching down to the bottom to incorporate any unmixed dry ingredients. Scrape about two-thirds of the batter into the prepared pan and spread it evenly with a small offset spatula. Scatter about two-thirds of the raspberries evenly over the batter. Scrape the remaining batter over the raspberries and spread it evenly. Scatter the remaining raspberries evenly over the batter and gently press them halfway into the batter. Sprinkle the topping evenly over the cake.

(continued on page 118)

Bake until a wooden toothpick inserted into the cake comes out clean, 55 to 60 minutes, covering the cake loosely with a sheet of aluminum foil for the last 20 minutes to prevent overbrowning. Set the pan on a wire rack to cool for 10 minutes. Using the parchment overhang as handles, lift the cake out of the pan and transfer it directly onto the rack to cool completely.

Peel away the parchment. Using a cake lifter, transfer the cake to a serving plate, and serve.

Storage: The cake is best the day it is made, but it will keep, wrapped airtight, at room temperature for up to 2 days.

SAKURA MADELEINES

My first trip to Paris had more or less the same purpose as that of any food blogger I know: to visit as many patisseries and chocolatiers as I could, to scour the flea markets for props, and to lose my mind (and half my travel money) at E. Dehillerin—the cookware mecca of Paris, open since 1820. I managed to cover maybe one-fifth of the places on my ambitious list and cried over the cakes, chocolates, and pastries I wasn't able to sample, but I came home with a suitcase full of ingredients to explore.

On my third day in Paris, on a sugar high thanks to the Jacques Genin salted butter caramels I was downing every ten minutes, we went to L'As du Fallafel—the most popular falafel joint in town, located in the heart of Le Marais—for a quick lunch. Slightly disappointed by the falafel, I opened my map to see what else was nearby. Two blocks away was Cuisinophile, a vintage kitchen store I had seen on David Lebovitz's blog, marked as a must-visit.

When my friend and I arrived at the shop, we found a note on the door saying they'd be back in 15 minutes, which I took to mean twice that in Parisian time. No problem; I was happy to linger for half an hour with my forehead plastered to the window, eyeing the eggbeaters, café au lait bowls, and glass milk bottles inside, deciding which pieces I must have and choosing fake favorites to inquire about first to soften up the shopkeeper before inquiring about the prices of the pieces I really wanted. As I was devising my master plan, my friend called from behind, asking if I'd be willing to have something to drink at the shop he was pointing to. I looked up and saw the sign: Mariage Frères. Willing? More like trembling!

Founded in 1854, Mariage Frères is a French fine tea company with salons and boutiques scattered throughout Paris. The one we were standing in front of, on rue du Bourg Tibourg, was where Henri Mariage, one of the founding brothers, had his offices more than 150 years ago. The place was stacked floor to ceiling with large black canisters of tea. Behind the counter were salesmen in white linen suits, presenting customers samples of tea to sniff. After inhaling the aromas of about a dozen teas, I settled for the two blends I liked most and started perusing the shop. I found the largest, plumpest, shiniest Tahitian vanilla beans I've ever seen and grabbed as many as my budget allowed. On my way to the cashier, rows of colorful boxes caught my eye. The white box with the silver and neon-pink flower on the front read "Sakura Thé Blanc—White Tea with Cherry Blossom Flavor." I had never before tasted either white tea or cherry blossom–flavored anything, and since it was a closed box there was no way of knowing how it smelled. So I had to buy it.

Later that day in my hotel room, I took a whiff of the tea and went straight back to my elementary school years. It had the exact scent of the Maya the Bee erasers I once couldn't stop smelling. I loved the scent, but I wasn't sure whether I wanted it in my tea. So when I arrived back home I put it away in a drawer and forgot about it. About a year later, I unearthed the box during a spring cleaning. It was kismet. Right around that time, I had been fighting with an Earl Grey madeleine recipe. No matter how much tea I used, I hadn't been able to infuse its intense flavor into the madeleine. When I unearthed the box, my mind went straight to that recipe. If there was a tea that wouldn't lose its oomph after being steeped in butter and baked into a madeleine, it was the Maya the Bee tea. I wasn't sure whether it would work, but I thought it would make a great story for my blog at the very least.

The verdict? If I had the chance, I'd hop on the first flight to Paris and buy the entire stock of Sakura Thé Blanc from Mariage Frères.

I know I'd get booed if I stopped there, as you may not easily find cherry blossom–flavored white tea, so I've come up with two great variations: lemon verbena and lavender. Oh, and if you have a tea you regret having purchased, now might be the time to use it.

(recipe on page 121)

Makes 12 madeleines

9 tablespoons (4.5 ounces; 125 grams) unsalted butter, plus more for pan

¼ cup plus 1 tablespoon (10 grams) sakura (cherry blossom) flavored white tea leaves

2 large eggs, at room temperature

⅓ cup plus 1 tablespoon (79 grams) granulated sugar

⅔ cup (93 grams) all-purpose flour, plus more for pan

½ teaspoon (2 grams) baking powder

¼ teaspoon (2 grams) fine sea salt

In a medium saucepan over medium heat, melt the butter. Stir in the tea leaves, remove the pan from the heat, cover, and let steep for 15 minutes. Scrape the infused butter into a fine-mesh strainer set over a glass measuring cup and strain, pressing hard on the leaves with a silicone spatula to extract as much butter as possible. Discard the tea leaves. You should have 7 tablespoons (3 ounces; 85 grams) of infused butter. If the yield is less than that, add melted butter to make up the difference.

Fit a large pastry bag with a ⅜-inch (1-cm) plain round tip (Ateco #804), twist the tip of the bag, place it in a tall glass, and fold the top of the bag down over the edge of the glass.

In the bowl of a stand mixer fitted with the whisk attachment, beat the eggs and sugar at high speed until pale and thick, about 4 minutes. With the mixer running, add the infused butter in a steady stream and beat until blended.

Remove the bowl from the mixer and sift together the flour, baking powder, and salt over the egg mixture. Using a large wire whisk, gently fold in the dry ingredients just until incorporated.

Scrape the batter into the prepared pastry bag, unfold the cuff, and twist to enclose the batter. Cover the glass with plastic wrap and refrigerate for at least 4 hours or up to 2 days. (For madeleines with their characteristic humps, the batter must chill for at least 24 hours.)

Set a rack in the middle of the oven and preheat the oven to 400°F (200°C).

Using a pastry brush, generously butter a nonstick, 12-shell (with a capacity of 2 tablespoons; 30 ml each) madeleine pan, reaching into the indentations and including the entire surface. Dust the pan with flour and tap out the excess.

Pipe the batter into the indentations, filling each one three-quarters full (1 ounce; 28 grams each).

Bake until the madeleines are golden and the tops spring back when lightly pressed, 12 to 14 minutes. Set the pan on a wire rack to cool for 5 minutes. Nudge the madeleines from the pan with a finger, transferring them directly onto the rack to cool completely.

Storage: The madeleines are best the day they are made, but they will keep, wrapped airtight, at room temperature for up to 2 days.

LEMON VERBENA MADELEINES

Replace the tea leaves with 2 cups (10 grams) loosely packed dried lemon verbena leaves, crumbled into small pieces.

LAVENDER MADELEINES

Replace the tea leaves with 2 tablespoons (3 grams) dried culinary lavender flowers.

CARROT CAKE WITH BLOND CHOCOLATE FROSTING

Before creating this recipe, I couldn't have imagined a carrot cake without walnuts. While developing it, when I added baking soda to soften the grated carrots, the cake's texture improved immensely but the walnuts in the cake turned almost black when baked. While contemplating other nuts to use, I thought of something better— something that would infuse every crumb of the cake with a nutty aroma: *beurre noisette*. The brown butter is made by cooking butter over low heat until the milk solids turn brown and give off a nutty aroma. Now I can't imagine a carrot cake made without it.

The cake turned out so great I couldn't stop there. You can find a Bundt cake variation without embellishments at the end of the recipe, but turning it into a festive layer cake couldn't be easier. The frosting is so simple, you'll have it ready even before the cake has cooled.

Please meet your new obsession: Brown butter carrot cake layers, slathered with a creamy blond chocolate and cream cheese frosting and crowned with toasted pumpkin seeds.

Serves 10 to 12

CAKE

17 tablespoons (8.5 ounces; 240 grams) unsalted butter, softened, plus more for pan

2 tablespoons (40 grams) honey

2 cups (280 grams) all-purpose flour

½ cup (40 grams) unsweetened shredded dried coconut

2 ½ teaspoons (10 grams) baking powder

2 teaspoons (6 grams) ground cinnamon

½ teaspoon (3 grams) baking soda

½ teaspoon (4 grams) fine sea salt

4 large eggs, at room temperature

1 ¾ cups (350 grams) granulated sugar

4 ¼ cups (12.3 ounces; 350 grams) loosely packed grated carrots (from about 1.1 pounds; 500 grams carrots)

1 tablespoon (18 grams) finely grated, peeled fresh ginger

GARNISH

¼ cup (38 grams) pumpkin seeds

To make the cake layers, in a medium saucepan over medium heat, cook the butter until the milk solids brown and the butter is golden, about 15 minutes, stirring occasionally and watching it closely toward the end to prevent scorching. Scrape the browned butter and milk solids into a small heatproof bowl, stir in the honey, and let cool completely.

Meanwhile, set a rack in the middle of the oven and preheat the oven to 350°F (175°C). If your oven isn't wide enough to accommodate two pans side by side, adjust two racks just above and below the middle.

Butter the bottoms and sides of two 8-inch (20.5-cm) round cake pans, line the bottoms with parchment rounds, and wrap dampened cake strips (see page 356) around the pans if you have them.

In a large bowl, stir together the flour, coconut, baking powder, cinnamon, baking soda, and salt.

In the bowl of a stand mixer fitted with the whisk attachment, beat the eggs and sugar at medium-high speed until the sugar dissolves and the whisk begins to leave a trail as it mixes, about 3 minutes. With the mixer running, add the browned butter mixture in a steady stream and beat until blended. Add the flour mixture in three equal parts, beating at the lowest speed just until incorporated after each addition.

Remove the bowl from the mixer and stir in the carrots and grated ginger with a large silicone spatula.

Divide the batter evenly between the prepared pans (about 26.5 ounces; 750 grams each) and level it with a small offset spatula.

Bake until a wooden toothpick inserted into the centers comes out clean, about 35 minutes, rotating the pans top to bottom after 20 minutes if they are on different levels. Set the pans on a wire rack to cool for 30 minutes. Leave the oven on.

To make the garnish, spread out the seeds on an unlined baking sheet in a single layer and bake until they are fragrant and the skins are golden brown, 8 to 10 minutes. Immediately transfer the toasted seeds to a plate to cool.

(ingredients and method continued on page 125)

12 ounces (340 grams) blond chocolate (preferably Valrhona Dulcey) or white chocolate, coarsely chopped

½ cup plus 1 tablespoon (135 grams) heavy cream

½ cup (100 grams) granulated sugar

14.1 ounces (400 grams) full-fat cream cheese

1¼ teaspoons (4 grams) ground cinnamon

Pressing firmly against the pans, run a small knife around the edges to loosen the cakes, invert onto wire racks, and remove the parchments. Invert the layers a second time onto the racks and let cool completely. (The cakes will keep, wrapped airtight, at room temperature for up to 2 days or in the freezer for up to 1 month. Thaw overnight in the refrigerator before using.)

To make the frosting, in a medium heatproof bowl set over a medium saucepan filled with 2 inches (5 cm) of barely simmering water, melt the chocolate, stirring occasionally with a silicone spatula.

Meanwhile, in a small saucepan over low heat, heat the cream and sugar until the sugar dissolves, stirring constantly.

Remove the bowl of melted chocolate from the pan and add the hot cream mixture, cream cheese, and cinnamon. Blend with an immersion blender (or in a food processor fitted with a metal blade) until smooth. You will have about 4 cups (33.9 ounces; 960 grams) of frosting. (The frosting will keep, wrapped airtight, in the refrigerator for up to 2 days. Whisk chilled frosting until smooth before using).

To assemble the cake, with a large serrated knife, trim away the thin, soft crusts from the tops of the cakes.

Dab a bit of frosting in the center of a serving plate to prevent the cake from sliding and center a cake layer over it, cut side up. Slide wide strips of parchment paper beneath the cake on all sides to protect the plate. Put 1 cup (8.5 ounces; 240 grams) of frosting on the cake and spread it with a large offset spatula evenly over the cake, going just past the edge. Place the second layer on top, cut side down. Put 1 cup (8.5 ounces; 240 grams) of frosting on top and again spread it evenly over the cake, going just past the edge. Cover the sides of the cake evenly with the remaining 2 cups (17 ounces; 480 grams) of frosting. Carefully slide the parchment strips out from under the cake.

Arrange the toasted pumpkin seeds along the top edge of the cake, pressing them gently into the frosting to secure them in place.

Cover the cake with an aluminum foil tent, poking holes in the foil with a fork to prevent condensation, and refrigerate for at least 1 hour before serving.

Storage: The cake will keep, covered with the foil tent, in the refrigerator for up to 3 days.

CARROT BUNDT CAKE

Set a rack in the lower third of the oven and preheat the oven to 350°F (175°C). Generously butter a 10-cup (2.4-liter) Bundt pan. If your pan has an intricate design, use a pastry brush to reach all the nooks and crannies. Prepare the cake batter as directed in the recipe. Scrape the batter into the prepared pan and smooth the top. Bake until a wooden toothpick inserted into the cake comes out clean, 55 to 60 minutes. Set the pan on a wire rack to cool for 10 minutes, then invert the cake directly onto the rack to cool completely. Using a cake lifter, transfer the cake to a serving plate, and serve.

Storage: The cake will keep, wrapped airtight, at room temperature for up to 3 days.

BANANA WALNUT MUFFINS

I don't like muffins. To me, they are artless little cakes. The muffin mixing method seems to prioritize ease over superior texture: wet ingredients are poured over dry ones before mixing with a casual stir. I believe it is this method and not their size, the ratios of ingredients, or the pan they're baked in that characterizes them as muffins. What else besides ease of mixing would cause anyone to prefer a dense and coarse crumb over a light and delicate one?

So why include a muffin recipe here? Because I love baking with bananas. Let me explain. My objective was to transform my favorite banana bread into a light and delicate cake, maximizing the number of bananas for intense banana flavor. I started on this endeavor immediately after finalizing the Deeply Appley Apple Cake (page 110). If successful, I was going to call it The Most Banana-y Banana Cake. Just as I baked the apples to evaporate most of their moisture, intensifying their flavor, I began by baking the bananas in their skins, first piercing them all over with a fork. You'd be surprised how much water a banana releases. Unfortunately, I wasn't able to lighten the cake, and I concluded that the banana's texture was the culprit. Baking them allowed me to use up to seven bananas instead of the usual three, but it didn't intensify the flavor. After a few trials, I accepted that bananas are destined to become quick breads.

But I wasn't done just yet. The failed cakes weren't as light as I'd have liked, but they all had something exceptionally tasty in common: toasty, almost crispy crust. All I had to do to maximize the crust area was to bake the banana bread as muffins. There's no need to bother with roasting the bananas, and I now have a muffin I actually like.

Makes 12 muffins

9 tablespoons (4.5 ounces; 125 grams) unsalted butter, melted and cooled, plus more for pan

1⅔ cups (233 grams) all-purpose flour, plus more for pan

1 tablespoon (12 grams) baking powder

10.6 ounces (300 grams) peeled ripe bananas (from 1 pound; 455 grams; about 3 large bananas)

¾ cup plus 2 tablespoons (175 grams) granulated sugar

⅓ cup (27 grams) unsweetened shredded dried coconut

2 large eggs, at room temperature

1 teaspoon (5 grams) pure vanilla extract

¼ teaspoon (2 grams) fine sea salt

1 cup (90 grams) walnut halves

Set a rack in the middle of the oven and preheat the oven to 375°F (190°C).

Generously butter the indentations and the surface of a nonstick, 12-cup (with a capacity of ½ cup; 120 ml each) muffin pan. Dust the pan with flour and tap out the excess.

Sift together the flour and baking powder into a large bowl.

In a separate large bowl, with an immersion blender (or in a food processor fitted with a metal blade), puree the bananas, melted butter, sugar, coconut, eggs, vanilla, and salt until smooth.

Pour the banana mixture over the flour mixture and stir with a large wire whisk just until combined. Do not overmix; the batter should be a bit lumpy.

Divide the batter evenly among the prepared muffin cups (2.8 ounces; 80 grams each). Break the walnut halves into large pieces and scatter them evenly over the tops.

Bake for 15 minutes, reduce the oven temperature to 350°F (175°C), and continue baking until the tops are golden and a wooden toothpick inserted into a muffin comes out clean, about 20 minutes. Set the pan on a wire rack to cool for 5 minutes, then transfer the muffins directly to the rack to cool completely.

Storage: The muffins are best the day they are made, but they will keep, wrapped airtight, at room temperature for up to 2 days.

ORANGE & POPPY SEED OLIVE OIL CAKE

When I first started baking, I came across a citrus and olive oil cake recipe and was puzzled, as I thought cakes were always started by creaming butter and sugar. But when I thought about flavor, pairing citrus with olive oil made sense.

Looking further into oil-based cakes, I learned that the choice between butter and oil wasn't solely about flavor. Butter does a better job of evenly distributing citrus zest and helps to incorporate air into the batter as you beat it with sugar, while oil coats the flour particles more effectively. The more thoroughly coated the flour, the less moisture it absorbs, resulting in a moister cake with a more tender crumb. This goes for all oils, but no other is as flavorful as a fruity olive oil.

To keep the cake moist longer—and to make use of the orange after zesting—I brush the cake with a quick orange glaze. You can use other citrus fruits for both the cake and glaze, but I wouldn't dream of omitting the crunchy poppy seeds.

Serves 10 to 12

CAKE

Butter, for pan

1 ¼ cups (175 grams) all-purpose flour

¾ cup plus 1 tablespoon (81 grams) blanched almond flour

3 tablespoons (30 grams) poppy seeds

½ teaspoon (2 grams) baking powder

¼ teaspoon (2 grams) fine sea salt

1 large orange

1 cup (200 grams) granulated sugar

4 large eggs, at room temperature

½ cup (120 grams) heavy cream, at room temperature

⅓ cup plus 2 teaspoons (81 grams) extra-virgin olive oil

Set a rack in the lower third of the oven and preheat the oven to 350°F (175°C).

Butter the bottom and sides of an 8 ½-by-4 ½-by-2 ¾-inch (21.5-by-11.5-by-7-cm; 6-cup) loaf pan. Line the pan with two overlapping strips of parchment paper that are long enough to cover the bottom and sides with 2 inches (5 cm) of overhang on each side. Butter the lower parchment to secure the top sheet.

To make the cake, in a large bowl, stir together the flour, almond flour, poppy seeds, baking powder, and salt.

Using a fine-tooth rasp grater, grate the zest of the orange (avoiding the bitter white pith) directly into the bowl of a stand mixer. Add the sugar and use your fingertips to rub the zest into the sugar. Add the eggs. Attach the bowl, fit the whisk attachment onto the mixer, and beat at medium-high speed until the sugar dissolves and the whisk begins to leave a trail as it mixes, about 4 minutes. Add the cream and olive oil and beat until blended, about 30 seconds. The batter will deflate a bit and liquefy. Add the flour mixture and beat at the lowest speed just until incorporated.

Remove the bowl from the mixer and scrape down the sides of the bowl with a silicone spatula, reaching down to the bottom to incorporate any unmixed dry ingredients. Scrape the batter into the prepared pan and smooth the top.

Bake until a wooden toothpick inserted into the cake comes out clean, about 1 hour, covering the cake loosely with a sheet of aluminum foil halfway through the baking time to prevent overbrowning. Set the pan on a wire rack to cool for 10 minutes. Using the parchment overhang as handles, lift the cake out of the pan and transfer it directly onto the rack to cool completely.

Peel away the parchment.

(ingredients and method continued on page 130)

GLAZE

½ cup (120 grams) freshly squeezed orange juice (from zested orange)

½ cup (100 grams) granulated sugar

To make the glaze, in a small saucepan over medium-high heat, bring the orange juice and sugar to a boil, stirring constantly until the sugar dissolves. Reduce the heat to medium and cook until the mixture has the consistency of runny jam or registers 220°F (105°C) on an instant-read thermometer, about 3 minutes. Immediately pour the glaze into a small bowl and let cool for 5 minutes.

Using a cake lifter, transfer the cake to a serving plate. Using a pastry brush, apply a generous amount of glaze on the cake, and serve.

Storage: The cake will keep under a cake dome at room temperature for up to 4 days.

My First Day in San Francisco

One foggy fall morning in 1998, sleepless from a twenty-hour, two-leg flight and stressed by the unpleasant wait for my student visa—which arrived only ten hours before my flight departed—my exhausted body and soul landed at San Francisco International Airport.

I caught a cab, told the driver the address with my last ounce of energy, and started watching the city I'd be living in for a long time. After a forty-minute ride through the foggiest and most depressing parts of town, the cab stopped in front of a small motel in the Richmond district, across from a deli with an annoying bell. A note attached to the management office door reading "back in 30" was the first of a series of tragic events.

I stacked my suitcases one upon the another, perched on top, and started watching the passersby. After what felt like an hour, a hulking woman with a cat the size of an overfed piglet in her lap appeared by my side. A cigarette was dangling from the corner of her mouth and the smoke was making her eyebrows frown, drawing attention to her non-existent grooming. Her contrastingly feminine fingers snatched a key to the room closest to the street—and to the deli's annoying bell.

Soon I was lying on a turquoise polyester blanket, trying to gather the energy to go on. After a quick rest, I got up, took a shower, grabbed my backpack, and crammed in a large folder with the paperwork necessary for registration. Before I went out the door, I realized I was clueless about where the school was, so I stopped by the management office to ask for directions. There she was, sitting on a sofa, cat on her lap, watching a show where people cursed and threw chairs at each other. She slowly got up, plodded to the front desk, and, without saying a word, pulled out a sheet of paper from the drawer and drew on it. With her poorly sketched map in my hand, I started walking to the school.

After registration, a quick tour of the school, and several stupid team-building exercises at the orientation, I was back on the road. I needed to open a bank account and start looking for a decent place to live right away, as the delay in my student visa had left me homeless, so I stopped by the bank before heading back to the motel. This detour would cost me big time.

Now, a side note here: When it comes to reading maps, finding an address, or simply put, directions, I am worse than a lab rat. I can write a paper on broadband signal processor chips or bake cream puffs shaped like swans, but I can't find my way around a block.

Imagine my surprise when I succeeded in finding the bank despite it being outside the map area. Unfortunately, I took a wrong turn on my way back to the motel and got lost. After an exhausting hour of mindless walking, I gave up on the useless map and asked for help. The first person I stopped turned out to be deaf and mute. I figured the universe was trying to tell me I should give up on finding the motel, so I walked into the first restaurant I spotted. Another mistake; after a greasy burger and limp French fries, my body protested even more, but I kept going.

Several hours later, I finally spotted the neon sign of the motel lighting up the street corner. Oh, how I

missed that polyester blanket! I took a quick shower, threw myself on the bed, and turned on the TV. And there they were: four familiar faces, eating cheesecake in their kitchen and listening to the story the eldest was telling. I knew these women. Ten years earlier, when I spent most of my time under the dinner table watching TV, *The Golden Girls* had been one of the shows I had looked forward to.

I was thousands of miles away from friends and family and everything felt unfamiliar, but suddenly I was filled with comfort and warmth. I knew that, with the girls by my side—and maybe a slice of cheesecake on my lap—everything was going to be fine. I forgot about my aching feet and back and slowly went to sleep, the show's theme song fading in my ears: "Thank you for being a friend."

CHOCOLATE CHEESECAKE

After my first day in San Francisco, *The Golden Girls* became an obsession. I had watched the show before—broadcast on Turkish national television and dubbed in Turkish—but now I was hearing Blanche's Southern accent for the first time. Can you imagine the show without it? I didn't remember how the government's station had translated the dirty jokes and plot lines surrounding Blanche's sexual escapades (and Sophia's naughty digs, for that matter) that dominate almost every episode, but I had a feeling I was finally watching the real thing. From then on, I followed the show religiously, thanks to Lifetime—six episodes a day during my school years and four episodes a day (missing morning episodes on work-days) for the rest of my years in San Francisco, almost without fail. And consequently, I developed another obsession: cheesecake.

What? Did you think I was going to watch their nightly cheesecake ceremonies with a handful of raisins?

After a while, catching all of the day's episodes became difficult. Back then the show wasn't available on DVD. There was a website built by fans with an online petition form to Buena Vista Home Entertainment urging them to release the show on DVD, and God knows how many times I signed it, with all the fake names I could come up with, but as the years passed, I lost hope and began recording the episodes on VHS. Nine eight-hour VHS cassettes were packed neatly between sweaters in my luggage on my way back to İstanbul.

I had managed to bring the girls home, but the ritual was never complete without a slice (or two) of cheesecake. I refused to eat the sad impostors sold in İstanbul bakeries, so a quart of ice cream quickly took its place. And then, thank heavens, I started baking. I hadn't baked any of the cheesecakes I'd eaten while watching the show in San Francisco, so I realized how important cream cheese was in my life only after baking my first cheesecake in İstanbul. Philadelphia cream cheese wasn't available in Turkey, and I wasn't fond of the alternatives, so I caved in and used Turkish labneh, a thick fresh cheese that isn't as creamy and rich as cream cheese.

Finally, the time came to develop my ultimate cheesecake recipe for this book. I won't bore you with details of the numerous cheeses and ratios I've tested. Suffice it to say that, over the course of a month or so, I had eaten so much cheesecake I couldn't have burned it off if I'd walked from İstanbul to San Francisco. I finally concluded that, however imperfect, Turkish cream cheese gave my cheesecake the most authentic flavor, so I adapted the recipe to the ingredient I had on hand. For this reason, I gravitate toward baking cheesecakes flavored with ingredients intense enough to leave the cream cheese in the shade. In this one, that happily means plenty of chocolate!

Serves 10 to 12

CRUST

3½ tablespoons (1.7 ounces; 50 grams) unsalted butter, melted and cooled, plus more for pan

1¾ cups (210 grams) Cocoa Wafer Crumbs (page 337)

CHEESECAKE

12.7 ounces (360 grams) bittersweet chocolate (70% cacao), finely chopped

¼ cup (25 grams) Dutch-processed unsweetened cocoa powder

2 teaspoons (10 grams) pure vanilla extract

¼ teaspoon (2 grams) fine sea salt

Set a rack in the lower third of the oven and preheat the oven to 350°F (175°C).

Butter the bottom and sides of a 9-inch (23-cm) springform pan and wrap the outer bottom and sides with a double layer of heavy-duty aluminum foil.

To make the crust, in a medium bowl, stir and mash the wafer crumbs and melted butter with a fork until the crumbs are evenly moistened. Scrape the mixture into the prepared pan and press it with the back of a spoon into an even layer on the bottom only. Bake until set, about 12 minutes. Set the pan on a wire rack to cool completely. Reduce the oven temperature to 300°F (150°C).

To make the cheesecake, in a medium heatproof bowl, combine the chocolate, cocoa powder, vanilla, and salt.

(ingredients and method continued on page 135)

1½ cups (360 grams) heavy cream

1⅓ cups (267 grams) granulated sugar

14.1 ounces (400 grams) full-fat cream cheese, at room temperature

4 large eggs, at room temperature

GARNISH

10 to 12 Fernando Rochers (page 279), optional

In a medium saucepan over medium-high heat, bring the cream and sugar to just below a boil, stirring constantly until the sugar dissolves. Take the pan off the heat, pour the hot cream over the chocolate mixture, and whisk until the chocolate melts and the cocoa powder dissolves. Let cool completely.

In the bowl of a stand mixer fitted with the whisk attachment, beat the cream cheese at medium speed until smooth, about 5 minutes. Add the eggs and beat until blended, about 2 minutes, scraping down the sides of the bowl as needed. Switch to the paddle attachment. Add the cooled chocolate mixture and beat at the lowest speed until blended, about 5 minutes. Meanwhile, put a kettle of water on to boil.

Scrape the batter into the prepared pan and spread it evenly with a small offset spatula.

Set the pan inside a large roasting pan and set it on the oven rack. Pour in boiling water until it reaches halfway up the sides of the pan. Close the oven door. Bake until the center of the cheesecake jiggles slightly when the pan is gently shaken, about 1 hour. Turn the oven off, prop the door slightly open with a wooden spoon, and let the cheesecake cool in the oven for 1 hour. Carefully remove the pan from the water bath, peel away the aluminum foil, and set the pan on a wire rack to cool completely. Cover the pan with a sheet of aluminum foil, poking holes in the foil with a fork to prevent condensation, and refrigerate for at least 5 hours, or preferably overnight.

To garnish and serve, remove the foil and wave a hairdryer set on low (or a small kitchen torch from a distance) over the sides of the pan. Pressing firmly against the pan, run a thin knife around the edge to loosen the cheesecake. Remove the sides of the pan and, if using them, evenly space Fernando rochers along the top edge of the cheesecake, using one to mark each slice. Alternatively, you can pipe a rosette of Crème Fraîche (page 338) or Crème Chantilly (lightly sweetened whipped cream; see page 160) onto each slice. Transfer the cheesecake on its base to a serving plate and serve cold.

Storage: The cheesecake will keep, covered with the aluminum foil tent, in the refrigerator for up to 5 days.

DEEPLY PUMPKINY PUMPKIN CHEESECAKE

Fitting 4.4 pounds of apples into a Bundt cake (Deeply Appley Apple Cake; page 110) felt like the biggest victory of my culinary adventure until I managed to squeeze 6.6 pounds of pumpkin into eight slices of cheesecake. That's right: you'll be eating close to a pound of pumpkin in every slice.

I owe this victory to *Cook's Illustrated.* The magazine's tip for achieving a concentrated flavor as well as a smooth and creamy texture in pumpkin cheesecake is genius—blotting canned pumpkin puree with paper towels to remove excess moisture before mixing it with the rest of the ingredients.

I always prefer to cook from scratch, so using canned pumpkin is out of the question for me. If you'd like to take a shortcut and have a favorite brand, feel free to use it, so long as you remove excess moisture as explained below.

Serves 8 to 10

CRUST

3½ tablespoons (1.7 ounces; 50 grams) unsalted butter, melted and cooled, plus more for pan

1¾ cups (210 grams) Cinnamon and Ginger Wafer Crumbs (page 337)

FILLING

6.6 pounds (3 kilograms) fresh pumpkin

1¼ cups (250 grams) granulated sugar

14.1 ounces (400 grams) full-fat cream cheese, at room temperature

3 large eggs, at room temperature

1 cup (240 grams) heavy cream, at room temperature

Set a rack in the middle of the oven and preheat the oven to 350°F (175°C).

Butter the bottom and sides of a 9-inch (23-cm) square baking pan. Line the pan with two overlapping strips of parchment paper that are the width of the pan bottom and long enough to cover the bottom and sides with 2 inches (5 cm) of overhang on each side. Butter the lower parchment to secure the top sheet.

To make the crust, in a medium bowl, stir and mash the wafer crumbs and melted butter with a fork until the crumbs are evenly moistened. Scrape the mixture into the prepared pan and press it with the back of a spoon into an even layer on the bottom only. Bake until set, about 12 minutes. Set the pan on a wire rack to cool completely. Leave the oven on.

To make the filling, peel, seed, and cut the pumpkin into 1½-inch (4-cm) pieces. Measure out 4 pounds (1.8 kilograms) of pumpkin flesh for the pumpkin puree (reserve the rest for another use, such as a soup). Arrange the pumpkin in an even layer on a large rimmed baking sheet lined with parchment paper. Bake for 1 hour 10 minutes, stirring once halfway through the baking time. Set the sheet on a wire rack and let cool for 10 minutes. Reduce the oven temperature to 325°F (160°C).

Transfer the baked pumpkin pieces in batches to a fine-mesh strainer set over a large heatproof bowl and press hard with a silicone spatula until only coarse fibers are left in the strainer. Discard the solids left in the strainer after each batch. Scrape any puree clinging to the bottom of the strainer into the bowl.

Scrape the strained pumpkin puree onto a rimless baking sheet lined with three layers of paper towels and spread it evenly with a small offset spatula. Place three layers of paper towels over the puree and press lightly to blot. Once the paper towels on top are completely wet, peel them away and place another three layers of paper towels on top. Place another rimless baking sheet over the towels and carefully flip the whole thing so that the bottom baking sheet is now on top. Remove the top baking sheet and peel away the wet paper towels. Continue to blot and flip until the paper towels come up with only traces of moisture. It will take 4 to 5 rounds. You will have about

(ingredients and method continued on page 139)

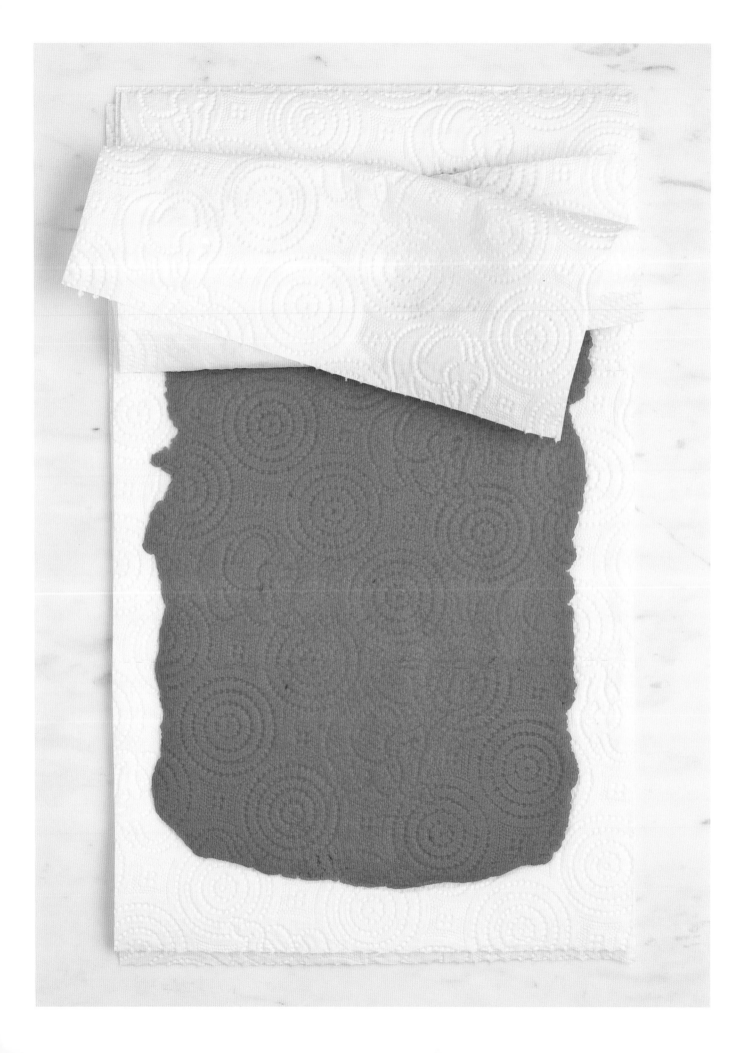

½ cup (120 grams) Crème Fraîche (page 338), lightly whipped

2 tablespoons (11 grams) blanched pistachio flour

1¾ cups (400 to 450 grams) of pumpkin puree. (The pumpkin puree will keep, wrapped airtight, in the refrigerator for up to 3 days or in the freezer for up to 1 month. Bring to room temperature before using.)

Measure out 1½ cups (390 grams) of the pumpkin puree (you may wish to sweeten the remaining puree to enjoy later as pumpkin butter), transfer it into a medium bowl, and stir in the sugar.

In the bowl of a stand mixer fitted with the whisk attachment, beat the cream cheese at medium speed until smooth, about 5 minutes. Add the sweetened pumpkin puree and beat until blended, about 3 minutes. Switch to the paddle attachment. Add the eggs and cream and beat at the lowest speed until blended, about 5 minutes, scraping down the sides of the bowl as needed. Meanwhile, put a kettle of water on to boil.

Scrape the batter into the prepared pan and spread it evenly with a small offset spatula.

Set the pan inside a large roasting pan and set it on the oven rack. Pour in boiling water until it reaches halfway up the sides of the pan. Close the oven door. Bake until the center of the cheesecake jiggles slightly when the pan is gently shaken, about 1 hour 15 minutes. Turn the oven off, prop the door slightly open with a wooden spoon, and let the cheesecake cool in the oven for 1 hour. Carefully remove the pan from the water bath and set the pan on a wire rack to cool completely. Cover the pan with a sheet of aluminum foil, poking holes in the foil with a fork to prevent condensation, and refrigerate for at least 5 hours, or preferably overnight.

To garnish and serve, using the parchment overhang as handles, lift the cheesecake out of the pan and transfer it to a cutting board. Cut the cheesecake in half, then cut each half crosswise into 4 or 5 equal rectangles. Transfer the pieces to a serving plate. Fit a small pastry bag with a medium closed 7-pointed star tip (Ateco #846), twist the tip of the bag, place it in a small glass, and fold the top of the bag down over the edge of the glass. Scrape the crème fraîche into the bag, unfold the cuff, and twist to enclose the crème fraîche. Holding the pastry bag at a 90-degree angle to the surface of the cheesecake, pipe a star onto one end of each rectangle. Sprinkle the pistachio flour evenly over the crème fraîche stars and serve cold.

Storage: The cheesecake slices will keep, covered with an aluminum foil tent (poke holes in the foil with a fork to prevent condensation), in the refrigerator for up to 5 days.

MATCHA & PISTACHIO NO-BAKE CHEESECAKE

About a year after I started my food blog, a friend's birthday came up and I took it upon myself to make the birthday cake. Matcha was all the rage among food bloggers back then, and I had been itching to use it in a recipe. My friend's birthday was the perfect occasion. I hadn't tasted anything made with matcha before, but the color of the cakes and buttercreams made with it looked so enticing on screen that I imagined it was impossible to produce anything short of impressive.

When it came to practice, things didn't go so smoothly. Most of the recipes I had been drooling over listed small amounts of matcha, nowhere near enough to paint my cheesecake the vibrant emerald green I had in mind. So I kept adding matcha until the batter matched the shade I envisioned and—silly me—didn't think to taste it before baking.

The next day, I brought the cake out to oohs and ahhs. Everyone was asking about the color and I was proudly explaining that I had added a very special ingredient that they couldn't have heard of. My friend blew out the candles, the cake was served, and I waited anxiously as he took the first bite. The moment I saw his face scrunch up and his eyebrows knit together, I knew it was a disaster. I took a bite and confirmed that it was inedible.

It was a colossal fail, and my friends have been quite diligent in making sure I never forget it. Now, I'm waiting impatiently for the tenth anniversary of the Great Matcha Cheesecake Disaster so that I can finally show them how it's really done, and hopefully shut them up once and for all.

Serves 10

CRUST

2 ½ tablespoons (1.2 ounces; 35 grams) unsalted butter, melted and cooled, plus more for pan

¾ cup (90 grams) Vanilla Wafer Crumbs (page 337)

½ cup (45 grams) blanched pistachio flour

½ teaspoon matcha

FILLING

8 ounces (225 grams) white chocolate, coarsely chopped

2 ⅔ cups (240 grams) blanched pistachio flour

1 tablespoon plus 2 teaspoons (10 grams) matcha

¼ teaspoon (2 grams) fine sea salt

½ cup (100 grams) granulated sugar

3 tablespoons (45 grams) water

1 pound (455 grams) full-fat cream cheese

Butter the bottom and sides of a 6 ½-inch (16.5-cm) springform pan.

To make the crust, in a medium bowl, stir together the wafer crumbs, pistachio flour, and matcha. Pour the melted butter over the dry ingredients, and stir and mash with a fork until they are evenly moistened. Scrape the crumb mixture into the prepared pan and press it with the back of a spoon into an even layer on the bottom only. Refrigerate, uncovered, until the filling is ready.

To make the filling, in a medium heatproof bowl set over a medium saucepan filled with 2 inches (5 cm) of barely simmering water, melt the chocolate, stirring occasionally with a silicone spatula. Remove the pan from the heat, leaving the bowl on top to keep the chocolate warm.

In the bowl of a food processor fitted with a metal blade, process 2 ⅓ cups (210 grams) of the pistachio flour, the matcha, and the salt until the pistachios release their oils and the mixture turns into a paste, about 5 minutes.

In a small saucepan over medium-high heat, bring the sugar and water to a boil, stirring occasionally. Take the pan off the heat, and with the food processor running, drizzle in the hot syrup through the feed tube. The pistachio puree may harden quickly, so immediately add the cream cheese and melted chocolate. Process until smooth and creamy, about 2 minutes, scraping down the sides of the bowl as needed. Scrape the filling in batches into a fine-mesh strainer set over a large bowl and strain, pressing it through with a silicone spatula. Scrape any filling clinging to the bottom of the strainer into the bowl. Discard the solids in the strainer. You will have about 3 ⅔ cups (900 grams) of filling.

Scrape the filling onto the chilled crust and spread evenly with a small offset spatula. Scatter the remaining ⅓ cup (30 grams) of

(continued on page 143)

pistachio flour over the filling and spread evenly with a small offset spatula, taking care not to apply too much pressure. Cover the pan with an aluminum foil tent, poking holes in the foil with a fork to prevent condensation, and refrigerate until the filling is firm, about 3 hours.

To unmold the cheesecake, remove the foil and wave a hairdryer set on low (or a small kitchen torch from a distance) over the sides of the pan. Pressing firmly against the pan, run a thin knife around the edge to loosen the cheesecake. Remove the sides of the pan. Transfer the cheesecake on its base to a serving plate and serve cold.

Storage: The cheesecake will keep, covered with the aluminum foil tent, in the refrigerator for up to 5 days.

DEVIL WEARS CHOCOLATE

Devil's food cake—or as I like to call mine, Devil Wears Chocolate—is the *ne plus ultra* of chocolate cake. Several years ago, I made the first incarnation of this cake for *Design*Sponge*'s "In the Kitchen With" column. It looked similar from the outside, but the filling was bittersweet and milk chocolate ganache combined with a jar of Biscoff spread. Called Speculoos in some parts of the world, Biscoff is a spread made from Belgian spice cookies. As much as it was spectacular, I now think that it betrayed the soul of the recipe. The devil must wear chocolate from head to toe. Now that I have a chance to atone for this sin, I've replaced the Biscoff spread with an ingredient that has zero chance of stealing the chocolate's thunder: water.

You won't believe how easy it is to prepare the chocolate filling: Pour boiling water over the dry ingredients, whisk until smooth, then blend in butter and cream. After about an hour in the refrigerator, you'll have the smoothest and lightest ganache ever. Replacing a large portion of the heavy cream in the conventional ganache recipe with water creates a lighter filling with a more intense chocolate flavor.

Presentation is everything, but it doesn't have to be laborious. Transforming the cake into a showstopper that could have come straight from a Parisian patisserie is just as easy. You simply melt chocolate, spread it on parchment paper, roll it into a tube, chill, and unroll. Listening to the chocolate break into shards as you unroll the tube is priceless. There will be enough shards to cover the cake completely, but if you'd prefer the luxury of choosing the best-looking ones, double the recipe and prepare two separate tubes. Leftover shards may be refrigerated for a long time and later melted for use in recipes, or may be used to garnish ice cream or other desserts.

You can take the traditional route for an equally exceptional presentation. After frosting the cake, prepare an extra half-batch of filling and dress the devil with chocolate swirls (see the end of the recipe). Unless I make it for a special occasion, that's what I usually do, as it allows me to serve and store the cake at room temperature. Since I don't temper the chocolate for the shards (tempered chocolate hardens too quickly to spread thinly and won't shatter as handsomely), they will sweat and soften at room temperature. If using them, decorate the cake immediately before serving and refrigerate the leftovers.

Whichever route you take, this cake is guaranteed to impress and delight even the most hardcore chocoholic.

Serves 10 to 12

CHOCOLATE SHARDS

6.3 ounces (180 grams) bittersweet chocolate (70% cacao), coarsely chopped

To make the chocolate shards, cut two 18-inch-long (45.5-cm) sheets of parchment paper and place one of them on a flat work surface.

In a medium heatproof bowl set over a medium saucepan filled with 2 inches (5 cm) of barely simmering water, melt the chocolate, stirring occasionally with a silicone spatula. Remove the bowl from the pan, wipe the bottom of the bowl with a cloth, and scrape the melted chocolate onto the parchment. Using a large metal offset spatula, spread it in an even layer, leaving a ⅜-inch (1-cm) border all around. Place the second sheet of parchment on top and gently press on it all over with your palm to release the air pockets. Starting with one short end, roll the parchment paper tightly into a 1-inch-wide (2.5-cm) tube, taking care not to apply too much pressure. Place the tube seam side down on a rimmed baking sheet, making sure both ends of the tube are supported by the rim to prevent it from unrolling. Refrigerate the tube until the chocolate sets, about 2 hours.

Line a large baking sheet with parchment paper. Place the tube on a flat surface. Press on the open seam with one hand and unroll the tube in one quick motion with your other hand. Remove the top sheet of parchment. Using a large offset spatula, go underneath the shards, pick them up, and transfer to the lined baking sheet. Cover the baking sheet loosely with plastic wrap and refrigerate until ready to use.

(ingredients and method continued on page 147)

CAKE

14 tablespoons (7 ounces; 200 grams) unsalted butter, softened, plus more for pan

⅔ cup (67 grams) Dutch-processed unsweetened cocoa powder

⅔ cup (160 grams) boiling water

⅓ cup (77 grams) plain full-fat strained (Greek-style) yogurt

2 teaspoons (10 grams) pure vanilla extract

1⅔ cups (233 grams) all-purpose flour

1 tablespoon (12 grams) baking powder

½ teaspoon (4 grams) fine sea salt

¼ teaspoon (2 grams) baking soda

1½ cups (300 grams) granulated sugar

3 large eggs, at room temperature

GANACHE

12.7 ounces (360 grams) bittersweet chocolate (70% cacao), finely chopped

¾ cup (150 grams) granulated sugar

⅔ cup (67 grams) Dutch-processed unsweetened cocoa powder

½ teaspoon (4 grams) fine sea salt

1 cup (240 grams) boiling water

5 tablespoons plus 1 teaspoon (2.7 ounces; 75 grams) unsalted butter, softened

⅔ cup (160 grams) heavy cream

To make the cake layers, set a rack in the middle of the oven and preheat the oven to 350°F (175°C). If your oven isn't wide enough to accommodate two pans side by side, adjust two racks just above and below the middle.

Butter the bottoms and sides of two 8-inch (20.5-cm) round cake pans, line the bottoms with parchment rounds, and wrap dampened cake strips (see page 356) around the pans if you have them.

In a medium heatproof bowl, whisk the cocoa powder and boiling water until the cocoa powder dissolves. Add the yogurt and vanilla and whisk until smooth.

Sift together the flour, baking powder, salt, and baking soda into a medium bowl.

In the bowl of a stand mixer fitted with the paddle attachment, beat the butter at medium-high speed until creamy, about 2 minutes. Add the sugar and beat until light and fluffy, about 5 minutes. Add the eggs, one at a time, and beat for 1 minute after each addition, scraping down the sides of the bowl as needed. Reduce the speed to low and beat in one-third of the flour mixture, followed by half of the chocolate mixture. Repeat with another third of the flour mixture and the remaining chocolate mixture. Finally, add the remaining flour mixture and beat just until incorporated.

Remove the bowl from the mixer and scrape down the sides of the bowl with a silicone spatula, reaching down to the bottom to incorporate any unmixed dry ingredients.

Divide the batter evenly between the prepared pans (about 21.1 ounces; 600 grams each) and spread them evenly with a small offset spatula.

Bake until a wooden toothpick inserted into the centers comes out clean, about 35 minutes, rotating the pans top to bottom after 20 minutes if they are on different levels. Set the pans on a wire rack to cool for 30 minutes. Pressing firmly against the pans, run a small knife around the edges to loosen the cakes, invert onto wire racks, and remove the parchments. Invert the layers a second time onto the racks and let cool completely. (The cakes will keep, wrapped airtight, at room temperature for up to 2 days or in the freezer for up to 2 months. Thaw overnight in the refrigerator before using.)

To make the ganache, in a medium heatproof bowl, combine the chocolate, sugar, cocoa powder, and salt. Pour the boiling water over the chocolate mixture and whisk until the chocolate melts and the cocoa powder dissolves. Add the butter and whisk until blended. Add the cream and whisk until blended. Cover the bowl tightly with plastic wrap, pressing it directly onto the surface of the ganache, and refrigerate until just thick enough to be easily spread while firmly holding its shape, 45 to 60 minutes. (Allowing it to get too thick risks damaging the cake layers.) You will have about 4 cups (36.8 ounces; 1.04 kilograms) of ganache.

To assemble the cake, dab a bit of ganache in the center of a serving plate to prevent the cake from sliding and center a cake layer over it, top side up. Slide wide strips of parchment paper beneath the cake on all sides to protect the plate. Put 1½ cups (13.8 ounces; 390 grams) of ganache on the cake and spread it with a large offset

(continued on page 149)

spatula evenly over the cake, going just past the edge. Refrigerate the cake, uncovered, until the ganache layer sets, about 15 minutes. For the duration of the assembly, keep the rest of the ganache at room temperature, covered with plastic wrap.

Place the second layer top side down on the chilled layer. Put 1 cup (9.2 ounces; 260 grams) of ganache on top and spread it in a thin, even layer over the top and sides of the cake. Don't worry about how the cake looks at this point; this is the crumb coat, which helps to trap the crumbs so that you may apply the final coating of ganache smoothly and cleanly. Refrigerate the cake, uncovered, until the crumb coat sets, about 15 minutes.

Place a pair of tweezers in the freezer to be used to avoid fingerprints and melting as you handle the shards. I also wrap a finger in plastic wrap for pressing the shards onto the cake sides.

Put the remaining 1½ cups (13.8 ounces; 390 grams) of ganache over the crumb-coated cake and spread it evenly over the top and sides of the cake. Carefully slide the parchment strips out from under the cake.

If you won't serve the cake immediately, you can keep it under a cake dome at room temperature for up to 2 days.

Decorate the cake immediately before serving. If the ganache has hardened, wave a hair dryer set to low over the frosting to soften it before sticking on the shards. Remove the chocolate shards from the refrigerator and the tweezers from the freezer. Using the frozen tweezers, pick up the largest shards and gently press them, curved sides facing the ganache, onto the sides of the cake with a plastic-wrapped finger. Sprinkle the smaller shards over the cake to cover the entire surface, and serve.

Storage: The cake will keep, covered with an aluminum foil tent (poke holes in the foil with a fork to prevent condensation), in the refrigerator for up to 4 days.

(variation on page 150)

DEVIL WEARS CHOCOLATE SWIRLS

This variation of Devil Wears Chocolate (page 144) omits the chocolate shards and uses an additional half recipe of the ganache. The ganache thickens as it stands. Rather than making a recipe and a half of ganache all at once and risk it becoming too thick to spread, assemble the cake, then prepare the additional half recipe to finish decorating it.

GANACHE (ADDITIONAL ½ RECIPE)

- 6.3 ounces (180 grams) bittersweet chocolate (70% cacao), finely chopped
- ¼ cup plus 2 tablespoons (75 grams) granulated sugar
- ⅓ cup (33 grams) Dutch-processed unsweetened cocoa powder
- ¼ teaspoon (2 grams) fine sea salt
- ½ cup (120 grams) boiling water
- 2 ½ tablespoons (1.2 ounces; 35 grams) unsalted butter, softened
- ⅓ cup (80 grams) heavy cream

Prepare the cake layers and ganache as directed on page 147, assembling the cake up to the point of attaching the shards and leaving the parchment strips in place. Refrigerate the cake, uncovered, until the ganache sets, about 15 minutes.

Make the additional ganache using the quantities for a half recipe (on the left) and the instructions in the recipe. Cover the bowl tightly with plastic wrap, pressing it directly onto the surface of the ganache, and refrigerate until just thick enough to be easily spread while firmly holding its shape, about 30 minutes for the half recipe.

Scrape the additional ganache over the chilled cake. Working quickly before the ganache becomes too firm, use the back of a spoon to swirl the ganache over the top and sides of the cake. Carefully slide the parchment strips out from under the cake and serve.

Storage: The cake will keep under a cake dome at room temperature for up to 2 days, or may be refrigerated, covered with an aluminum foil tent (poke holes in the foil with a fork to prevent condensation), for up to 4 days.

TRIPLE RASPBERRY & LEMON BIRTHDAY CAKE

The first buttercream-layered cake I made when I started baking reminded me of the birthday cake of my childhood. It had two layers of white cake that tasted of nothing and were so dry you had to squash the lifeless raspberries perched between the layers with a fork and wait for the juices to moisten the cake. The cake was layered with a buttercream-like frosting that had no taste of butter yet left a stubborn layer of grease on the roof of your mouth. The only bearable component was the thin blanket of pink glaze, decorated with twisted threads and beads of white royal icing. I was the politest child you can imagine and didn't complain for years. Then I discovered that being insistent once a year wasn't the end of the world, and the birthday cakes got better, but it is that pink raspberry cake that brings back memories when I see similar ones on display at patisseries around İstanbul.

The first one I baked for myself was much better, but I wasn't sold on the Swiss meringue buttercream. I loved the smooth texture and buttery taste, but not so much how rich and sweet it was. I had to find a way to love it unconditionally.

The answer came when I accidentally over-reduced a raspberry sauce I was working on for a cheesecake recipe. I had intended for a tangy sauce to balance the cheesecake's richness, but it turned out way too sour on its own, and almost half of it stuck to the pan. The sauce was beyond saving, but it gave me a clue for solving the Swiss buttercream puzzle. I turned it into an even more insanely tart puree and added it to a batch of plain buttercream. It balanced the sweetness of the meringue, cut the richness of the pound of butter it was made with, and painted the buttercream a soft pink, eliminating the need for food coloring. It gave me what should have been the birthday cake of my childhood—four layers of moist, lemon-scented butter cakes, generously filled with a perfectly balanced raspberry buttercream, layered with a pound of fresh raspberries, and covered with crumbled freeze-dried raspberries for a crunchy, puckery finish.

Serves 10 to 12

CAKE

14 tablespoons (7 ounces; 200 grams) unsalted butter, softened, plus more for pan

2 cups (280 grams) all-purpose flour

1 tablespoon plus 1 teaspoon (16 grams) baking powder

½ teaspoon (4 grams) fine sea salt

⅔ cup (160 grams) whole milk, at room temperature

⅓ cup (77 grams) plain full-fat strained (Greek-style) yogurt, at room temperature

2 teaspoons (10 grams) pure vanilla extract

3 lemons

1¼ cups (250 grams) granulated sugar

4 large egg whites, at room temperature

To make the cake layers, set a rack in the middle of the oven and preheat the oven to 350°F (175°C). If your oven isn't wide enough to accommodate two pans side by side, adjust two racks just above and below the middle.

Butter the bottoms and sides of two 8-inch (20.5-cm) round cake pans, line the bottoms with parchment rounds, and wrap dampened cake strips (see page 356) around the pans if you have them.

Sift together the flour, baking powder, and salt into a medium bowl.

In a medium bowl, whisk the milk, yogurt, and vanilla until smooth.

Using a fine-tooth rasp grater, grate the zest of the lemons (avoiding the bitter white pith) directly into the bowl of a stand mixer. Add the sugar and use your fingertips to rub the zest into the sugar.

Attach the bowl and fit the paddle attachment onto the mixer. Add the butter and beat at medium-high speed until light and fluffy, about 3 minutes. Add the egg whites and beat until blended, about 3 minutes, scraping down the sides of the bowl as needed. Reduce the speed to low and beat in one-third of the flour mixture, followed by half of the milk mixture. Repeat with another third of the flour mixture and the remaining milk mixture. Finally, add the remaining flour mixture and beat just until incorporated.

Remove the bowl from the mixer and scrape down the sides of the bowl with a silicone spatula, reaching down to the bottom to incorporate any unmixed dry ingredients.

(ingredients and method continued on page 155)

2¼ cups (9.5 ounces; 270 grams)
fresh raspberries

1¼ cups plus 6 tablespoons
(325 grams) granulated sugar

2 tablespoons (30 grams) freshly
squeezed lemon juice (from
zested lemon)

7.4 ounces (210 grams; about
6 large) egg whites

1 pound (455 grams) unsalted
butter, cut into large pieces
and softened

Divide the batter evenly between the prepared pans (about
19.8 ounces; 560 grams each) and spread them evenly with a small
offset spatula.

Bake until a wooden toothpick inserted into the centers comes
out clean, about 30 minutes, rotating the pans top to bottom after
20 minutes if they are on different levels. Set the pans on a wire rack
to cool for 30 minutes. Pressing firmly against the pans, run a small
knife around the edges to loosen the cakes, invert onto wire racks,
and remove the parchments. Invert the layers a second time onto the
racks and let cool completely. (The cakes will keep, wrapped airtight,
at room temperature for up to 2 days or in the freezer for up to 2
months. Thaw overnight in the refrigerator before using.)

To make the raspberry buttercream, in a medium bowl, mash
the berries and 6 tablespoons (75 grams) of the sugar with a silicone
spatula and let stand until the berries release their juices and the sugar
dissolves, about 15 minutes. Scrape the berries and their juices into
a fine-mesh strainer set over a medium saucepan and strain, pressing
hard with the spatula until only the seeds are left in the strainer.
Scrape any puree clinging to the bottom of the strainer into the pan.
Discard the seeds. You will have about 1 cup (240 grams) of sweetened
berry puree.

Add the lemon juice to the puree, set the pan over medium-high
heat, and bring to a boil, stirring frequently. Reduce the heat to
medium and cook until the juices thicken and the puree is reduced
to a little over ½ cup (130 grams), about 12 minutes, frequently
stirring and scraping the bottom of the pan with a silicone spatula to
prevent scorching. Scrape the puree into a small heatproof bowl and
let cool for 15 minutes, stirring occasionally. Cover the bowl tightly
with plastic wrap, pressing it directly onto the surface of the puree to
prevent a skin from forming. Keep at room temperature while you
make the meringue. (The raspberry puree will keep in the refrigerator
for up to 1 month. Let stand at room temperature for 20 minutes and
whisk until smooth before using.)

In the bowl of a stand mixer set over a medium saucepan filled
with 2 inches (5 cm) of barely simmering water, whisk the egg whites
and the remaining 1¼ cups (250 grams) of sugar until the sugar
dissolves and the mixture registers 162°F (72°C) on an instant-read
thermometer, 10 to 15 minutes.

Attach the bowl and fit the whisk attachment onto the mixer and
beat at medium-high speed until the meringue is thick, glossy, and
completely cool, about 10 minutes. Add the butter in five equal parts,
beating until blended after each addition. After the last addition, beat
until the buttercream is thick and smooth, about 5 minutes. Add
the raspberry puree and beat until blended, about 1 minute. You will
have about 5½ cups (34 ounces; 965 grams) of buttercream. (The
buttercream will keep, wrapped airtight, at room temperature for
up to 24 hours, or in the refrigerator for up to 5 days. Bring to room
temperature and whisk at medium-low speed until smooth before
using.)

(ingredients and method continued on page 157)

3¾ cups (1 pound; 455 grams)
   fresh raspberries

2 cups (2.1 ounces; 60 grams)
   freeze-dried raspberries

To assemble and decorate the cake, with a large serrated knife, trim away the top crusts of the cakes and slice each cake in half horizontally. You will have two layers with a bottom crust and two with no crust.

Dab a bit of buttercream in the center of a serving plate to prevent the cake from sliding and center a bottom-crust cake layer over it, cut side up. Slide wide strips of parchment paper beneath the cake on all sides to protect the plate. Put 1 cup (6.2 ounces; 175 grams) of buttercream on the cake and spread it with a large offset spatula evenly over the cake, going just past the edge. By hand, gently halve one-third of the fresh raspberries (5.3 ounces; 150 grams) lengthwise (top to bottom) and evenly arrange them, cut side down, on the buttercream, leaving a ½-inch (1.3-cm) border all around. Repeat these steps twice more using the no-crust layers and all of the raspberries, then top the cake with the bottom-crust layer, placing it crust side up. Put 1 cup (6.2 ounces; 175 grams) of buttercream on top and spread it in a thin, even layer over the top and sides of the cake. Don't worry about how the cake looks at this point; this is the crumb coat, which helps to trap the crumbs so that you may apply the final coating of buttercream smoothly and cleanly. Refrigerate the cake, uncovered, until the crumb coat sets, about 15 minutes.

Put the remaining 1½ cups (9.3 ounces; 265 grams) of buttercream on top of the crumb-coated cake and spread it evenly over the top and sides of the cake.

Put the freeze-dried raspberries into a mesh strainer set over a medium bowl and use your fingertips to gently break them into small pieces. Shake the strainer over the bowl to strain out any fine powder (enjoy it with yogurt or add it to a smoothie). Scatter the berry pieces in the strainer over the cake to cover the top. To cover the sides, grab small handfuls of berry pieces and gently press them into the buttercream, rotating the cake as you go. Carefully slide the parchment strips out from under the cake.

Serve at room temperature or slightly chilled.

Storage: The cake will keep under a cake dome at room temperature for up to 24 hours, or may be refrigerated, covered with an aluminum foil tent (poke holes in the foil with a fork to prevent condensation), for up to 2 days. Before serving, let the chilled cake stand at room temperature, uncovered, until the buttercream softens, about 45 minutes.

MONTE BIANCO

Oh, the things my friends have called you! Some have asked if you were a giant bowl of whole-wheat spaghetti. Others have wrinkled up their noses and called you a mound of worms! I'm so glad you have no ears.

I wonder what they would have thought of your companion on the day it arrived at my doorstep in a thousand pieces. I had bought it specially for you. I picked up the pieces with tweezers, one by one, and sent them off to the ceramics hospital. A few months later the glorious pedestal returned, reborn from its own dust. You were meant for each other.

Have I ever told you that you're the most delicious thing a chestnut could ever be? You are so perfect I don't dare rain even a drop of chocolate on you. The moment my friends hear this, they'll realize how perfect you are, so I hold my tongue. Just so you are all mine, always and forever.

Serves 8 to 10

CHESTNUT PUREE

2.2 pounds (1 kilogram) fresh chestnuts

2¾ cups (660 grams) whole milk, plus more if needed

1 cup (200 grams) granulated sugar

11 tablespoons (5.5 ounces; 155 grams) cold unsalted butter, cut into small pieces

To make the chestnut puree, bring a large saucepot of water to a boil. With a chestnut (or bird's beak) knife, make a horizontal slit on the fat side of each chestnut, cutting through the tough outer shell and the thin skin underneath, but avoiding the meat.

Boil the first quarter of the chestnuts for 10 minutes. Chestnuts are easiest to peel while they're hot, so I boil them in batches, peeling them as I go. I can peel a quarter of the chestnuts in 10 minutes—the time it takes the next batch to boil. If you are slower, boil the chestnuts in smaller batches. With a slotted spoon, transfer the boiled chestnuts to a colander. While they are still hot, peel away their outer shells and skins and transfer the meats to a cutting board. (It's helpful to place a bowl of ice water nearby to cool your fingers as you peel.) Repeat to boil and peel all of the chestnuts. You will have about 1.66 pounds (750 grams) of chestnut meat. If they yield less, adjust the other ingredients accordingly. (The peeled chestnuts will keep in an airtight container in the refrigerator for up to 3 days, or in the freezer for up to 2 months. Thaw overnight in the refrigerator before using.)

Finely chop the chestnut meats, transfer them to a large saucepot, and add the milk and sugar. Bring the mixture to a boil over medium-high heat, then reduce the heat to medium and cook until the chestnuts soak up almost all of the milk and the mixture turns into a thick chunky puree, about 30 minutes, stirring frequently and scraping the bottom of the pot with a silicone spatula to prevent scorching.

Take the pan off the heat and puree the mixture with an immersion blender (or in a food processor fitted with a metal blade) until smooth. Add the butter and puree until blended. You will have about 5 cups (1.3 kilograms) of puree. Check the consistency; the puree should be thick enough to firmly hold its shape when piped, but soft enough to be piped without too much pressure. If it appears too thick or stiff—and keeping in mind that it will thicken further as it cools— blend in more milk, 2 tablespoons (30 grams) at a time, to reach the desired consistency. If it is too soft, cook over low heat until it reaches the desired consistency, stirring and scraping the bottom of the pot frequently to help evaporate excess moisture.

Scrape the puree into a large bowl, cover with plastic wrap, and refrigerate until cold, about 3 hours.

(ingredients and method continued on page 160)

CRÈME CHANTILLY

1½ cups (360 grams) cold heavy cream

3 tablespoons (30 grams) confectioners' sugar

To assemble the Monte Bianco, fit a large pastry bag with a ¼-inch (6-mm) plain round tip (Ateco #10), twist the tip of the bag, place it in a tall glass, and fold the top of the bag down over the edge of the glass. Scrape half of the chestnut puree into the bag, unfold the cuff, and twist to enclose the puree. Start piping the puree into a mountain-like mound on a serving plate or shallow bowl, starting 8 inches (20.5 cm) wide at the bottom and gradually tightening the circle as you go along. Repeat with the remaining puree to complete the mountain. If you won't be serving the Monte Bianco until later in the day, cover the chestnut mountain with an aluminum foil tent (poke holes in the foil with a fork to prevent condensation) and keep it in the refrigerator until serving.

Shortly before serving, *make the crème Chantilly.* In the chilled bowl of a stand mixer fitted with the whisk attachment, beat the cream at medium speed until it starts to thicken, about 1 minute. Add the sugar and beat until stiff peaks form (when you invert the whisk, the peak should point straight up), about 1 minute.

Fit a large pastry bag with a small closed 6-pointed star tip (Ateco #34), twist the tip of the bag, place it in a tall glass, and fold the top of the bag down over the edge of the glass. Scrape half of the crème Chantilly into the bag, unfold the cuff, and twist to enclose the crème Chantilly. Starting at the top, pipe little stars to cover about two-thirds of the chestnut mountain, leaving a section at the bottom bare. Serve cold, with the remaining crème Chantilly in a bowl on the side.

Storage: Monte Bianco is best the day it is made, but it will keep, covered with an aluminum foil tent (poke holes in the foil with a fork to prevent condensation), in the refrigerator for up to 3 days.

MANGO & RED CURRANT PAVLOVAS

Pavlova is a study in the art of harmonizing textures and flavors. Mine starts with coconut-flecked meringue clouds, fragile and crunchy on the outside and light and chewy on the inside. Nestled in the clouds is the best thing that has ever happened to a mango—a smooth, rich, sweet, and tangy curd, looking for the meringue's slightest crack to slide into. Finally, beads of red currants will shock you like a note played *sforzando*. Oh, how apparent that this dessert was created in honor of a great ballerina.

Serves 6

MERINGUE NESTS

5 ounces (140 grams; about 4 large) egg whites, at room temperature

1 cup (200 grams) granulated sugar

2 tablespoons (10 grams) unsweetened shredded dried coconut

MANGO CURD

1 large (1 pound; 455 grams) ripe mango, peeled, pitted, flesh cut into large pieces

8 large egg yolks, at room temperature

⅔ cup (133 grams) granulated sugar

⅓ cup (80 grams) freshly squeezed lemon juice

7 tablespoons (3.5 ounces; 100 grams) unsalted butter, cut into small pieces and softened

To make the meringue nests, set two racks just above and below the middle of the oven and preheat the oven to 250°F (120°C).

Draw three 4½-inch (11.5-cm) circles on each of two sheets of parchment paper, leaving about 2 inches (5 cm) between them.

In the bowl of a stand mixer fitted with the whisk attachment, beat the egg whites at medium-low speed until foamy, about 2 minutes. Raise the speed to medium and beat until the whisk begins to leave a trail as it mixes, about 2 minutes. Gradually beat in the sugar over the next minute. Raise the speed to medium-high and beat until the sugar dissolves completely and stiff peaks form (when you invert the whisk, the peak should point straight up), about 4 minutes.

Dab meringue on the four corners of two baking sheets. Line the sheets with the prepared parchment, writing side down, pressing on the corners to secure it in place.

Using a large spoon, drop the meringue in mounds onto the circles (about 2 ounces; 55 grams each). Using the back of the spoon, shape each mound into a nest by creating a 1⅜-inch-deep (3.5-cm) indentation in the center and a 1-inch-thick (2.5-cm) raised rim. Sprinkle the coconut evenly over the meringue nests.

Bake until the nests are crisp and dry to the touch, about 50 minutes, rotating the sheets top to bottom and side to side halfway through the baking time. While rotating, check to see if the nests are taking on any color; if they are, reduce the oven temperature to 230°F (110°C) for the remaining baking time. When they are ready, turn the oven off, leaving the nests in the oven to cool and dry, about 5 hours or overnight. (The meringue nests will keep, wrapped airtight, at room temperature for up to 2 days.)

To make the mango curd, in a medium bowl, puree the mango flesh with an immersion blender (or in a food processor fitted with a metal blade) until smooth.

In a large heatproof bowl, whisk the egg yolks and sugar until pale and thick, about 5 minutes. Measure out 1 cup (240 grams) of the mango puree (enjoy the remaining puree with yogurt or add it to a smoothie) and whisk it into the yolk mixture along with the lemon juice. Set the bowl over a medium saucepan filled with 2 inches (5 cm) of barely simmering water and whisk until thickened and the mixture registers 170°F (75°C) on an instant-read thermometer, about 25 minutes.

(ingredients and method continued on page 163)

6 small stems (about 4.2 ounces; 120 grams) fresh red currants

Scrape the curd into a fine-mesh strainer set over a medium heatproof bowl and strain, pressing hard with a silicone spatula until there is only pulp left in the strainer. Scrape any curd clinging to the bottom of the strainer into the bowl. Discard the pulp. Add the butter and whisk until blended.

Fill a medium bowl with cold water and ice. Place the bowl with the strained curd over the ice bath and stir the curd until it is completely cool, about 10 minutes. Remove the bowl from the ice bath. Cover tightly with plastic wrap, pressing it directly onto the surface of the curd, and refrigerate for at least 4 hours. You will have about 2¼ cups (520 grams) of mango curd. (The curd will keep in the refrigerator for up to 3 days, or in the freezer for up to 1 month. Thaw overnight in the refrigerator before using.)

Just before serving, ***assemble and garnish the pavlovas***. Using an offset spatula, carefully lift and transfer the meringue nests to six serving plates. Divide the curd evenly among the nest indentations (about ⅓ cup plus 1 tablespoon; 85 grams each). Garnish each pavlova with a small stem of red currants, and serve.

Storage: Store each component separately, assembling the pavlovas immediately before serving to retain the meringue's crispy texture.

ETON MESS

There are two similar stories about the origin of the Eton mess. Both take place at the annual cricket match at Eton College and involve a damaged strawberry pavlova. One claims that it was the doing of a clumsy delivery guy; the other blames a bouncy Labrador retriever for the mess. I choose to believe that it was the Labrador retriever and would like to offer my belated commendation: Good boy!

It may have been named after a mess, but to me it is pure genius. If you've ever eaten a pavlova, you know that it will *become* a mess with the first cut of a knife. Eton Mess may not look as grand as a pavlova when served, but arranging all the elements in bite-size pieces, and in just the right proportions, offers your guests a neater and more balanced mess.

The classic recipe consists of meringue, whipped cream, and fresh strawberries. For mine, I macerate the strawberries, using the drained juices as a syrup drizzled over the mess at the last minute. I prefer a lightly sweetened whipped cream (crème Chantilly), and I sprinkle toasted almonds slices between the layers for flavor and crunch. Macerating the berries intensifies their flavor, but it also makes the assembly time sensitive: macerate them too long and they will become limp. The meringue and almonds may be prepared ahead of time, but macerate the fruit and make the syrup about two hours before assembly, and put everything together at the last minute for the best texture.

Serves 6 to 8

MERINGUE

3.7 ounces (105 grams; about 3 large) egg whites, at room temperature

¾ cup (150 grams) granulated sugar

TOASTED ALMONDS

½ cup (50 grams) sliced blanched almonds

To make the meringue pieces, set a rack in the middle of the oven and preheat the oven to 270°F (130°C).

In the bowl of a stand mixer fitted with the whisk attachment, beat the egg whites at medium-low speed until foamy, about 2 minutes. Raise the speed to medium and beat until the whisk begins to leave a trail as it mixes, about 2 minutes. Gradually beat in the sugar over the next minute. Raise the speed to medium-high and beat until the sugar dissolves completely and stiff peaks form (when you invert the whisk, the peak should point straight up), about 4 minutes.

Dab meringue on the four corners of a baking sheet. Line the sheet with parchment paper, pressing on the corners to secure it in place.

Scrape the meringue onto the parchment and, using an offset spatula, flatten it into a 1-inch-high (2.5-cm) rectangle measuring about 6 by 9 inches (15 by 23 cm).

Bake until the meringue is crisp and dry to the touch, about 50 minutes, rotating the sheet halfway through the baking time. While rotating, check to see if the meringue is taking on any color; if it is, reduce the oven temperature to 250°F (120°C) for the remaining baking time. When it is ready, turn the oven off, leaving the meringue in the oven to cool and dry, about 5 hours or overnight. (The meringue will keep, wrapped airtight, at room temperature for up to 2 days.)

To toast the almonds, set a rack in the middle of the oven and preheat the oven to 350°F (175°C). Spread out the almonds on an unlined baking sheet in a single layer and bake until fragrant and golden, 8 to 10 minutes. Immediately transfer the toasted almonds to a plate to cool. Alternatively, you can toast them in an ungreased nonstick pan over medium heat, shaking the pan and tossing the almonds frequently to prevent them from scorching.

(ingredients and method continued on page 167)

FRUIT & SYRUP

5 ½ cups (1.46 pounds; 660 grams) fresh strawberries, hulled

½ cup (100 grams) granulated sugar

CRÈME CHANTILLY

1 ½ cups (360 grams) cold heavy cream

2 tablespoons (20 grams) confectioners' sugar

About 2 hours before assembling the dessert, ***prepare the fruit and syrup.*** Cut the larger strawberries lengthwise (top to bottom) into quarters and the smaller ones lengthwise in half. In a large bowl, toss the berries with the sugar and let stand until the berries release their juices and the sugar dissolves, about 1 hour, occasionally stirring them gently with a silicone spatula. Scrape the berries and their juices into a mesh strainer set over a large bowl and let drain for 20 minutes, gently shaking the strainer to help drain the juices. Transfer the berries to a bowl, cover with plastic wrap, and refrigerate until assembly.

Pour the drained juices into a medium saucepan and bring to a boil over medium-high heat. Reduce the heat to medium and cook until the syrup has the consistency of runny jam or registers 220°F (105°C) on an instant-read thermometer, about 7 minutes. Immediately pour the syrup into a small pitcher and let cool for 15 minutes. Skim off and discard the foamy top layer. Cover with plastic wrap and refrigerate until assembly.

Shortly before assembling the Eton mess, ***make the crème Chantilly.*** In the chilled bowl of a stand mixer fitted with the whisk attachment, beat the cream at medium speed until it starts to thicken, about 1 minute. Add the sugar and beat until stiff peaks form (when you invert the whisk, the peak should point straight up), about 1 minute.

Just before serving, ***assemble the Eton mess.*** Break one-third of the meringue into large pieces and scatter them in a wide 2-quart (2-liter) serving bowl. Spoon dollops of crème Chantilly between the meringue pieces. Scatter one-third of the macerated strawberries and toasted almonds evenly over the top. Repeat twice more to use all the components. Drizzle a couple tablespoons of the berry syrup over the top and serve immediately, serving the remaining syrup on the side. Alternatively, you can assemble the dessert in individual serving glasses.

Storage: Store each component separately, assembling the Eton mess immediately before serving to retain the meringue's crispy texture. The meringue and almonds may be prepared ahead, but wait to prepare the fruit until about 2 hours before assembly, and whip the cream just before serving.

TARTS, GALETTES, PIE, QUICHE, COBBLER & CRUMBLE

BLANCHE

I just had to name this timeless tart after another—Golden Girl Blanche Devereaux, who once said, "Like the fatal blossom of the graceful jimson weed, I entice with my fragrance but can provide no succor."

Except this time, she does.

Serves 9

2 ½ cups (650 grams) chilled
Vanilla Pastry Cream (page 320)

17 ounces (480 grams) Vanilla Bean
Short Tart Dough (page 333),
fully baked as a 9-inch (23-cm)
square tart crust or a 10¼-inch
(26-cm) round tart crust and
cooled

1 cup (4.2 ounces; 120 grams) fresh
strawberries, hulled and halved
lengthwise (top to bottom)

½ cup (2.7 ounces; 75 grams) fresh
blackberries

1 cup (4.2 ounces; 120 grams) fresh
raspberries

¾ cup (3.5 ounces; 100 grams)
fresh blueberries

½ cup (2.8 ounces; 80 grams)
stemmed fresh red currants

12 to 15 sprigs fresh chocolate mint
(*Mentha x piperita f. citrata*)

Whisk the chilled pastry cream until smooth and scrape it into the cooled tart crust. Spread evenly with a small offset spatula. Gently shake the pan to fill the corners of the crust and to smooth the top.

Starting with the larger pieces and working your way to the smaller berries and currants, arrange the fruits over the pastry cream, making sure that each slice will get its fair share of all varieties.

Pluck the young and tender top leaves from the mint sprigs and tuck them evenly among the fruits.

Set the tart in its pan on an overturned flat-bottomed bowl (or a wide can) and gently release the ring. Slip the tip of a small knife between the crust and the bottom of the tart pan and run it all around the edge to loosen the crust. Carefully slide the tart onto a serving plate, and serve.

Storage: Blanche is best shortly after she is made, but she will keep, wrapped airtight, in the refrigerator for up to 2 days.

RASPBERRY, WHITE CHOCOLATE & YOGURT TART

Fold tangy strained yogurt into a silky white chocolate ganache, and you'll have a filling that rivals Vanilla Pastry Cream (page 320) in ten minutes flat.

I like to match the sweet, rich filling with tart fruits, such as raspberries and sour cherries, but I suspect roasted pluots or apricots would complement it equally well. If you use sweeter fruits, you might want to omit the added sugar in the filling. You may also replace the white chocolate with blond chocolate (see page 81)—its biscuit-y flavor yearns for bananas and caramel-covered nuts (see page 45).

Serves 8 to 10

FILLING

2 tablespoons (30 grams) water, at room temperature

1½ teaspoons (6 grams) powdered gelatin

½ cup (120 grams) heavy cream

7 ounces (200 grams) white chocolate, finely chopped

3 tablespoons (38 grams) granulated sugar

1 cup plus 1 tablespoon (244 grams) plain full-fat strained (Greek-style) yogurt

3⅓ cups (14.1 ounces; 400 grams) fresh raspberries

CRUST

17 ounces (480 grams) Almond Short Tart Dough (page 335), fully baked as a 10¼-inch (26-cm) round tart crust and cooled

GLAZE

⅓ cup (110 grams) Pomegranate Jam (page 298) or seedless raspberry jam

1 tablespoon (15 grams) water

To make the filling, pour the water into a small bowl, sprinkle the gelatin evenly over the top, and let stand until the gelatin blooms and absorbs the water, about 5 minutes.

In a medium saucepan over medium heat, bring the cream to just below a boil, stirring frequently. Reduce the heat to low and add the chocolate, sugar, and bloomed gelatin. Stir gently with a silicone spatula until the chocolate melts and the gelatin dissolves, about 3 minutes. Take the pan off the heat, add the yogurt, and whisk until smooth.

Scrape the filling into the cooled tart crust and gently shake and swirl the pan to spread the filling evenly. Transfer the tart in its pan to a baking sheet. Cover the tart with a sheet of aluminum foil, poking holes in the foil with a fork to prevent condensation, and refrigerate until the filling is firm, about 2 hours.

Remove the foil from the chilled tart. Arrange the berries over the filling in tight concentric circles.

To make the glaze, in a small saucepan, stir the jam and water over medium heat until runny. Take the pan off the heat, scrape the glaze into a small bowl, and let cool for 10 minutes.

Using a small pastry brush, gently dab the glaze all over the berries.

Set the tart in its pan on an overturned flat-bottomed bowl (or a wide can) and gently release the ring. Slip the tip of a small knife between the crust and the bottom of the tart pan and run it all around the edge to loosen the crust. Carefully slide the tart onto a serving plate, and serve.

Storage: The tart is best the day it is made, but it will keep, covered with an aluminum foil tent (poke holes in the foil with a fork to prevent condensation), in the refrigerator for up to 3 days.

CHOCOLATE & SALTED CARAMEL TART

This tart needs no explanation—the photo says it all—but I'll indulge anyway. Starting at the bottom, a buttery, rich, sweet cocoa crust. On the crust rests a layer of salty, oozy caramel, waiting impatiently to be discovered when you cut through its cloak of silky bittersweet chocolate ganache. The top is dressed with salt crystals hand-harvested from the salt marshes of Guérande in Brittany, France—fleur de sel: "flower of salt," the Chanel of salts.

Serves 10 to 12

SALTED CARAMEL

½ cup (120 grams) heavy cream

1¾ cups (350 grams) granulated sugar

⅓ cup (80 grams) water

7 tablespoons (3.5 ounces; 100 grams) cold unsalted butter, cut into large pieces

¼ teaspoon (2 grams) fine sea salt

CRUST

17 ounces (480 grams) Cocoa Short Tart Dough (page 335), fully baked as a 10¼-inch (26-cm) round tart crust and cooled

GANACHE

8.5 ounces (240 grams) bittersweet chocolate (70% cacao), finely chopped

1 cup (240 grams) heavy cream

GARNISH

½ teaspoon (2 grams) fleur de sel de Guérande or flaky sea salt, such as Maldon

To make the salted caramel, in a small saucepan over medium heat, bring the cream to just below a boil, stirring frequently. Take the pan off the heat and cover to keep the cream warm.

Put the sugar in a medium heavy-bottomed saucepan and shake the pan to level the sugar. Pour the water around the inside edge of the pan. Set the pan over medium-high heat and cook without stirring until the caramel turns a dark amber color, 20 to 25 minutes (it should register 383°F [195°C] on an instant-read thermometer). Take the pan off the heat and, holding it at arm's length, immediately pour in the warm cream and whisk until blended. Be careful; the caramel will bubble up vigorously and hot steam will rise. Add the butter and salt, whisking until blended.

Strain the caramel through a mesh strainer set over a medium heat-proof bowl. Scrape any caramel clinging to the bottom of the strainer into the bowl. Immediately scrape the strained caramel into the tart crust. Gently shake and swirl the pan to evenly spread the caramel. (If you have a helping hand, you can strain the caramel directly into the tart crust.) Transfer the tart in its pan to a baking sheet and refrigerate, uncovered, until the caramel is firm, about 20 minutes.

Meanwhile, **make the ganache.** Put the chocolate in a large heatproof bowl. In a medium saucepan over medium heat, bring the cream to just below a boil, stirring frequently. Take the pan off the heat and pour about one-third of the hot cream over the chocolate. Stir gently with a silicone spatula until blended. Add another third of the hot cream and stir until blended. Add the rest of the hot cream and stir until smooth and the chocolate melts completely.

Scrape the ganache over the firmed caramel layer. Gently shake and swirl the pan to spread it evenly and to smooth the top. Refrigerate the tart, uncovered, until the ganache is firm, about 30 minutes.

To garnish and serve, set the tart in its pan on an overturned flat-bottomed bowl (or a wide can) and gently release the ring. Slip the tip of a small knife between the crust and the bottom of the tart pan and run it all around the edge to loosen the crust. Carefully slide the tart onto a serving plate. Sprinkle the fleur de sel evenly over the tart. Serve cold, or let stand at room temperature for about 30 minutes before serving to slightly soften the caramel and ganache.

Storage: The tart will keep, covered with an aluminum foil tent (poke holes in the foil with a fork to prevent condensation), in the refrigerator for up to 3 days.

PISTACHIO FRANGIPANE & APRICOT TART

I wish you'd had the chance to shop at a farmers' market with my father. With him by my side, my Tuesday market routine would turn into a lesson in how to pick the best produce and how to establish long-lasting friendships with the people who grow it. I called him the produce whisperer. He could smell the season's most fragrant apricots a mile away. Even the grumpiest vendor would smile and soften like a brioche dough the moment he cracked his first joke. He would then talk his way into the back of the stall, go through the farmer's "secret stash" reserved for special customers, and pick the best fruits and vegetables, one by one.

One of his favorite fruits was *şekerpare* apricots—a small variety with firm, pale-orange flesh, yellow-orange skin with prominent red cheeks, and honey-like flavor. He came to the market prepared for these with empty plastic boxes, in which he would arrange the fruits in neatly packed rows, red cheeks facing up. When I couldn't join him, he never failed to bring me a box.

Amazing fruits like that don't need much, but then again, you could arrange apricot halves on a pistachio frangipane–filled tart shell, bake until the frangipane puffs up and half buries them, then revive them with a lick of vanilla-specked apricot jam. The final touches are a dollop of cold, lightly whipped crème fraîche to cut through the sweetness and a sprinkling of pistachio flour. OK, I think we've done them justice.

Look for an apricot variety that is sweet, juicy, flavorful, and on the firm side when ripe so that they retain their shape after baking.

Serves 8

FILLING
¾ cup (68 grams) blanched pistachio flour

¼ cup (40 grams) confectioners' sugar

¼ teaspoon (2 grams) fine sea salt

3½ tablespoons (1.7 ounces; 50 grams) cold unsalted butter, cut into small pieces

1 large egg yolk

¼ cup (60 grams) heavy cream

8 small (about 8 ounces; 225 grams) firm-ripe fresh apricots

2 tablespoons (40 grams) strained Vanilla Bean and Apricot Jam (page 302) or any apricot jam

CRUST
12.7 ounces (360 grams) Vanilla Bean Short Tart Dough (page 333), partially baked as a 13¾-by-4¼-inch (35-by-11-cm) rectangular tart crust and cooled

GARNISH
1 cup (240 grams) Crème Fraîche (page 338) or heavy cream, lightly whipped

2 teaspoons (4 grams) blanched pistachio flour

Set a rack in the middle of the oven and preheat the oven to 340°F (170°C).

To make the filling, in the bowl of a food processor fitted with a metal blade, process the pistachio flour, sugar, and salt until blended, about 30 seconds. Add the butter and process until the mixture becomes a paste, about 30 seconds. Add the egg yolk and process until blended, about 30 seconds, scraping down the sides of the bowl as needed. Scrape the mixture into a medium bowl, add the cream, and whisk until blended. Scrape the filling into the cooled tart crust and spread it evenly with a small offset spatula.

Cut the apricots in half lengthwise (top to bottom), remove and discard the pits, and arrange the fruit halves cut side up over the filling in two rows, pressing them gently into the filling to secure them in place.

Bake until the pistachio frangipane sets and the edges of the crust are golden, 25 to 30 minutes. Slide the pan onto a wire rack to cool completely.

Use a pastry brush to glaze the apricots with the strained jam.

Set the tart in its pan on three evenly spaced overturned shot glasses and gently release the outer rim. Slip the tip of a small knife between the crust and the bottom of the tart pan and run it all around the edge to loosen the crust. Carefully slide the tart onto a serving plate.

To garnish and serve, cut the tart into 8 slices and top each with a dollop of lightly whipped crème fraîche and a sprinkling of pistachio flour. Serve warm or at room temperature, with the rest of the whipped crème fraîche in a serving bowl on the side.

Storage: The tart is best the day it is made, but it will keep, covered with an aluminum foil tent (poke holes in the foil with a fork to prevent condensation), in the refrigerator for up to 2 days. Before serving, reheat in a preheated 325°F (160°C) oven until warmed through, 10 to 15 minutes, and refresh the apricots with extra strained jam.

It's a Small World

●

A year after I moved back to İstanbul from San Francisco, despite being at my new job for less than a year, I snagged a two-week summer vacation and spent it in San Francisco.

It was as if I'd never said goodbye. I no longer had a place to call my own, but Özlem—one of my oldest and closest friends, and with whom I shared a house in San Francisco for many years—was still living there. She had just moved into her new place, a five-minute walk from my old box of a studio apartment on Chestnut Street. As soon as she'd leave for work, I'd walk to the coffee shop across from my old place, grab a cup of coffee and a chocolate cupcake, perch on the bench outside, and have breakfast while staring at my old blinds. Then, I'd hop on a bus and visit every neighborhood I had lived in. After a few days of reminiscing, it was time to shop. I had just started my food blog and was having difficulty finding the right equipment in the cookbooks in İstanbul. Forget a madeleine mold or tart pans with removable bottoms—I didn't even own a silicone spatula. I'd come back to Özlem's place at the end of the day, carefully pack what I'd bought into my luggage, determine how much space I had left, and spend the following days filling it up.

The day before I left was a Saturday, and we decided to go to Chinatown. I didn't have space left for even a hazelnut in any of my bags. As I was going through the stacks of molds in a kitchen store, I stumbled upon a mooncake mold carved in the shape of a Buddha with an oversized forehead. I waved it to Özlem at the other end of the store and asked what she thought. She grabbed it from my hand and went straight to the register to pay for it. "Just a small gift for you to remember me when you bake in İstanbul," she said, smiling with every muscle of her face as she always does.

Back home, I made cinnamon Buddha cookies by adding cinnamon to Dorie Greenspan's Sweet Tart Dough in *Baking: From My Home to Yours* and published it on my blog. A few weeks later, my baking heroine left a comment on my blog, telling me how intrigued she was by my using her tart dough to make cookies. Such a small world, I thought to myself, having no idea how small it actually was.

Several years later, I received an e-mail from a Turkish reader on her way to San Francisco with her family, asking me the address of the store where I'd bought the Buddha mold. Having forgotten all about a Canadian reader who had already tracked down the shop and had been kind enough to share its name and address on my English language blog, I told her I had no idea which store it was exactly and wished her luck. A week after that e-mail, dearest Ebru wrote back, giving me the good news that she had located the store. Most of the stores were closed the first time she visited Chinatown, so she had gone back the morning of her flight, miraculously finding the same Buddha at the bottom of a mountain of molds. What shocked her even more was the slip of paper placed in her bag by the store owner; it was the recipe for Cinnamon Buddha Cookies I had published on my blog, complete with credits to me and Dorie Greenspan and a small black-and-white photo. It turns out they were including the recipe every time they sold that mold.

I now know that the name of the store is The Wok Shop, located at 718 Grant Avenue in San Francisco. During my last visit, I stopped by and introduced myself to the owner, Tane Chan, who was as surprised as she was excited. We took the obligatory selfie, and I bought up all the Buddha molds in the store, thinking they'd make great gifts for the launch of my cookbook. Who knows, maybe you're holding one. It's a small world.

If you do have the Buddha or a similar mold, you should know that the dough for the Vanilla Bean Short Tart Dough on page 333 also makes great cookies. To make them into cinnamon Buddha

cookies, replace the vanilla seeds with 2 teaspoons (6 grams) of ground cinnamon. Heavily dust the cavity of the mold with flour, tapping out the excess. Press enough chilled dough into the cavity to fill it, cutting away excess dough. Holding the mold at a 45-degree angle to the counter with the cavity facing down, repeatedly slam the bottom edge of the mold against the counter to release the dough. Bake in a preheated 350°F (175°C) oven until the cookies are light brown on the edges, about 30 minutes.

LEMON MERINGUE TARTS

I had other plans for the lemon tart beneath that wave of torched meringue. I'd planned to sprinkle a thin layer of sugar over the lemon curd and torch it until it caramelized, like a crème brûlée—shattering that amber crust before digging into the silky curd is one of the world's great joys. But then I stumbled on a video in which Philippe Conticini, co-founder and head pastry chef of La Pâtisserie des Rêves in Paris, taught two kids how to make his signature lemon meringue tart. He spread thin layers of lemon confit and lemon curd in a sweet pastry shell, then one of his apprentices turned the tart upside down, pressed it onto a mound of meringue, and slowly raised the tart, leaving a dome leaning to one side. I love when simple techniques create such exquisite effects, so out went the brûléed top and in came the meringue wave.

Serves 8

LEMON CURD

1 cup (240 grams) heavy cream

3 lemons

¾ cup plus 2 tablespoons (175 grams) granulated sugar

4 large eggs

4 large egg yolks

½ cup (120 grams) freshly squeezed lemon juice (from zested lemons)

CRUST

17 ounces (480 grams) Vanilla Bean Short Tart Dough (page 333), fully baked as eight 4¼-inch (11-cm) round tart crusts

MERINGUE

3.7 ounces (105 grams; about 3 large) egg whites

¾ cup (150 grams) granulated sugar

Set a rack in the middle of the oven and preheat the oven to 250°F (120°C).

To make the lemon curd, in a small saucepan over medium heat, bring the cream to just below a boil, stirring frequently. Take the pan off the heat and cover to keep the cream hot.

Using a fine-tooth rasp grater, grate the zest of the lemons (avoiding the bitter white pith) directly into a medium saucepan. Add the sugar and use your fingertips to rub the zest into the sugar. Add the eggs, yolks, and lemon juice, whisking until the eggs lighten in color and the sugar dissolves, about 3 minutes. While continuing to whisk the egg mixture constantly, drizzle in about half of the hot cream. Add the rest of the cream all at once. Set the pan over medium heat and cook until the curd thickens slightly and registers 162°F (72°C) on an instant-read thermometer, 5 to 10 minutes, constantly stirring and scraping the bottom of the pan with a silicone spatula.

Pour the curd through a mesh strainer into a large glass measuring cup and scrape any curd clinging to the bottom of the strainer into the cup.

Divide the curd evenly among the baked tart crusts (⅓ cup; 90 grams each). Transfer the pans to a baking sheet and bake until the centers jiggle slightly when the pans are gently shaken, about 25 minutes. Slide the pans onto a wire rack to cool completely.

Transfer the pans back to the baking sheet, cover the tarts with a large piece of plastic wrap, pressing it directly onto the surfaces of the tarts, and refrigerate for 2 hours.

Shortly before assembly, ***make the meringue.*** In the bowl of a stand mixer set over a medium saucepan filled with 2 inches (5 cm) of barely simmering water, whisk the egg whites and sugar until the sugar dissolves and the mixture registers 162°F (72°C) on an instant-read thermometer, 6 to 8 minutes. Attach the bowl and fit the whisk attachment onto the mixer. Beat at medium-high speed until the meringue is thick, glossy, and completely cool, about 6 minutes. Scrape the meringue into a large shallow bowl.

(continued on page 184)

Shortly before serving, ***assemble the tarts.*** Set the tarts pans on overturned shot glasses and gently release their rings. Slip the tip of a small knife between the crust and bottom of each tart pan and run it all around the edges to loosen the crusts. Carefully slide the tarts from their bases onto the baking sheet.

Using a small offset spatula, spread a big dollop of meringue over the surface of each tart in an even layer. Shape the meringue remaining in the bowl into a mound. Invert and press the tarts, one by one, onto the meringue mound, slowly raising them as you rotate the bowl with your other hand to create a pointed meringue swirl. Transfer the tarts to serving plates. Using a kitchen torch, toast the meringue tops until golden brown, and serve.

Storage: The tarts are best shortly after they are made, but they will keep, on a baking sheet covered with an aluminum foil tent (poke holes in the foil with a fork to prevent condensation), in the refrigerator for up to 8 hours.

PEACH & SOUR CHERRY COBBLER

I don't remember when I baked my first cobbler, but I'm certain that I would have liked to have it in my baking repertoire earlier. I liken cobbler to a one-pot meal with the bread baked on top, and I find it odd that it has been so foreign to Turkey, where dunking bread into one-pot meals is deeply seated in our culture. Making up for lost time, I make cobbler every chance I get once ripe peaches hit the market. I like to mix sweet fruits with sour ones for balance, so I always throw sour cherries into my cobblers. On the rare occasions when I have drunken sour cherries left over from the previous year's sour cherry liqueur (page 288), I throw in a few as boozy surprises.

This recipe is straightforward, but I have one piece of important advice: To prevent the bottom of the biscuits from becoming soggy, the juices released from the fruits must stay below the fruit pieces throughout baking. The key to achieving this is using the right size baking dish—a slightly smaller one will be fine, but in a larger one, the fruit pieces will not be packed tightly enough to hold the biscuits aloft.

Serves 8

BISCUITS

7 tablespoons (3.5 ounces; 100 grams) cold unsalted butter

1½ cups (210 grams) all-purpose flour, plus more for shaping dough

⅓ cup (67 grams) granulated sugar

1¾ teaspoons (7 grams) baking powder

¼ teaspoon (2 grams) fine sea salt

½ cup (120 grams) cold heavy cream

FILLING

3.3 pounds (1.5 kilograms; 6 to 7 large) fresh peaches

3 cups (14.8 ounces; 420 grams) pitted fresh sour cherries (from about 1.1 pounds; 500 grams sour cherries with pits and stems)

½ cup plus 2 tablespoons (125 grams) granulated sugar

1 tablespoon plus 2 teaspoons (13 grams) cornstarch

1 tablespoon (15 grams) freshly squeezed lemon juice

To make the biscuits, cut the butter into ¾-inch (2-cm) pieces and freeze for 15 minutes.

In a large bowl, whisk the flour, sugar, baking powder, and salt until blended. Add the butter pieces and toss to coat them in flour. Using a pastry blender, cut the butter into the flour until most of the butter pieces are the size of fat peas. Pour the cream evenly over the mixture and stir with a fork until clumps form.

Heavily dust a large sheet of parchment paper with flour. Scrape the mixture onto the parchment and dust it heavily with flour. Using your hands, gently press the clumps together and shape the dough into a 1-inch-thick (2.5-cm) rectangle measuring 4 by 8 inches (10 by 20.5 cm). Wrap the dough tightly with the parchment. Smooth the top with a rolling pin and the sides with the palms of your hands. Transfer the wrapped dough to a baking sheet and freeze until firm, about 30 minutes. (Once firm, you can cut the dough into eight 2-inch (5-cm) squares, individually wrap them airtight, and refrigerate for up to 2 days or freeze for up to 2 months. No need to thaw, though you may need to add 5 to 10 minutes to the baking time.)

Set a rack in the middle of the oven and preheat the oven to 400°F (200°C).

While the dough chills, **make the filling.** Peel the peaches, cut them in half lengthwise (top to bottom), remove and discard the pits, and cut the halves lengthwise into ½-inch-thick (1.3-cm) slices. In a 13-by-9-inch (33-by-23-cm) rectangular baking dish that is at least 2¾ inches (7 cm) deep, gently toss the peach slices with the cherries, sugar, cornstarch, and lemon juice. Spread the filling evenly in the pan. (For individual servings, use eight 4-inch [10-cm] round baking dishes that are at least 2¾ inches [7 cm] deep and divide the filling evenly among the dishes.)

Bake for 20 minutes, stirring once halfway through the baking time.

(ingredients and method continued on page 189)

2 tablespoons (30 grams) heavy
    cream

1 tablespoon (13 grams) granulated
    sugar

Three-Bean Vanilla Ice Cream
    (page 247), optional

While the filling bakes, ***glaze the biscuits.*** Unwrap the chilled dough and place it on a flat surface. Cut the dough in half lengthwise, then cut each half crosswise into 4 equal pieces to make eight 2-inch (5-cm) square biscuits. Using a pastry brush, brush the biscuit tops with the cream. Sprinkle the sugar evenly over the biscuits. Refrigerate the glazed biscuits, uncovered, until the filling is ready.

Remove the baking dish from the oven, stir the filling, and spread it evenly with the back of a spoon. Arrange the chilled biscuits evenly over the fruit, making 2 rows of 4 biscuits each. (For individual servings, top the fruit in each baking dish with one biscuit.)

Return the baking dish to the oven and bake until the tops of the biscuits are golden, about 35 minutes, rotating the dish halfway through the baking time.

Set the dish on a wire rack to cool for 15 minutes. Scoop the filling into serving bowls and top each one with a biscuit. Serve warm, with vanilla ice cream if you wish.

Storage: The cobbler should be served the day it is made. Before serving later in the day, reheat in a preheated 350°F (175°C) oven until warmed through, about 10 minutes.

STRAWBERRY & RASPBERRY CRUMBLE

I don't know what I'd do without fruit crumbles. They are the perfect comforting dessert when you have only time and energy enough to slice fruits, mix them with sugar, and spread them in a baking dish. If you keep a stash of topping in your freezer, a crumble for one or a crowd will be ready for the oven before it is heated. Pop it in when you sit down for dinner, and by the time you are itching for something sweet, berries will be bubbling in their juices beneath a crispy topping.

I like to mix sweet fruits with tart ones for balance, and I select the topping ingredients to complement the fruits. My favorite combination is berries with an almond streusel topping, but tropical fruits with coconut streusel or fall fruits paired with hazelnuts are equally comforting.

Whatever you choose, make sure to have great vanilla ice cream nearby when the bubbling subsides.

Serves 6

TOPPING

14 tablespoons (7 ounces; 200 grams) cold unsalted butter

1½ cups (210 grams) all-purpose flour

¾ cup plus 1 tablespoon (163 grams) granulated sugar

¾ cup (75 grams) blanched almond flour

¼ teaspoon (2 grams) fine sea salt

FILLING

3¾ cups (15.9 ounces; 450 grams) fresh strawberries, hulled

2½ cups (10.6 ounces; 300 grams) fresh raspberries

¼ cup (50 grams) granulated sugar

2 teaspoons (5 grams) cornstarch

2 teaspoons (10 grams) freshly squeezed lemon juice

SERVING

Three-Bean Vanilla Ice Cream (page 247), optional

To make the topping, cut the butter into ½-inch (1.3-cm) pieces and freeze for 15 minutes.

Set a rack in the middle of the oven and preheat the oven to 375°F (190°C).

In a large bowl, whisk together the flour, sugar, almond flour, and salt. Add the frozen butter pieces and toss to coat with the flour mixture. Using a pastry blender, cut the butter into the dry ingredients until most of the pieces are the size of green lentils. Cover with plastic wrap and freeze for 15 minutes. (The topping will keep in an airtight container in the refrigerator for up to 3 days or in the freezer for up to 2 months. No need to thaw.)

To make the filling, cut larger strawberries lengthwise (top to bottom) into quarters and smaller ones lengthwise in half. In a large bowl, gently toss the strawberries and raspberries with the sugar, cornstarch, and lemon juice. Spread the filling evenly in a 15¾-by-8¾-inch (40-by-22-cm) oval or 13-by-9-inch (33-by-23-cm) rectangular baking dish that is at least 1½ inches (4 cm) deep. Sprinkle the topping evenly over the filling. (For individual servings, use six 4-inch [10-cm] round baking dishes that are at least 1½ inches [4 cm] deep, dividing the filling and topping evenly among the dishes. Baking and cooling times are the same for individual baking dishes.)

Set the baking dish on a baking sheet lined with aluminum foil and bake until the topping is golden, 50 to 55 minutes, rotating the dish halfway through the baking time.

Set the dish on a wire rack to cool for 15 minutes. Serve warm, with vanilla ice cream if you wish.

Storage: The crumble is best shortly after it is made, but it will keep, wrapped airtight, in the refrigerator for up to 24 hours. Before serving, reheat in a preheated 350°F (175°C) oven until warmed through, 10 to 15 minutes.

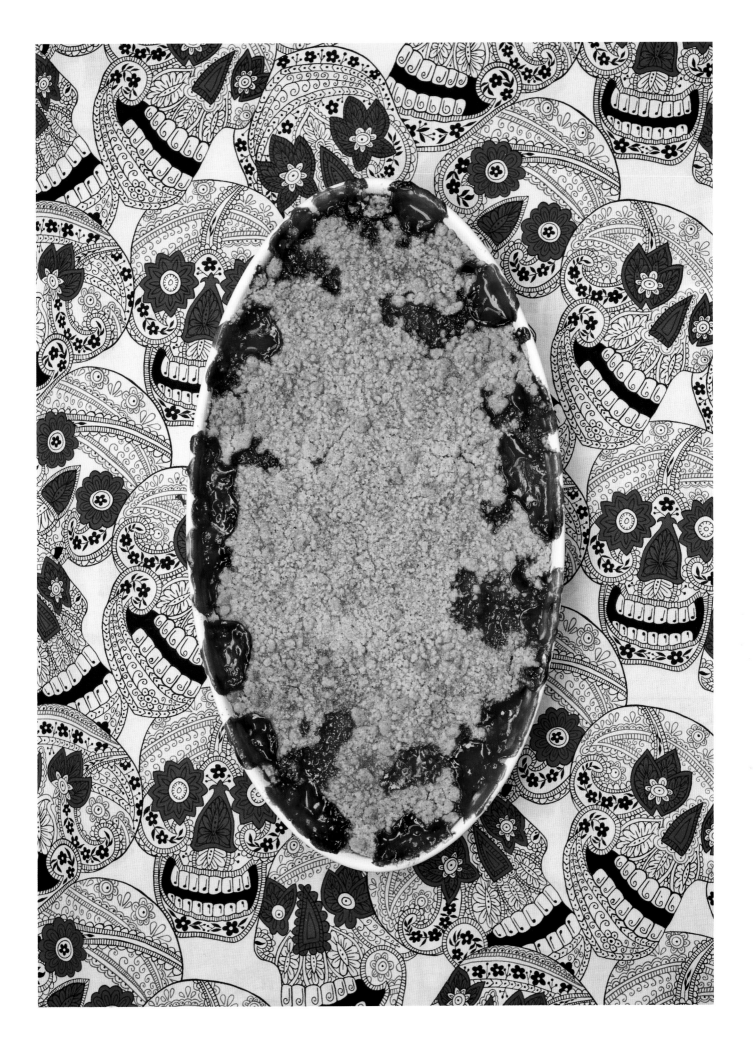

RASPBERRY JEWEL PLUOT GALETTE

Two years before opening Chez Panisse, Alice Waters, together with her friend from the Montessori Centre, began a journey in London that ended in a remote village in Turkey. In the middle of nowhere, they ran out of gas and asked for help from a big-eyed boy. The boy mimed that there was no gas left to pump, but when they asked for food he led them to his house. He built a fire out of pinecones, put on a teapot, and came back with a tiny piece of cheese, which he cut into microscopic portions to serve them.

Realizing the big-eyed boy had given them everything he had, expecting nothing in return, Alice was deeply moved. In an essay she contributed to the collection *The Kindness of Strangers* by Don George, she recounts the incident as "A small miracle of trust, and a lesson in hospitality that changed my life forever."

Forty years passed, and another big-eyed boy from Turkey dined at Alice's restaurant. She offered me no cheese nor gave me everything she had, but she did serve up a feast to remember.

About a month later, Chez Panisse celebrated its fortieth anniversary with a series of gatherings around the Bay Area. Hundreds of people who had worked in the restaurant and café gathered together alongside dozens of culinary legends. Glued to my monitor, I devoured every pixel of every photo from the event that was shared online, but I stopped dead in my tracks when I saw David Lebovitz's post picturing a brush dripping with glaze promenading over pluot slices fanned out on a flaky crust. It was love at first sight. Thank God I can bake, I told myself. If not, after seeing what I saw I might have just died.

With the next morning's first light, I was out the door hunting for pluots. David's post had no recipe, but I could see what the folks at Chez Panisse were doing. They must have found the most fragrant pluots of the season and realized instinctively that they were destined for a tart—filled using as few ingredients as possible. Actually, just two: pluots and sugar.

I don't know for sure whether this was indeed what they had intended, but if it was I must say it was genius, because the galette needs nothing more. You see, pluots are rich in pectin, and forty-five minutes in the oven with sugar means instant jam. Yes, this galette creates its own filling! The sugar draws moisture from the pluots, the heat turns it into a syrup, and that pectin in the pluots quickly turns that syrup to jam.

The same logic applies to the glaze: grate two pluots into a pot, add sugar, and seven minutes later the glaze is ready. If you've made Raspberry Jewel Pluot Jam (page 305), you can use about half a cup of that instead, but I can't recommend any other substitutions. It would be a crime to glaze this beauty any other way.

The Raspberry Jewel pluot has firm, sweet, red flesh, balanced by a hint of acid. If you can find another variety that shares these characteristics, you may try it in its place.

Serves 8 to 10

FILLING

1.32 pounds (600 grams; about 6 large) firm-ripe fresh Raspberry Jewel pluots

3 tablespoons plus 1 teaspoon (42 grams) granulated sugar

1 tablespoon (0.5 ounces; 15 grams) unsalted butter, melted

CRUST

17 ounces (480 grams) Flaky Pie Dough (page 328), rolled out as a 13-inch (33-cm) galette dough and chilled

Set a rack in the middle of the oven and preheat the oven to 375°F (190°C).

To make the filling, cut the pluots in half lengthwise (top to bottom), remove and discard the pits, and cut the halves lengthwise into ¼-inch-thick (6-mm) slices.

Peel away the plastic wrap and top parchment sheet from the chilled dough. Sprinkle 1 tablespoon (13 grams) of the sugar evenly over the surface, leaving a 1½-inch (4-cm) border all around. Arrange the pluot slices over the sugar in slightly overlapping concentric circles. Sprinkle 2 tablespoons (25 grams) of the sugar evenly over the slices. Working from the outside in, roll up the border of the dough in a tight cylinder until it touches the fruit. Brush the edges with the melted butter and sprinkle the remaining 1 teaspoon (4 grams) of sugar evenly over the rim.

(ingredients and method continued on page 195)

7 ounces (200 grams; about 2 large) firm-ripe fresh Raspberry Jewel pluots

½ cup (100 grams) granulated sugar

Three-Bean Vanilla Ice Cream (page 247), optional

Bake until the crust is golden and the juices released from the fruit have thickened, about 45 minutes, rotating the sheet halfway through the baking time.

Meanwhile, ***make the glaze.*** Without peeling them, grate the pluots into a medium saucepan using the largest holes of a box grater. Stir in the sugar and let stand until the pluots release their juices and the sugar dissolves, about 10 minutes.

Set the pan over high heat and bring the mixture to a boil. Reduce the heat to medium-high and cook until it has the consistency of runny jam, about 7 minutes, stirring occasionally. Scrape the mixture into a fine-mesh strainer set over a medium heatproof bowl and strain, pressing hard with a silicone spatula until there is only pulp left in the strainer. Scrape any glaze clinging to the bottom of the strainer into the bowl. Discard the pulp.

When the galette is ready, slide it onto a wire rack to cool for 10 minutes, then transfer it to a serving plate. Using a pastry brush, apply the glaze generously over the pluot slices and serve immediately, with vanilla ice cream if you wish.

Transfer the remaining glaze to a small bowl, cover tightly with plastic wrap, and store in the refrigerator.

Storage: The galette is best shortly after it is made, but it will keep, wrapped airtight, in the refrigerator for up to 2 days. Before serving, reheat in a preheated 325°F (160°C) oven until warmed through, about 10 minutes, and refresh the fruit layer with leftover glaze warmed in a small saucepan over low heat. You can substitute leftover glaze for the raspberry syrup in Raspberry Lemonade (page 292) to make pluot lemonade.

FIG, THYME & BLUE CHEESE GALETTE

The inspiration for this galette was a fruit plate my parents used to prepare for me when I was a child. At the start of fall, when the fig and fresh walnut seasons intersect, my mom would crack open walnuts and peel off their skins, then my father would stuff them into the season's ripest figs and drizzle them with a little honey before bringing them to my room. What took them thirty minutes to prepare would be gone in thirty seconds.

This is a grown-up galette version of that fruit plate, with the addition of a silky blue cheese filling that takes three minutes to prepare. Delicate, newly harvested walnuts get lost among the strong flavors, so there's no need to seek them out for this recipe. A drizzle of thyme honey at the last minute accentuates the fresh thyme and binds the salty and sweet elements.

Being both sweet and savory, this galette can stand in for both the cheese and the dessert course at the end of a meal.

Serves 8 to 10

CRUST

17 ounces (480 grams) Flaky Pie Dough (page 328), rolled out as a 13-inch (33-cm) galette dough and chilled

FILLING

4.2 ounces (120 grams) full-fat cream cheese

2.1 ounces (60 grams) Roquefort or Danish blue cheese

3 tablespoons (45 grams) heavy cream

1.1 pounds (500 grams; about 5 medium) fresh black figs

½ cup (45 grams) walnut halves

3 tablespoons (60 grams) thyme honey or other mild-flavored honey

2 tablespoons (2 grams) loosely packed fresh thyme leaves (10 to 15 medium sprigs)

Set a rack in the middle of the oven and preheat the oven to 375°F (190°C).

Peel away the plastic wrap and top parchment sheet from the chilled dough. Flute the edges of the dough by using your index finger to push it inward about ¾ inch (2 cm) all around, spacing the flutes about ¾ inch (2 cm) apart. Lay the parchment paper back on top. Cut a sheet of aluminum foil twice the size of the dough, fold it in half and place it over the parchment. While pressing down on the center with your palm, pull up the sides of the foil about 1 inch (2.5 cm) to create a raised rim just inside the fluted edge. Fill the foil with pie weights or dried beans.

Bake the crust for 25 minutes. Lift out the parchment, foil, and pie weights. Return the crust to the oven and bake until it is golden, about 15 minutes.

Slide the crust onto a wire rack to cool completely. If you won't be serving the galette until later in the day, once cooled, slide the crust onto a serving plate, cover with plastic wrap, and keep at room temperature until assembly.

Shortly before serving, **make the filling** and **assemble the galette.** In a medium bowl, puree the cream cheese, Roquefort, and cream with an immersion blender (or in a food processor fitted with a metal blade) until smooth.

Slide the baked crust onto a serving plate and scrape the filling into the center of the crust. Spread the filling evenly over the crust with a small offset spatula, leaving a 1-inch (2.5-cm) border around the edge.

Trim away the stem ends of the figs and quarter the figs lengthwise (top to bottom). Arrange the fig pieces over the filling in two concentric circles with the stem ends all facing the same direction. Break the walnut halves into large pieces and scatter them between the figs. Drizzle the honey over the filling. Sprinkle the thyme leaves evenly over the filling, and serve.

Storage: The galette should be served shortly after it is made, as with time the filling will cause the crust to soften. To make ahead, keep the components separate and assemble the galette just before serving.

PEEL-TO-STEM APPLE PIE

After discovering the gelling power of apple pectin (see page 296), I knew I had to revisit my apple pie recipe. I had buried the recipe in the "maybe" pile long before I started working on my book. Now it was time to polish it.

I had always imagined cinnamon-specked apple slices suspended in a thick, gooey sauce under a golden-brown shell that shatters with each bite. The best I had achieved was having the fruit swim in a pool of sauce that left the bottom crust soggy. I hoped that the pectin stock I would make with the apple peels and cores would thicken the sauce for the pie of my dreams.

I baked what I had in mind, waited impatiently for the pie to cool, cut a slice, and was disappointed. There was improvement, but the filling still wasn't as thick as I had hoped. I returned the recipe to the "maybe" pile until I thought of another ingredient: *salep.*

Salep is a powder made from dried tubers of terrestrial orchids that grow in parts of Anatolia. The plant contains a nutritious polysaccharide (complex carbohydrate) called glucomannan, which gives Turkish ice cream its silky, elastic texture. Salep also refers to a wintertime drink in Turkey made with milk and sugar, thickened with salep powder, and topped with cinnamon. To distinguish it from the drink, the ingredient is referred to as *saf* ("pure") salep.

Pure salep turned my apple stock into a silky, gooey sauce and thickened it enough to hold the distinct layers of apple slices tightly together.

Sadly, the orchids from which salep is made are endangered, and it is illegal to export pure salep, so your chances of finding it are slim. Happily, my dear friend Rachel Boller, who tested almost every recipe in this book, had great success substituting glutinous rice flour.

If you are curious about salep and ever find yourself in İstanbul, look for it at the Spice Bazaar. It is expensive, so be sure to buy it from a reliable source, like Ucuzcular Baharat in the Spice Bazaar (see page 365). Do steer clear of the boxed instant salep mixes (usually with a photo of a steaming cup on the front)—these contain the smallest amount of pure salep needed to include it on the label and are loaded with starches and thickeners.

Serves 8 to 10

CRUST

2.12 pounds (960 grams) Flaky Pie Dough (page 328), rolled out as two 13-inch (33-cm) rounds for a double-crust pie and chilled

FILLING

2.2 pounds (1 kilogram; 4 to 5 large) Granny Smith apples

2.2 pounds (1 kilogram; 4 to 5 large) sweet and firm apples, such as Fuji or Gala

1 cup (200 grams) granulated sugar

⅓ cup (80 grams) freshly squeezed lemon juice

3 tablespoons (23 grams) cornstarch

2 teaspoons (6 grams) ground cinnamon

1½ cups (360 grams) water

3½ tablespoons (1.7 ounces; 50 grams) unsalted butter

To make the crust, peel away the parchment from one of the dough rounds, leaving the other round in the refrigerator. Center the dough over a 10¼-inch (26-cm) fluted pie dish that is 2⅜ inch (6 cm) deep, easing it across the bottom and up the sides without pressing the edges onto the sides of the dish. Trim the edges of the dough to leave a ½-inch (1.3-cm) overhang. Cover with plastic wrap and refrigerate until needed.

To make the filling, peel, core, and cut both types of apples in half lengthwise (top to bottom). Do not discard the cores and peels. Use a mandoline or sharp knife to slice the apples crosswise into 1/16- to ⅛-inch-thick (2- to 3-mm) slices. Transfer the slices into a bowl large enough to comfortably toss them. Add the sugar, lemon juice, cornstarch, and cinnamon, tossing them gently to avoid breaking up the apple slices too much. Let the apples macerate until they release their juices, about 20 minutes.

Meanwhile, coarsely chop the apple cores and peels and transfer them to a medium saucepan. Add the water, cover, and bring to a boil over high heat. Reduce the heat to medium and cook, partially covered, until ½ inch (1.3 cm) of liquid is left in the pan, 10 to 15 minutes. Remove the pan from the heat and strain the mixture through a mesh strainer into a separate medium saucepan, pressing on the solids to extract all of the apple stock.

(ingredients and method continued on page 201)

2 teaspoons (5 grams) pure salep
  or glutinous rice flour
  (see headnote)

¼ teaspoon (2 grams) fine sea salt

GLAZE

1 large egg yolk

1 tablespoon (15 grams) heavy
  cream

1 tablespoon (13 grams) granulated
  sugar

SERVING

Salted Caramel Ice Cream
  (page 248), optional

Set mesh strainers over two large bowls, roughly divide the macerated apple slices with their juices between the strainers, and let them drain for 30 minutes.

Transfer the apple slices from the strainers to a large bowl, cover with plastic wrap, and refrigerate until needed. Scrape the juices from the two bowls into the apple stock in the pan, and cook over medium-high heat, stirring occasionally, until it is reduced to ½ cup (160 grams), 15 to 30 minutes, depending on how much juice the apples have released. Watch closely toward the end to prevent scorching.

Remove the pan from the heat, immediately add the butter, salep, and salt, and whisk until blended. (***If using glutinous rice flour,*** cook an additional 2 minutes, whisking constantly.) Scrape the apple sauce into a bowl and refrigerate, uncovered, until it reaches room temperature, 15 to 20 minutes. Once cool, the mixture will be sticky and as thick as porridge.

To assemble the pie, stack about one-quarter of the chilled apple slices in concentric circles over the bottom of the chilled crust. Spread about one-third of the apple sauce evenly over the slices. Continue layering in this manner until you have used all of the apples and sauce, ending with apple slices. The slices will rise about 1 inch (2.5 cm) above the lip of the dish. If the edges of the dough are very soft, freeze the pie before continuing, uncovered, until the edges are firm, about 10 minutes.

Meanwhile, ***make the glaze.*** In a small bowl, whisk the egg yolk and heavy cream with a fork until blended.

Remove the pie from the freezer and the second dough round from the refrigerator, peel away the parchment, and center the dough over the filling. If needed, trim the dough to make a 1-inch (2.5-cm) overhang. Tuck the overhang under the bottom crust and press the dough firmly onto the fluted edges of the pie pan to seal it. Brush the dough with the glaze and sprinkle the sugar evenly over the top. Starting about 1 inch (2.5 cm) from the center, cut 4 evenly spaced slits 2 inches (5 cm) long as steam vents on the top crust. Freeze the pie, uncovered, for 30 minutes.

Meanwhile, set a rack in the lower third of the oven, center a rimmed baking sheet lined with aluminum foil on the rack, and preheat the oven to 400°F (200°C).

Set the pie on the baking sheet in the oven and bake for 20 minutes, then reduce the oven temperature to 350°F (175°C) and continue baking until the crust is golden brown and the juices are bubbling up through the slits, about 55 minutes longer.

Transfer the pie to a wire rack and let cool for at least 3 hours. Serve warm or at room temperature, with salted caramel ice cream if you wish.

Storage: The pie is best the day it is made, but it will keep, wrapped airtight, at room temperature for up to 2 days or in the refrigerator for up to 4 days. Before serving, reheat in a preheated 350°F (175°C) oven until warmed through, 15 to 20 minutes.

TOMATO CONFIT & PESTO QUICHE

When I think of summer, I think of tomatoes and basil. And when I think of tomatoes and basil, I think of this quiche, which brings the two together into one of their most delicious forms.

As you'll notice, it is made from four separate recipes—pie dough, confit tomatoes, pesto, and crème fraîche. But don't roll your eyes just yet—each of these recipes is a must-have for summer, and the recipes will provide you with plenty of leftovers. If you've made a double recipe of the dough, as I always do, thaw the remaining pie dough overnight and you'll have a fruit galette on the table in no time. Keep a bowl of crème fraîche in the fridge, and soon a big dollop of it alongside a bowl of berries will become your favorite summer snack. Freeze batches of pesto and you'll thank yourself for its fresh flavor in fall and winter. Prepare the confit tomatoes, and you'll thank me as they melt in your mouth—or curse me when you devour an entire loaf of bread while sopping up the tomato-infused oil.

Serves 8 to 10

CRUST

17 ounces (480 grams) Flaky Pie Dough (page 328), partially baked as a 10¼-inch (26-cm) quiche crust

1.8 ounces (50 grams) Parmigiano-Reggiano, finely grated

FILLING

½ cup (120 grams) Crème Fraîche (page 338) or heavy cream

1 large egg

1 large egg yolk

⅓ cup plus 2 tablespoons (110 grams) Pesto (page 343)

1 ounce (28 grams) Parmigiano-Reggiano, finely grated

7 (about 10.6 ounces; 300 grams) confit tomato halves, drained (see Tomato Confit, page 340)

When preparing the quiche crust, immediately after transferring it from the oven to a wire rack, sprinkle the cheese evenly over the bottom of the crust. Reduce the oven temperature to 270°F (130°C).

To make the filling, in a medium bowl, whisk the crème fraîche, egg, yolk, and ⅓ cup (80 grams) of the pesto with a fork until blended, taking care not to incorporate too much air. Scrape the filling into the crust, sprinkle the cheese evenly over it, and arrange the confit tomato halves on top.

Bake until the filling sets around the edges but jiggles slightly in the center when the pan is gently shaken, about 1 hour.

Slide the pan onto a wire rack and cool for 20 minutes.

Set the quiche in its pan on an overturned flat-bottomed bowl (or a wide can) and gently release the ring. Slip the tip of a small knife between the crust and the bottom of the pan and run it all around the edge to loosen the crust. Carefully slide the quiche onto a serving plate. Spread the remaining 2 tablespoons (30 grams) of pesto in the center and around each confit tomato half, and serve right away.

Storage: The quiche is best shortly after it is made, but it will keep, wrapped airtight, in the refrigerator for up to 24 hours. Before serving, reheat in a preheated 325°F (160°C) oven until warmed through, 10 to 15 minutes.

BREADS & PASTRIES

BRIOCHE

You may not be surprised to learn that the first bread I attempted was brioche. I remember it as if it were yesterday. I knew I was in trouble long before I pulled it from the oven. The smell of yeast and butter filled the kitchen, rendering me powerless. That rich and tender crumb was impossible to resist, and I finished the entire loaf before the day was through.

I haven't changed a bit in terms of my inability to resist it, but the way I make brioche now is considerably different. I rely on a quick sponge to get a head start, add the smallest amount of yeast possible, and use the best butter I can find.

Brioche dough needs long beating in a powerful stand mixer, which inevitably warms it. If the dough gets too warm, it might prove difficult to blend in the softened butter without it melting. Using cold eggs helps prevent that, but the temperature of the butter is important, too. You should easily leave a deep indentation by pressing your finger into the butter, but it should not melt from the heat of your finger.

Brioche stales quickly, so unless you're as powerless as I am, you must come up with ideas for making use of leftovers. French toast would be an obvious choice for me, especially at the end of summer when I can cut its richness with a tangy sour cherry syrup.

Makes 1 standard loaf

SPONGE

½ cup (70 grams) bread flour

1¼ teaspoons (5 grams) instant yeast

¼ cup (60 grams) whole milk, at room temperature

DOUGH

3 cold large eggs

1½ cups (210 grams) bread flour, plus more for shaping

2 tablespoons (25 grams) granulated sugar

1 teaspoon (8 grams) fine sea salt

10 tablespoons plus 2 teaspoons (5.3 ounces; 150 grams) unsalted butter, cut into large pieces and softened, plus more for bowl and pan

To make the sponge, in the bowl of a stand mixer, stir together the flour and yeast. Pour in the milk and stir with a silicone spatula until well blended. Cover the bowl tightly with plastic wrap and let the dough rest at room temperature for 1 hour.

To make the dough, in a small bowl, beat the eggs with a fork until well blended. Add the beaten eggs to the sponge and whisk until blended. Add the flour, sugar, and salt and stir with the spatula until the flour is absorbed.

Attach the bowl and fit the dough hook onto the mixer and beat at medium speed for 5 minutes. With the mixer running, add the butter in five equal parts, beating until completely blended after each addition, about 1 minute each time. After the last addition, beat until the dough starts to pull away from the sides of the bowl, 8 to 10 minutes. The dough will be smooth, sticky, and elastic. Scrape the dough into a generously buttered large bowl, cover tightly with lightly buttered plastic wrap, and let rise at room temperature until almost tripled in size, about 2 hours.

Deflate the dough by pressing down in the center with your fist. Lightly butter your palm and slide it under the dough so that about half of it rests on your palm. Stretch the dough up and fold it over onto itself. Repeat the stretching and folding three times, giving the bowl a quarter turn each time. Roll the dough into a ball in the bowl, cover tightly with plastic wrap, and refrigerate overnight.

The next day, generously butter the bottom and sides of an 8½-by-4½-by-2¾-inch (21.5-by-11.5-by-7-cm; 6-cup) loaf pan.

Deflate the chilled dough by pressing down in the center with your fist. Turn the dough out onto a lightly floured work surface and divide it into 8 equal pieces (about 2.7 ounces; 75 grams each). Roll each piece into a tight ball by pulling the sides to the bottom and pinching them together. Roll each ball on the work surface under your cupped palm until they are perfectly round and the bottoms are sealed.

(ingredients and method continued on page 208)

GLAZE
1 large egg

Pinch of fine sea salt

Place the balls sealed side down in the prepared pan, making two rows of four balls. Cover the pan loosely with lightly buttered plastic wrap and let rise at room temperature until the dough reaches the lip of the pan, about 2 hours.

About 30 minutes before the dough is ready, set a rack in the middle of the oven and preheat the oven to 375°F (190°C).

To make the glaze, in a small bowl, beat the egg and salt with a fork until frothy. Using a pastry brush, apply a thin coating of glaze to the dough, taking care not to deflate it. Wait for 5 minutes, then gently apply a second coating.

Bake until the top is golden brown and an instant-read thermometer inserted into the center registers 190°F (88°C), about 35 minutes.

Set the pan on a wire rack to cool for 20 minutes, then unmold the brioche directly onto the rack to cool until it is barely warm.

Storage: Brioche is best the day it is made, but it will keep, wrapped airtight, at room temperature for up to 2 days.

ROSEMARY & SEA SALT FOCACCIA

It doesn't feel like summer until I have baked the season's first focaccia and used it to sop up meltingly tender confit tomatoes and their infused oil (page 340). You might believe there's already enough olive oil in the recipe and think of me as overindulgent, but trust me, this bread stands ready to soak up more. Yes, there is olive oil in, under, and on the dough, plus an extra lick as it emerges from the oven, but the dimples on top and the hungry holes inside need their share, too. I'm sure you'll be generous.

Makes one 10-by-15-inch (25.5-by-38-cm) loaf

DOUGH

3¼ cups (455 grams) all-purpose flour

1½ teaspoons (6 grams) instant yeast

1¼ cups (300 grams) water, at room temperature

2 tablespoons plus 1 teaspoon (32 grams) extra-virgin olive oil, plus more for bowl, pan, and shaping

1¼ teaspoons (10 grams) fine sea salt

TOPPING

2 tablespoons (28 grams) extra-virgin olive oil

3 tablespoons (5 grams) loosely packed, coarsely chopped fresh rosemary (4 large sprigs)

1 teaspoon (5 grams) flaky sea salt, such as Maldon

To make the dough, in the bowl of a stand mixer, stir together the flour and yeast. Add the water, 1 tablespoon (14 grams) of the olive oil, and the salt. Stir with a silicone spatula until the flour is absorbed.

Attach the bowl and fit the dough hook onto the mixer and beat at medium speed until a sticky dough forms, about 5 minutes. Scrape the dough into a generously oiled large bowl, flip it over to coat completely with oil, cover tightly with plastic wrap, and let the dough rise at room temperature until doubled in size, 1 hour to 1 hour 30 minutes.

Pour the remaining 1 tablespoon plus 1 teaspoon (18 grams) of olive oil into a 15-by-10-inch (38-by-25.5-cm) jelly-roll pan and spread it evenly with your fingers.

Lightly oil your hand and use it to deflate the dough by pressing down in the center with your fist. Generously oil your palm and slide it under the dough so that about half of it rests on your palm. Stretch the dough up and fold it over onto itself. Repeat three times, giving the bowl a quarter turn each time. Scrape the dough into the center of the prepared pan, lightly oil the top with your palm, cover loosely with plastic wrap, and let the dough relax for 10 minutes.

Using generously oiled hands, press and stretch the dough to fill the pan. If it resists, cover the dough with plastic wrap and leave it to relax a couple of minutes longer before continuing. Lightly oil the dough with your palm, cover loosely with plastic wrap, and allow the dough to rise at room temperature until it reaches the lip of the pan, 45 to 60 minutes.

About 30 minutes before the dough is ready, set a rack in the middle of the oven and a broiler tray or roasting pan on the lowest shelf. Preheat the oven to 450°F (230°C).

Put on a kettle of water to boil.

To make the topping, in a small bowl, stir 1 tablespoon (14 grams) of the olive oil with the rosemary. Gently spread the mixture evenly over the dough with the palm of your hand, taking care not to deflate the dough. Dimple the dough all around by gently pressing on the dough with your fingertips. Sprinkle the flaky salt evenly over the dough.

(continued on page 211)

Pour 4 cups (960 grams) of boiling water into the broiler tray and reduce the oven temperature to 400°F (200°C). Bake the focaccia until the top is golden brown, about 30 minutes.

Take the pan out of the oven and use a large metal offset spatula to transfer the focaccia to a wire rack. Brush the top with the remaining 1 tablespoon (14 grams) of olive oil and let cool until it is barely warm, about 20 minutes.

Storage: Focaccia is best the day it is made, but it will keep, wrapped airtight, at room temperature for up to 24 hours.

SOURDOUGH SİMİT

I haven't met a single person who has visited İstanbul without making an instant connection with *simit*, our beloved ring-shaped bread encrusted with sesame seeds. If you've ever been to my city, you must have seen street vendors selling simit from their baskets or trolleys, or even from a tray expertly balanced on their heads. That's the real deal, also called *sokak simidi* ("street-style simit"), which has a dense crumb and a faint sweetness from a dip in grape molasses and water before being covered with sesame seeds and baked.

Here's something you won't find in the streets of İstanbul: sourdough simit.

I made my first sourdough starter right after purchasing a copy of *Tartine Bread*. Recreating the wildly popular San Francisco bakery's basic country bread at home was one of my greatest baking accomplishments. I baked many great breads with that starter, but then my Turkish cookbook project took hold of me so strongly I couldn't find the time to care for it, and eventually we parted ways. Years later, while working on this manuscript, food-writing guru Dianne Jacob visited İstanbul after her workshop in Alaçatı—a small village on the Aegean Sea eastern shoreline—and brought me the most thoughtful gift anyone from the Bay Area could bring to a San Francisco–obsessed home baker in İstanbul: San Francisco sourdough starter culture, which contains the *Lactobacillus sanfranciscensis* bacteria named after my home away from home. It is with great pleasure that I've been baking İstanbul's beloved simit using San Francisco's bacteria ever since.

You'll want the sourdough starter to be at its peak vitality (what I call "mature" in the ingredients list), which is right before it should be fed. If you store your starter in the refrigerator, you'll need to bring it to room temperature and give it two to three feedings before using it. I maintain my starter at 100 percent hydration (equal weights of water and flour). If you're using measuring cups rather than weighing, stir the starter well before measuring.

This recipe, leavened only with sourdough starter, takes two days to make. At the end of the recipe I've included a variation using instant yeast, which reduces the total time to about three hours.

My favorite way to enjoy simit is with thick slices of salty, sharp aged *Trakya kaşar* cheese (similar to Pecorino Romano) tucked between the slices and cherry tomatoes on the side with olive oil and dried thyme. (You can find my savory cookie version of this sandwich on page 72.) Simit doesn't keep well, so the next day I slice a couple of them across the equator, sprinkle the cut sides with cheese and a dash of cayenne pepper, and bake them open-faced under the broiler until the cheese is bubbly. The rest become simit crumbs for pasta and gratin dishes or croutons for soups and salads.

Makes 6 simits

DOUGH

1¼ cups (11.5 ounces; 325 grams) mature 100%-hydration sourdough starter (see headnote)

⅔ cup (160 grams) water, at room temperature

3¼ cups (455 grams) bread flour, plus more for proofing (and shaping, if needed)

1¼ teaspoons (10 grams) fine sea salt

To make the dough, in the bowl of a stand mixer, stir together the starter and water until the starter dissolves. Add the flour and salt, stirring until most of the flour is absorbed.

Attach the bowl and fit the dough hook onto the mixer and beat at medium-low speed until a smooth, stiff, slightly sticky dough forms, about 12 minutes. Cover the bowl with plastic wrap and let the dough relax for 15 minutes.

Line two baking sheets with parchment paper and lightly flour the parchment.

Turn the dough out onto an unfloured work surface and divide it into 12 equal pieces (about 2.7 ounces; 75 grams each). Roll each piece under the palms of your hands into an 18-inch-long (45.5-cm) strand that is about ¾ inch (2 cm) thick. The dough will be slightly sticky, but try not to flour the work surface or the dough so that the strands can stick together tightly when proofed. If you have trouble rolling out the dough, lightly flour the work surface, but make sure to brush off the excess flour after shaping.

(ingredients and method continued on page 215)

COATING

¼ cup (80 grams) grape molasses or light molasses

½ cup (120 grams) boiling water

1¼ cups (200 grams) brown sesame seeds

Place two strands of dough parallel and close to one another, place your palms over each end, and roll the ends in opposite directions to twist the strands 7 to 8 times. Pinch the two ends together to form a 6-inch (15-cm) ring with a 4-inch (10-cm) hole in the center. Place the ring on one of the prepared sheets. Repeat with the remaining strands, evenly spacing 3 rings on each sheet. Lightly flour the tops, cover loosely with plastic wrap, and let proof at room temperature for 3 hours. The rings will puff up slightly. Refrigerate the rings on the sheets for 12 to 14 hours.

At least 30 minutes before baking, set a rack in the middle of the oven and preheat the oven to 500°F (260°C).

To make the coating, in a shallow bowl slightly wider than a ring of dough, whisk together the molasses and water with a fork. Put the sesame seeds in a similar size bowl.

Transfer the chilled dough rings with their parchment to a work surface. Line the baking sheets with clean parchment paper.

Carefully peel away one of the rings, holding it with both hands to prevent it from stretching, and dip it into the molasses mixture. Flip it over to coat the second side, lift it with both hands, and hold it over the bowl for a few seconds to allow excess liquid to drain. Lightly press the ring into the sesame seeds, flipping it to encrust both sides. Sprinkle any uncoated parts with sesame seeds to cover the ring completely. Place the coated ring on one of the prepared sheets. The ring will stretch slightly to measure about 6½ inches (16.5 cm) in diameter with a 4½-inch (11.5-cm) hole in the center. Repeat with the remaining dough rings, arranging half of them on each sheet with about 1 inch (2.5 cm) all around them.

Reduce the oven temperature to 400°F (200°C) and bake one sheet of simits until they are golden brown on top and an instant-read thermometer inserted into a simit registers 212°F (100°C), about 25 minutes. Transfer the simits together with the parchment to a wire rack and let cool until they are barely warm. Repeat to bake the second batch.

Storage: Simits are best the day they are baked, but they will keep, wrapped airtight, at room temperature for up to 24 hours.

(variation on page 216)

YEASTED SİMİT

Makes 6 simits

DOUGH

4 cups (560 grams) bread flour, plus more for resting (and shaping, if needed)

¾ teaspoon (3 grams) instant yeast

1⅓ cups (320 grams) water, at room temperature

1¼ teaspoons (10 grams) fine sea salt

COATING

¼ cup (80 grams) grape molasses or light molasses

½ cup (120 grams) boiling water

1¼ cups (200 grams) brown sesame seeds

To make the dough, in the bowl of a stand mixer, stir together 2 cups (280 grams) of the flour and yeast. Add the water and stir until the flour is absorbed. Cover the bowl with plastic wrap and let the dough rest at room temperature until bubbly and frothy on the surface, about 1 hour 30 minutes.

Add the remaining 2 cups (280 grams) of flour and the salt, stirring until the flour is absorbed. Attach the bowl and fit the dough hook onto the mixer and beat at medium speed until a smooth and slightly sticky dough forms, about 5 minutes. Turn the dough out onto a lightly floured work surface, cover with plastic wrap, and let it relax for 15 minutes.

Meanwhile, set a rack in the middle of the oven and preheat the oven to 500°F (260°C). Line two baking sheets with parchment paper.

To make the coating, in a shallow bowl slightly wider than a ring of dough, whisk together the molasses and water with a fork. Put the sesame seeds in a similar size bowl.

Divide the dough into 12 equal pieces (about 2.5 ounces; 70 grams each). Roll each piece under the palms of your hands into an 18-inch-long (45.5-cm) strand that is about ¾ inch (2 cm) thick. The dough will be slightly sticky, but try not to flour the work surface or the dough so that the strands can stick together tightly when baked. If you have trouble rolling, lightly flour the work surface, but make sure to brush off the excess flour after shaping.

Place two strands of dough parallel and close to one another, place your palms over each end, and roll the ends in opposite directions to twist the strands 7 to 8 times. Pinch the two ends together to form a 6-inch (15-cm) ring with a 4-inch (10-cm) hole in the center. Repeat with the remaining strands.

Dip one of the rings into the molasses mixture, then flip it over to coat the second side. Lift the ring and hold it over the bowl for a few seconds to allow excess liquid to drain. Lightly press the ring into the sesame seeds, flipping it to encrust both sides. Sprinkle any uncoated parts with sesame seeds to cover the ring completely. Place the coated ring on one of the prepared sheets. The ring will stretch slightly to measure about 6½ inches (16.5 cm) in diameter with a 4½-inch (11.5-cm) hole in the center. Repeat with the remaining dough rings, arranging half of them on each of the prepared sheets with about 1 inch (2.5 cm) all around them.

Reduce the oven temperature to 400°F (200°C) and bake one sheet of simits until they are golden brown on top and an instant-read thermometer inserted into a simit registers 212°F (100°C), about 25 minutes. Transfer the simits together with the parchment to a wire rack and let cool until they are barely warm. Repeat to bake the second batch.

Storage: Simits are best the day they are baked, but they will keep, wrapped airtight, at room temperature for up to 24 hours.

WHOLE-WHEAT & KEFIR PULLMAN LOAF

One of the golden rules for great bread is the slower the fermentation, the better the flavor. But that doesn't mean you can't bake great bread quickly; you just have to rely on other things for flavor. I developed this recipe for occasions when I don't have the time and patience to make a bread that requires multiple days to coax the most flavor from the flour but don't want to sacrifice flavor. This bread relies on butter, kefir, honey, and a variety of seeds for flavor, and it takes about three-and-a-half hours to make, start to finish, including an inactive hour of baking time and two hours of resting and proofing—meaning just twenty minutes of actual work. As a bonus, the dough is easy to work with, doesn't require arduous kneading, and comes together in a single bowl—two if you count a small bowl to combine the seeds. It requires no stand mixer or floured work surface, making for easy cleanup.

It is my go-to bread for a late-night grilled cheese sandwich or a quick morning toast topped with a thick layer of butter and homemade jam. Because it slices so beautifully, it is an excellent candidate for seeded toasts to serve alongside dips and spreads, or to use for *canapés*.

Makes 1 large loaf (about 28 slices)

2 ½ cups (350 grams) bread flour

2 ¼ cups (315 grams) whole-wheat flour

1 ⅓ cups (320 grams) unflavored milk kefir, at room temperature

½ cup (120 grams) water, at room temperature

6 tablespoons (3 ounces; 85 grams) unsalted butter, melted and cooled, plus more for pan

3 tablespoons (60 grams) honey

1 tablespoon plus ½ teaspoon (14 grams) instant yeast

3 tablespoons (30 grams) flax seeds

3 tablespoons (26 grams) sunflower seeds

2 tablespoons (20 grams) sesame seeds

2 tablespoons (20 grams) poppy seeds

2 ½ teaspoons (20 grams) fine sea salt

Stir together the bread and whole-wheat flours in a large bowl. Stir in the kefir and water. Knead with one hand until the flour is completely absorbed, 3 to 5 minutes. Cover the bowl tightly with plastic wrap and let rest at room temperature for 30 minutes.

Tear the rested dough into walnut-size pieces, leaving them in the bowl. Add the melted butter, honey, and yeast, and knead until incorporated, 3 to 5 minutes. Cover the bowl tightly with plastic wrap and let the dough rest at room temperature for 30 minutes.

Again, tear the dough into walnut-size pieces. In a small bowl, stir together the flax, sunflower, sesame, and poppy seeds. Reserve 1 tablespoon (10 grams) of the seed blend, stir the salt into the remaining seeds, and add to the dough. Knead until the seeds are evenly incorporated, 3 to 5 minutes.

Generously butter the inside and underside of the lid of a 13-by-4-by-4-inch (33-by-10-by-10-cm) Pullman loaf pan.

Turn the dough out onto an unfloured work surface and stretch it into a 9-by-16-inch (23-by-40.5-cm) rectangle, with a long side facing you. Fold the short sides 1 inch (2.5 cm) inward, pinching the seams to seal. Starting with the side facing you, roll the dough into a tight log and pinch the seam to seal.

Put the dough, sealed side down, into the prepared pan. To ensure an even rise, gently pat down the dough until the top is level and the ends touch the pan on both ends. Sprinkle the reserved seed blend evenly over the dough. Secure the lid, leaving about ½ inch (1.3 cm) of space at one end to observe the rise, and let the dough rise until it is almost touching the underside of the cover, about 1 hour.

(continued on page 219)

At least 20 minutes before the dough is ready, set a rack in the middle of the oven and preheat the oven to 350°F (175°C).

Fully secure the lid and bake until golden brown on top and an instant-read thermometer inserted into the loaf registers 203°F (95°C), 1 hour to 1 hour 10 minutes. Start checking for doneness after 50 minutes by sliding open the lid without removing the pan from the oven.

Take the pan from the oven and remove the lid. Unmold the loaf onto a wire rack to cool completely.

Storage: The loaf will keep, wrapped airtight, at room temperature for up to 3 days or in the refrigerator for up to 1 week.

CROISSANTS & PAINS AU CHOCOLAT

The first time I visited Paris, my expectations for the city's croissants were high. I wasn't disappointed, but my excitement did not reach the same heights as when I took my first bite of Pierre Hermé's Mogador macaron or Franck Kestener's Atlantique chocolate tablet, or when Jacques Genin's mango and passion fruit caramel melted in my mouth. That got me thinking: could I—a home baker from İstanbul, who didn't grow up eating croissants and has made at most a dozen batches in his life—have been making better croissants than the savants of Paris? Absolutely not, but the reason I preferred mine was simple: The best croissant is the one that comes fresh from your oven.

I'm not minimizing the importance of quality ingredients and the grasp of technique that comes only through experience, but the croissant that will make you feel weak in the knees is the one that you'll bake yourself. Isn't that *merveilleux*? All you need is high-quality butter and a reliable recipe that works at home, which I'm here to provide to you.

Croissants depend on distinct layers made by rolling and folding dough and butter that retain the same consistency throughout preparation. It's easy to gauge the consistency of the dough from start to finish, but once the butter is locked inside, it becomes difficult to know how stiff it is. It should be firm enough that it doesn't melt and become absorbed by the dough, but soft enough to easily roll. This ideal consistency is achieved through a long rest in the refrigerator while the dough relaxes, followed by a short time in the freezer to solidify the butter before each fold. Stick patiently to the resting times in the recipe and I promise everything will go smoothly.

If you plan ahead, you can divide the recipe into multiple days, working at a more relaxed pace that fits your schedule. The first day is easiest, taking an hour at most to make the dough, then chilling it overnight. You'll need the better half of the following day to prepare the butter block, laminate the dough, shape the croissants, and proof the dough—about nine hours total. I freeze the dough briefly before baking, but you can leave it in the freezer overnight to bake the following morning.

Don't let the length of the recipe scare you; my instructions at the end for pains au chocolat made with the same dough, and for making croissants with half of the dough and pains au chocolat with the other half, make it look longer.

And how will you know your croissants are as good as I've promised? Wait fifteen minutes after pulling them from the oven and take a big bite—if you barely notice that you're covered in buttery flakes, you've done it.

Makes 8 croissants, 10 pains au chocolat, or 4 croissants and 6 pains au chocolat

DOUGH

3½ cups (490 grams) all-purpose flour, plus more for rolling and shaping

3 tablespoons (38 grams) granulated sugar

2½ teaspoons (10 grams) instant yeast

2 teaspoons (16 grams) fine sea salt

1¼ cups (300 grams) whole milk, at room temperature

5 tablespoons (2.5 ounces; 70 grams) unsalted butter, melted and cooled, plus more for bowl

The day before making the croissants and/or pains au chocolat, **make the dough.**

In a large bowl, stir together the flour, sugar, yeast, and salt. Add the milk and melted butter, stirring until the flour is completely absorbed. Turn the mixture out onto an unfloured work surface and knead to make a rough, slightly sticky dough (photo 1, page 223), about 4 minutes. Avoid adding more flour; the dough will become easier to handle as you knead. Form the dough into a ball, cover with plastic wrap (photo 2, page 223), and let rest at room temperature for 45 minutes. The dough will puff up slightly (photo 3, page 223). Transfer the dough to a generously buttered medium bowl, flip it over to coat with butter completely, cover tightly with plastic wrap, and refrigerate overnight.

(ingredients and method continued on page 222)

BUTTER BLOCK

3 sticks (12 ounces; 340 grams) cold unsalted butter, cut into small pieces

¼ cup (35 grams) all-purpose flour

The next day, *make the butter block.* Cut a 20-inch-long (51-cm) sheet of parchment paper. Fold the parchment in half lengthwise, then fold over the three open sides to create an 8-inch (20.5-cm) square envelope (see photos for making and using the envelope on page 74, keeping in mind that the center will now be an 8-inch square).

In the bowl of a stand mixer fitted with the paddle attachment, beat the butter and flour at medium speed until blended, about 1 minute.

Unfold the envelope and scrape the butter mixture into the center of the square. Leaving about a ½-inch (1.3-cm) border all around, spread out the butter mixture in the square with a small offset spatula as evenly as possible. Fold the envelope, creasing it firmly, and flip it so that the open sides are secured. Roll out the butter mixture from the center to the edges to create an 8-inch (20.5-cm) even slab that is about ¼ inch (6 mm) thick (photo 4). Transfer the wrapped butter block to a baking sheet and refrigerate until firm enough to leave just a slight indentation when you press your finger into it, 30 to 45 minutes.

Meanwhile, turn the chilled dough out onto a lightly floured work surface and roughly shape it into a small rectangle with your hands. Lightly flour the dough and roll it out into a 9-by-15¾-inch (23-by-40-cm) rectangle that is about ⅜ inch (1 cm) thick. Gently stretch out the rounded corners occasionally to make a neat rectangle, taking care not to tear the dough. Transfer the dough to a baking sheet lined with parchment paper, cover with plastic wrap, and freeze for 10 minutes.

For the first fold, place the dough from the freezer on a lightly floured work surface with a short side facing you. Unfold the chilled butter envelope, peel away the parchment, and center the butter block on the dough. Fold the top and bottom sides of the dough over the butter so that the ends meet in the middle (photo 5). Pinch the seam closed (photo 6). Pinch closed the right and left open sides of the dough to fully enclose the butter block in a neatly sealed square.

Turn the dough 90 degrees so that the sealed center seam is perpendicular to you. Working from the center outward on both sides, roll out the dough into a 9½-by-15¾-inch (24-by-40-cm) rectangle, about ⅝ inch (1.6 cm) thick. Lightly flour the work surface and the dough as needed, brushing off the excess flour between folds.

Divide the dough with your eyes lengthwise into three equal pieces. Fold the top third down over the center (photo 7) and the bottom third up over the top (photo 8) to make a 6-by-9½-inch (15-by-24-cm) rectangle (photo 9). Transfer the dough to a baking sheet lined with parchment and cover tightly with plastic wrap. Refrigerate for 1 hour, then freeze for 20 minutes longer.

For the second fold, place the chilled dough on the work surface with a short side facing you. Again, roll out the dough into a 9½-by-15¾-inch (24-by- 40 cm) rectangle, then fold the top third down over the center and the bottom third up over the top. Return the dough to the lined baking sheet and cover tightly with plastic wrap. Refrigerate for 1 hour, then freeze for 20 minutes longer.

(ingredients and method continued on page 226)

For the final fold, place the dough on the work surface with a short side facing you and roll out the dough into a 9½-by-15¾-inch (24-by-40-cm) rectangle. This time, fold the top and bottom sides of the dough almost to the center, leaving about a ¾ inch (2 cm) gap in the middle (photo 10). Fold the bottom up over the top as if you were closing a book. You will have a rectangle that measures 4 by 9½ inches (10 by 24 cm) (photo 11). Return the dough to the lined baking sheet and cover tightly with plastic wrap. Refrigerate for 1 hour, then freeze for 20 minutes.

Place the dough on the work surface with a long side facing you. Roll out the dough into a 9¾-by-20½-inch (25-by-52-cm) rectangle that is about ½ inch (1.3 cm) thick, lightly flouring the work surface and the dough as needed. Trim the dough into a neat 9½-by-20-inch (24-by-51-cm) rectangle. The dough is now ready to form into croissants, pains au chocolat, or both following the instructions below for each.

To form croissants, using diagram A as a guide, use the tip of a paring knife to mark the top edge of the dough every 5 inches (12.5 cm). Starting 2½ inches (6.5 cm) from the left, mark the bottom edge of the dough every 5 inches (12.5 cm). Position a ruler to connect the top left corner with the first mark on the bottom and cut the dough along that line. Pivot the ruler to connect the end of the bottom cut with the next mark along the top and cut the dough along that line. Continue to pivot and connect each ending point to the next point on the opposite side of the dough, making 8 cuts in all. Place the two smaller end pieces with their straight edges together and pinch the seam together to make a triangle matching the others (photo 12); flip it over and pinch the seam on the reverse to seal the pieces together. You will now have 8 matching triangles.

Transfer the triangles to the lined baking sheet, cover tightly with plastic wrap, and freeze until firm, about 15 minutes. Line a baking sheet with parchment paper.

Place a partially frozen triangle on a lightly floured work surface with the base facing you. Roll to lengthen the triangle until it is 12½ inches long (32 cm) and about ¼ inch (6 mm) thick (photo 13). Fold the corners of the base upward and inward about 1 inch (2.5 cm) (photo 14). Roll the triangle from the base to the last 1½ inches (4 cm) of the tip. While holding the dough in place with one hand, stretch the tip of the dough slightly with your other hand to reach it up and tuck it under the front of the roll (photo 15). Repeat with the remaining triangles, arranging them tucked end down on the prepared baking sheet with 2 inches (5 cm) all around them. Cover the sheet loosely with plastic wrap and let rise at room temperature until 1½ times their volume, 2 hours 30 minutes to 3 hours, then freeze for 20 minutes. The croissants are now ready to bake; you may skip to page 230 for instructions.

(ingredients and method continued on page 228)

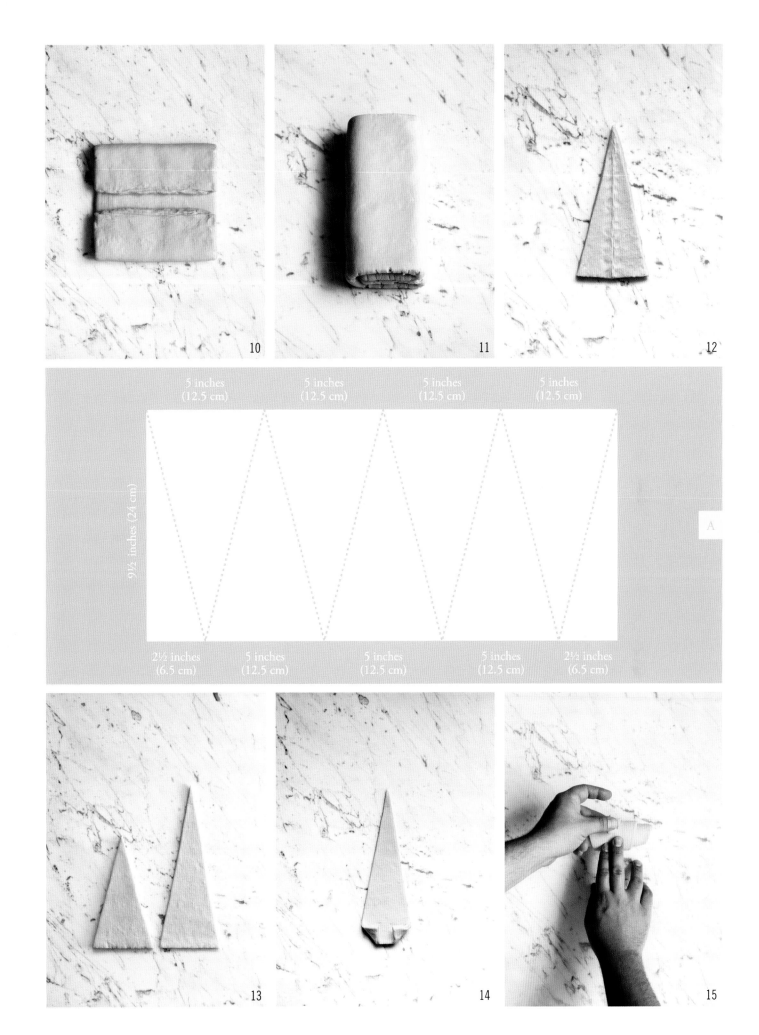

10

11

12

5 inches
(12.5 cm)

5 inches
(12.5 cm)

5 inches
(12.5 cm)

5 inches
(12.5 cm)

9½ inches (24 cm)

A

2½ inches
(6.5 cm)

5 inches
(12.5 cm)

5 inches
(12.5 cm)

5 inches
(12.5 cm)

2½ inches
(6.5 cm)

13

14

15

6.3 ounces (180 grams) bittersweet chocolate (70% cacao), in batons, pistoles, or fèves (or coarsely chopped)

To form pains au chocolat, using diagram B as a guide, cut the dough in half horizontally, then make vertical cuts every 4 inches (10 cm) to make 10 rectangles measuring 4 by 4¾ inches (10 by 12 cm).

Transfer the rectangles to the lined baking sheet, cover tightly with plastic wrap, and freeze until firm, about 15 minutes. Line a baking sheet with parchment paper.

Place a partially frozen rectangle on a lightly floured work surface with a short side facing you. Roll to lengthen the rectangle until it is 4¼ by 8 inches (11 by 20.5 cm) and about ¼ inch (6 mm) thick (photo 16). Arrange 0.6 ounces (18 grams) of chocolate in a 1-inch-thick (2.5-cm) line about 1 inch (2.5 cm) above the base and extending slightly beyond both sides. Fold the base of the dough up and over the chocolate, then roll the dough upward to the top edge (photo 17). Repeat with the remaining rectangles, arranging them tucked end down on the prepared baking sheet with 2 inches (5 cm) all around them. Cover the sheet loosely with plastic wrap and let rise at room temperature until 1½ times their volume, 2 hours 30 minutes to 3 hours, then freeze for 20 minutes. The pains au chocolat are now ready to bake; you may skip to page 230 for instructions.

To form both croissants and pains au chocolat, using diagram C as a guide, cut the chilled dough vertically 9½ inches (24 cm) from the left to form two pieces, a 9½-inch (24-cm) square on the left and a 9½-by-10½ inch (24-by-26.5 cm) rectangle on the right. ***To form croissants with the left piece,*** use the tip of a paring knife to mark the dough in the center at the top (4¾ inches; 12 cm from the left edge) and starting 2⅜ inches (6 cm) from the left and right on the bottom (4¾ inches; 12 cm between the marks). Cut the croissants following the steps on the previous page, patching together the two smaller pieces to make a fourth triangle. ***To form pains au chocolat with the right piece,*** cut the dough in half horizontally, then make vertical cuts every 3½ inches (9 cm) to make 6 rectangles measuring 3½ by 4¾ inches (9 by 12 cm).

Transfer the triangles and rectangles to the lined baking sheet, cover tightly with plastic wrap, and freeze until firm, about 15 minutes. Line a baking sheet with parchment paper.

Roll and shape the partially frozen triangles and squares using the instructions above, rolling to extend the partially frozen triangles to 12½ inches (32 cm) and the rectangles to 3¾ by 8 inches (9.5 by 20.5 cm). Arrange the pastries, tucked end down, on the prepared baking sheet with 2 inches (5 cm) all around them. Cover the sheet loosely with plastic wrap and let rise at room temperature until 1½ times their volume, 2 hours 30 minutes to 3 hours, then freeze for 20 minutes.

(ingredients and method continued on page 230)

4¾ inches (12 cm)

4¾ inches (12 cm)

4 inches (10 cm) 4 inches (10 cm) 4 inches (10 cm) 4 inches (10 cm) 4 inches (10 cm) 4 inches (10 cm)

B

16

17

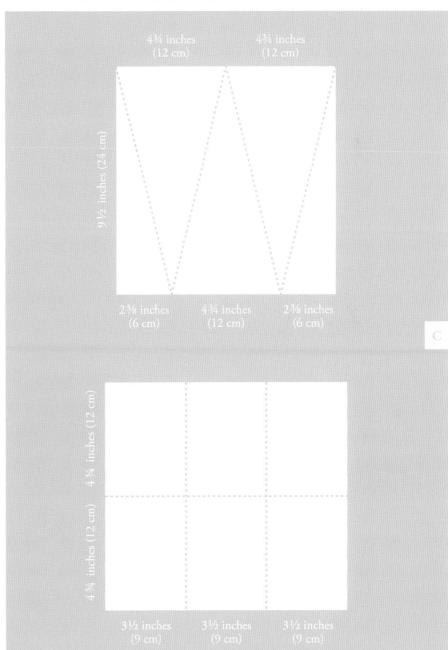

4¾ inches (12 cm)

4¾ inches (12 cm)

9½ inches (24 cm)

2⅜ inches (6 cm)   4¾ inches (12 cm)   2⅜ inches (6 cm)

C

4¾ inches (12 cm)

4¾ inches (12 cm)

3½ inches (9 cm)   3½ inches (9 cm)   3½ inches (9 cm)

GLAZE

1 large egg

1 tablespoon (15 grams) whole milk

Pinch of fine sea salt

To bake, set a rack in the middle of the oven and preheat the oven to 350°F (175°C). Line a baking sheet with parchment paper.

Arrange half of the partially frozen croissants and/or pains au chocolat on the prepared baking sheet, leaving 4 inches (10 cm) all around them. Keep the rest of the pastries in the refrigerator.

To make the glaze, in a small bowl, beat the egg, milk, and salt with a fork until frothy. Using a pastry brush, gently apply a thin coating of glaze to the pastries, taking care not to deflate them.

Bake until the tops are golden brown, 35 to 40 minutes. Transfer the pastries to a wire rack to cool for 15 minutes, then serve warm. Repeat to bake the remaining pastries.

Storage: To hold and bake later, freeze the formed and risen pastries until solid, then individually wrap them with plastic wrap and freeze in a resealable plastic freezer bag for up to 1 month. No need to thaw, though you may need to add a couple of minutes to the baking time. The croissants and pains au chocolat are best shortly after they are made, but they will keep, wrapped airtight, at room temperature for up to 24 hours. Reheat in a 350°F (175°C) oven until warmed through, about 8 minutes.

PROFITEROLES

You should have seen my first outline for this book. It included all the classic pastry doughs and the pastries you can make with each of them, with a list of flavor combinations to match each pastry. I was determined to develop every recipe in that list, but after a few months it started to feel like a project. I wanted my book to be an intimate tale about my baking journey and not a baking encyclopedia, so I narrowed down the recipes to the ones that have gained permanent status in my life. In the end, I was quite happy with what I'd accomplished, but some of the recipes I had cut began to haunt me.

About a week before I turned in my manuscript, I had been struggling with the introduction, which I deliberately had left to the last minute. I had too many things to say, and it seemed impossible to figure out where to start and end. I decided to take a few days' break, and my mind went straight to the list of recipes and flavor combinations that hadn't made it into the book. I took one last look at the list and the desserts under the Pâte à Choux heading looked particularly enticing. I had already nailed down the recipe for the master dough, so I thought I'd give a couple of the recipes a try to see if I could have them ready for publication. I had to let go of intricate desserts like Gâteau Saint-Honoré and Paris-Brest because of the time constraint, but profiteroles seemed achievable, especially since the filling—a silky Vanilla Pastry Cream (page 320)—was already in the book. All that was left was to come up with a chocolate sauce and take a photo—two of my greatest pleasures.

After my book hit the stands and readers started sharing photos online of the things they'd baked, my social media accounts were tagged with bowl after bowl of profiteroles. I knew I'd made the right decision.

Makes 45 profiteroles; serves 15

CHOCOLATE SAUCE

½ cup (100 grams) granulated sugar

¼ cup (60 grams) water

1¼ cups (300 grams) whole milk

¼ cup (25 grams) Dutch-processed unsweetened cocoa powder

5.3 ounces (150 grams) bittersweet chocolate (70% cacao), coarsely chopped

CREAM PUFFS

2½ cups (650 grams) chilled Vanilla Pastry Cream (page 320)

Pâte à Choux (page 344), baked as 45 cream puff shells

To make the chocolate sauce, put the sugar in a medium heavy-bottomed saucepan and shake the pan to level the sugar. Pour the water around the inside edge of the pan. Set the pan over medium-high heat and cook without stirring until the sugar syrup registers 275°F (135°C) on an instant-read thermometer or forms firm yet pliable threads when a bit is dropped into cold water (soft-crack stage), 8 to 10 minutes. Add the milk and cocoa powder and whisk until the sugar threads melt and the cocoa powder dissolves, about 3 minutes. Take the pan off the heat, add the chocolate, and whisk until the chocolate melts. Scrape the sauce into a medium heatproof bowl and let cool for 20 minutes. Cover the bowl tightly with plastic wrap, pressing it directly onto the surface of the sauce, and refrigerate for at least 2 hours. You will have about 2 cups (540 grams) of chocolate sauce. (The sauce will keep in the refrigerator for up to 4 days.)

Just before serving, ***assemble the profiteroles.*** Fit a large pastry bag with a ⅜-inch (1-cm) plain round tip (Ateco #804), twist the tip of the bag, place it in a tall glass, and fold the top of the bag down over the edge of the glass. Scrape the pastry cream into the bag, unfold the cuff, and twist to enclose the cream.

With the tip of a paring knife, poke a small hole in the bottom of each cream puff shell. Insert the tip of the pastry bag into the hole of one shell and squeeze the bag to fill it with the pastry cream. Repeat to fill all the shells.

(continued on page 233)

Whisk the chilled chocolate sauce until smooth and pour it into a sauce boat.

For the most impressive presentation, pile all of the filled puffs into a 2-quart (2-liter) serving bowl. Alternatively, arrange three puffs each in individual serving bowls. Pour a generous amount of chocolate sauce over the puffs and serve immediately, with the remaining sauce on the side.

Storage: Profiteroles are best shortly after they are made, but they will keep, wrapped airtight, in the refrigerator for up to 2 days. For individual servings, store the filled shells and chocolate sauce separately.

MOCHA ÉCLAIRS

After adding profiteroles to the book at the last minute (see page 231), I started itching for an éclair. I already had the master dough recipe, and I could easily make a variation of the Vanilla Pastry Cream (page 320)—especially when I had been dying to combine coffee and chocolate in a dessert.

Turning the vanilla pastry cream into a mocha pastry cream couldn't have been easier—pour hot coffee over chocolate, stir, and blend into the pastry cream. The bitter punch from coffee needed a soft, sweet pairing: biscuit-y blond chocolate (see page 81) was the perfect candidate. I finished them off with a sprinkle of cacao nibs, an addictive finish thanks to their delicate crunch.

Makes 16 éclairs

ÉCLAIRS
3 cups (800 grams) chilled Mocha Pastry Cream (page 322)

Pâte à Choux (page 344), baked as 16 éclair shells

GLAZE
5.3 ounces (150 grams) blond chocolate (preferably Valrhona Dulcey) or white chocolate, coarsely chopped

¼ cup (27 grams) cacao nibs

Just before serving, **assemble the éclairs.** Fit a large pastry bag with a ⅜-inch (1-cm) plain round tip (Ateco #804), twist the tip of the bag, place it in a tall glass, and fold the top of the bag down over the edge of the glass. Scrape the pastry cream into the bag, unfold the cuff, and twist to enclose the cream.

With the tip of a paring knife, poke small holes in both ends of each éclair shell. Insert the tip of the pastry bag into a hole on one end and squeeze the bag to fill the shell halfway; insert the bag in the other end and fill the shell. Repeat to fill all the shells.

To make the glaze, in a medium heatproof bowl set over a medium saucepan filled with 2 inches (5 cm) of barely simmering water, melt the chocolate, stirring occasionally with a silicone spatula. Scrape the melted chocolate into a narrow, shallow container long enough to hold a shell.

Hold one of the filled shells upside down, dip it halfway into the glaze, then tilt it to let the excess glaze drip back into the container. Place the éclair, glazed side up, on a serving tray. Repeat to glaze the remaining shells. Sprinkle the cacao nibs evenly over the éclairs. Refrigerate, uncovered, until the glaze is firm, about 15 minutes. Serve cold.

Storage: Éclairs are best shortly after they are made, but they will keep, wrapped airtight, in the refrigerator for up to 2 days.

GRANOLA

The only morning over the last few years that I woke up happy and lively was the morning of my flight to San Francisco. I am not, nor have I ever been, a morning person. Unless I'm flying to San Francisco that morning, don't call me, don't talk to me, and especially, don't ask me a question before I've had three cups of coffee and spent an hour pretending to scan the news but really just staring at the furniture and the Golden Gate Bridge photo in my living room.

Due to my sluggish and cranky demeanor, I've never been a breakfast person. I ought to be ashamed because I had the best breakfast role model. My father awakened at the break of dawn, put in an hour's exercise, and ate the following every morning for as long as he lived: three black olives, three green olives, one slice each of Turkish feta cheese and *gravyer* cheese (sounds like Gruyère but looks and tastes like Emmental), a slice of toasted bread, six cherry tomatoes skinned by my poor mother (or a large, juicy heirloom tomato when in season), and a cup of tea sweetened with the honey left on the spoon after he'd downed it before starting his breakfast. I, on the other hand, have only the energy to start the coffee machine.

What I really should be ashamed of are the things I eat before I go to bed: an ice cream croissant sandwich if I have frozen croissants (see page 220) in the freezer or grilled cheese sandwiches if I've recently baked a Whole-Wheat and Kefir Pullman Loaf (page 217). Even if I haven't baked a thing that week, I'll have at least a few slices of sourdough bread stashed in the freezer. I'll toast a slice, quickly prepare a pistachio paste as it toasts to slather on it, top it with a few pieces of chocolate, put it under the broiler for half a minute, and sprinkle it with fleur de sel. I can go on and on about my nighttime guilty pleasures, but I won't, because I want to tell you about the granola recipe that made me into a breakfast person.

First of all, I use old-fashioned rolled oats, which bake faster and provide a lighter, crispier texture than those labeled thick or extra-thick. I am not a fan of dried fruit, so you won't see any in my recipe; if you like it, wait until after you've baked the granola to stir it in. As long as you stick to the ratio of dry ingredients to wet, you can use any nuts and seeds you like. A great variation would be to make it with just hazelnuts and mix in a big handful of chopped milk chocolate and a couple tablespoons of cacao nibs after it has cooled.

And here is the unique part of my recipe: I prepare a smooth oatmeal with a small portion of the oats and water, add the sugar and oil, and cook it until it becomes a hot, sticky glue. I work that glue into the dry ingredients for granola that bakes into perfect little clusters that retain their crunch right up until the last spoonful.

(recipe on page 239)

Makes 5 ½ cups (600 grams); serves 8 to 10

3 cups (240 grams) old-fashioned rolled oats

1 cup (100 grams) sliced blanched almonds

½ cup (40 grams) unsweetened shredded dried coconut

⅓ cup (50 grams) pumpkin seeds

¼ cup (35 grams) sunflower seeds

2 tablespoons (20 grams) flax seeds

1 teaspoon (3 grams) ground cinnamon

¾ cup (180 grams) water

½ cup (100 grams) granulated sugar

3 tablespoons plus 1 teaspoon (45 grams) extra-virgin olive oil

½ teaspoon (4 grams) fine sea salt

Set a rack in the middle of the oven and preheat the oven to 325°F (160°C).

In a large bowl, toss 2½ cups (200 grams) of the oats with the almonds, coconut, pumpkin seeds, sunflower seeds, flax seeds, and cinnamon.

In a medium saucepan over medium-high heat, cook the remaining ½ cup (40 grams) of oats with the water until smooth and creamy, about 5 minutes, constantly stirring and pressing the oats against the bottom of the pan with a silicone spatula. Add the sugar, oil, and salt and cook until the sugar dissolves, about 1 minute, stirring constantly.

Scrape the hot mixture over the dry ingredients in the bowl and stir with a large silicone spatula. Once the mixture is cool enough to handle, work the wet ingredients into the dry ones with your hands to evenly coat them.

Scrape the mixture into an unlined 15-by-10-inch (38-by-25.5-cm) jelly-roll pan and spread it in an even layer. Bake until the granola is golden brown, about 1 hour, stirring the outer parts toward the center and spreading it back evenly in the pan every 15 minutes for even baking. (If you use a larger pan, start checking for doneness after 45 minutes.)

Set the pan on a wire rack and let the granola cool completely.

Storage: The granola will keep in an airtight container at room temperature for up to 2 weeks.

ICE CREAMS,
FROZEN YOGURT & SORBETS

Everywhere I Turn, There's Ice Cream

I've been eating ice cream almost every day for as long as I can remember. In fact even now, as I write about eating ice cream, I'm eating ice cream.

Ice cream is to me what water is to you. Your body weight is 60 percent water; mine is probably 60 percent ice cream. About 70 percent of the earth's surface is covered with water; more than 70 percent of my tongue's surface is regularly covered with ice cream.

I haven't been making ice cream at home for as long as I can remember, but I'm certain I've made enough to last a more typical person's lifetime. I always say that if I moved to San Francisco, with so many great bakeries within arm's reach, I wouldn't bake as much as I do in İstanbul. There are many great ice cream shops in San Francisco, too, but even if I moved there, I'd still constantly be making ice cream at home because I am very specific when it comes to certain flavors. Chocolate ice cream must have the right proportion of chocolate to custard so that I can keep eating for as long as I wish. Vanilla has to be extravagant, flecked with a million vanilla seeds. Any caramel in ice cream must be cooked darker than most people dare. Strawberry ice cream should have an intense fresh strawberry flavor and be packed with sweet, sticky pieces of roasted strawberries. Sorbets ought to capture the essence of the fruit and be balanced with acid without an invasive taste of lemon. And homemade frozen yogurt should be as creamy as ice cream without using thickeners. The recipes in this chapter satisfy my high expectations. The ice creams

are all custard based. The only exception is Isabella Grape and Kefir Ice Cream, thickened with cornstarch instead of egg yolks, because I find that grapes don't play well with eggs.

You may be surprised to learn that I don't own an ice cream maker. I have yet to find a model that I like in Turkey with a built-in compressor, so instead I use the ice cream maker attachment of my trusty KitchenAid mixer. It requires me to keep the bowl in the freezer at all times, but that is easily justified by the counter space I save by not having an ice cream maker.

Consumer-grade ice cream makers work slower than professional machines, trapping less air in the ice cream while churning. Less air means more intense flavor, but also a more firm, dense texture. Home freezers operate at a temperature range that is much lower than the ideal serving range of between 7°F and 10°F (-14°C and -12°C). For these reasons, ice cream you make at home won't be as airy and soft as those bought at an ice cream shop, unless you use the ice cream–maker attachment of a stand mixer, which can be set to run as fast as you like. Most will be scoopable for 48 hours after popping them in the freezer. To serve later, let the container stand at room temperature for 10 to 15 minutes before scooping for ideal consistency.

If I were you, I'd be very interested in trying the recipes of an ice cream-aholic like me, and I would do so without making the slightest change.

CHOCOLATE ICE CREAM

I'm sure we've all been asked to list three things we'd want if stranded on a desert island. My answer was always: enough chocolate ice cream to last a lifetime, a humongous freezer to store it, and a spoon to eat it. Then I grew up and realized that some things were more important than manners. If you asked me today, I'd still choose the ice cream and freezer, but I would definitely let go of the spoon in exchange for a solar-powered laptop loaded with all the episodes of *The Golden Girls*.

Since I'll be spending the rest of my life on that island, I'll need a chocolate ice cream I'll never tire of eating. This is that ice cream. It starts with an intensely flavored chocolate base made simply by pouring boiling water over chocolate, cocoa powder, vanilla extract, and salt—the cocoa deepens the flavor and darkens the color, salt suppresses the chocolate's natural bitterness, and boiling water brings the chocolate flavor forward.

Those who know my tendency to go overboard with chocolate in recipes will be surprised to see that, considering my standards, I've been somewhat skimpy with it here. The reason is simple: I wasn't aiming to maximize the amount of chocolate in the recipe, but rather to find the ideal amount that would compel me to keep eating it forever. The answer is below.

Makes about 1 quart (1 liter)

5.6 ounces (160 grams) bittersweet chocolate (70% cacao), finely chopped

2 tablespoons (13 grams) Dutch-processed unsweetened cocoa powder

1 teaspoon (5 grams) pure vanilla extract

¼ teaspoon (2 grams) fine sea salt

½ cup (120 grams) boiling water

1 cup (240 grams) whole milk

⅔ cup (160 grams) heavy cream

½ cup plus 2 tablespoons (125 grams) granulated sugar

3 large egg yolks

In a large heatproof bowl, combine the chocolate, cocoa powder, vanilla, and salt. Pour the boiling water over the chocolate mixture and whisk until smooth. Set a fine-mesh strainer over the bowl.

In a medium saucepan over medium-high heat, bring the milk, cream, and ½ cup (100 grams) of the sugar to just below a boil, stirring frequently.

Meanwhile, in a separate medium saucepan, use a narrow wire whisk to mix the yolks with the remaining 2 tablespoons (25 grams) of sugar until the yolks lighten in color, 2 to 3 minutes. While whisking the egg mixture constantly, drizzle in about half of the hot milk mixture. Add the rest of the hot milk mixture all at once. Cook the custard over medium heat until it is thick enough to coat a silicone spatula (running a finger down the back should leave a clear track) or registers 176°F (80°C) on an instant-read thermometer, about 5 minutes, constantly stirring and scraping the bottom of the pan with the spatula.

Scrape the custard through the strainer into the bowl with the chocolate mixture. Scrape any custard clinging to the bottom of the strainer into the bowl and whisk until blended. Cover the bowl with plastic wrap and refrigerate for at least 8 hours or overnight.

Whisk the chilled custard until smooth, scrape it into the bowl of an ice cream maker, and churn according to the manufacturer's instructions.

Scrape the ice cream into a heavy-duty plastic container with a tight-fitting lid and cover with plastic wrap, pressing it directly onto the surface of the ice cream. Cover and freeze for at least 8 hours or overnight before serving.

Storage: The ice cream will keep in the freezer for up to 1 week. Before serving, let the container stand at room temperature until the ice cream is soft enough to scoop, 20 to 30 minutes.

THREE-BEAN VANILLA ICE CREAM

Some desserts are incomplete without vanilla ice cream. Can you imagine summer berries bubbling underneath a golden crisp topping without the cold, creamy slap of vanilla ice cream? Picture a tender biscuit perched on a pool of sweet peaches and sour cherries; isn't it infinitely better to sop up their juices when it's marbled with vanilla ice cream?

Whether or not it accompanies a dessert, classic vanilla ice cream can easily be transformed into something extravagant by using more vanilla beans. The most outrageous version I've encountered is Sherry Yard's Seven-Bean Vanilla Ice Cream, which I made for the fifth anniversary of my blog and ate in a single sitting. I've come to learn that three is the optimal number of vanilla beans for a single batch of extravagant vanilla ice cream, but you are welcome to try it with more.

Makes about 1¼ quarts (1.25 liters)

2 cups (480 grams) whole milk

3 vanilla beans, split and seeds scraped (see page 32)

¾ cup (180 grams) heavy cream

6 large egg yolks

¾ cup (150 grams) granulated sugar

¼ teaspoon (2 grams) fine sea salt

In a medium saucepan over medium-high heat, bring the milk and the vanilla seeds and pods to a simmer. Take the pan off the heat, cover, and let steep for 30 minutes.

Retrieve the vanilla pods from the milk, rinse thoroughly with cold water, and let dry out completely before using them to make Vanilla Sugar (page 326), if desired.

Fill a large bowl with ice and cold water. Place a large bowl over the ice bath with the bottom touching the water. Set a fine-mesh strainer on top.

Add the cream to the vanilla-infused milk, set the pan over medium heat, and bring to just below a boil, stirring occasionally.

Meanwhile, in a separate medium saucepan, use a narrow wire whisk to mix the yolks, sugar, and salt until the yolks lighten in color, 2 to 3 minutes. While whisking the egg mixture constantly, drizzle in about half of the hot milk mixture. Add the rest of the hot milk mixture all at once. Cook the custard over medium heat until it is thick enough to coat a silicone spatula (running a finger down the back should leave a clear track) or registers 176°F (80°C) on an instant-read thermometer, 5 to 7 minutes, constantly stirring and scraping the bottom of the pan with the spatula.

Scrape the custard through the strainer into the bowl set over ice water. Scrape any custard clinging to the bottom of the strainer into the bowl. Stir the custard frequently to cool to room temperature, about 10 minutes. Remove the bowl from the ice water, cover with plastic wrap, and refrigerate for at least 8 hours or overnight.

Whisk the chilled custard until smooth, scrape it into the bowl of an ice cream maker, and churn according to the manufacturer's instructions.

Scrape the ice cream into a heavy-duty plastic container with a tight-fitting lid and cover with plastic wrap, pressing it directly onto the surface of the ice cream. Cover and freeze for at least 8 hours or overnight before serving.

Storage: The ice cream will keep in the freezer for up to 1 week. Before serving, let the container stand at room temperature until the ice cream is soft enough to scoop, 10 to 15 minutes.

SALTED CARAMEL ICE CREAM

The morning after I'd decided to add chopped salted butter caramels to the salted caramel ice cream I was churning, I swallowed a big spoonful, rested the spoon on the counter, gazed at the container of ice cream beginning to melt around the edges, and wanted to scream and cry for the years I'd spent without it.

It wasn't just the caramel pieces that kept melting in my mouth long after the ice cream was gone. It was also the fact that I'd taken the caramel further into darkness than most others would dare. The magic temperature was 400°F (204°C)—the fine line between the darkest possible shade of brown and burnt black. This recipe alone justifies the purchase of an instant-read thermometer.

Makes about 1¼ quarts (1.25 liters)

1⅓ cups (320 grams) whole milk

1¼ cups (300 grams) heavy cream

1 cup (200 grams) granulated sugar

¼ cup (60 grams) water

6 large egg yolks

½ teaspoon (3 grams) pure vanilla extract

½ teaspoon (4 grams) fine sea salt

4 Salted Butter Caramels (page 270), optional

In a medium saucepan over medium-high heat, bring the milk and cream to just below a boil, stirring frequently. Take the pan off the heat and cover to keep warm.

Put the sugar in a medium heavy-bottomed saucepan and shake the pan to level the sugar. Pour the water around the inside edge of the pan. Set the pan over medium-high heat and cook without stirring until the caramel turns a very dark brown, just short of black, or registers 400°F (204°C) on an instant-read thermometer, 13 to 15 minutes. Take the pan off the heat and, holding it at arm's length, immediately pour in about one-third of the warm milk mixture. Be careful; the caramel will bubble up vigorously and hot steam will rise. Add the rest of the warm milk mixture, set the pan over medium-low heat, and whisk until the caramel melts completely. Take the pan off the heat and cover to keep the mixture hot.

Fill a large bowl with ice and cold water. Place a large bowl over the ice bath with the bottom touching the water. Set a fine-mesh strainer on top.

In a medium saucepan, use a narrow wire whisk to mix the yolks until they lighten in color, 2 to 3 minutes. While whisking the yolks constantly, drizzle in about one-third of the hot caramel mixture. Add the rest of the hot caramel mixture together with the vanilla and salt. Cook the custard over medium heat until it is thick enough to coat a silicone spatula (running a finger down the back should leave a clear track) or registers 176°F (80°C) on an instant-read thermometer, about 8 minutes, constantly stirring and scraping the bottom of the pan with the spatula.

Scrape the custard through the strainer into the bowl set over ice water. Scrape any custard clinging to the bottom of the strainer into the bowl. Stir the custard frequently to cool to room temperature, about 10 minutes. Remove the bowl from the ice water, cover with plastic wrap, and refrigerate for at least 8 hours or overnight.

If you are using salted butter caramels, unwrap and freeze them for 5 minutes, then cut them into ¼-inch (6-mm) pieces with an oiled knife.

(continued on page 250)

Whisk the chilled custard until smooth, scrape it into the bowl of an ice cream maker, and churn according to the manufacturer's instructions, mixing in the caramel pieces during the last few minutes if using.

Scrape the ice cream into a heavy-duty plastic container with a tight-fitting lid and cover with plastic wrap, pressing it directly onto the surface of the ice cream. Cover and freeze for at least 8 hours or overnight before serving.

Storage: The ice cream will keep in the freezer for up to 1 week.

PISTACHIO ICE CREAM

When I started to work on this recipe, I struggled with making an intensely flavored pistachio custard. Steeping ground pistachios in milk and then straining them for a smooth custard yielded a weak pistachio flavor that became even weaker when frozen. Trying to find a solution, I remembered the jar of Bronte pistachio cream my friend Sara Rosso of the blog *Ms. Adventures in Italy* had gifted me many years ago. Even though it had only a 40 percent pistachio content, the nutty aroma was unbelievably intense. So I decided to prepare my own pistachio cream with emerald-green pistachios from Gaziantep—the pistachio capital of Turkey.

Turning the edible emeralds into pistachio cream allows you to incorporate a larger amount of nuts without sacrificing texture. Once strained, you'll see that the amount of pistachio solids left behind in the strainer is scant.

When I sat down to write about the ice cream, I realized that, though that intense nutty aroma I associated with the pistachio cream my friend had gifted me was so deeply etched into my mind, it had never occurred to me during many trials to toast the pistachios. I had to make another batch. I spread out the pistachios on an unlined baking sheet and toasted them in the oven for ten minutes. That was the only thing I changed, but the outcome was completely different. Blanched pistachios provide wonderful pistachio taste and a bright green color (see photo), while toasted pistachios contribute a nutty aroma and shift the color of the ice cream to a pale yellow green. Both are amazing and it's hard to choose, so I'll leave that decision to you.

Makes about 1 quart (1 liter)

1⅔ cups (225 grams) whole blanched pistachios

¼ teaspoon (2 grams) fine sea salt

¾ cup (150 grams) granulated sugar

3 tablespoons (45 grams) water

½ cup (120 grams) heavy cream

2 cups (480 grams) whole milk

3 large egg yolks

If you prefer a deep, toasted pistachio flavor, set a rack in the middle of the oven and preheat the oven to 350°F (175°C). Spread out the pistachios on an unlined baking sheet in a single layer and bake until the pistachios are fragrant and turn pale yellow-green, 8 to 10 minutes. Immediately transfer the toasted nuts to a plate to cool. ***If you prefer a milder, raw pistachio flavor,*** skip the toasting process.

In the bowl of a food processor fitted with a metal blade, process 1⅓ cups (180 grams) of the pistachios with the salt until the pistachios release their oils and the mixture turns into a paste, about 5 minutes.

In a small saucepan over medium-high heat, bring ½ cup (100 grams) of the sugar and the water to a boil, stirring occasionally. Take the pan off the heat, and with the food processor running, drizzle in the hot syrup through the feed tube. The pistachio puree may harden quickly, so immediately add the cream. Process until smooth and creamy, about 2 minutes, scraping down the sides of the bowl as needed.

Fill a large bowl with ice and cold water. Place a large bowl over the ice bath with the bottom touching the water. Set a fine-mesh strainer on top.

In a medium saucepan over medium-high heat, bring the milk to just below a boil, stirring frequently.

Meanwhile, in a separate medium saucepan, use a narrow wire whisk to mix the yolks with the remaining ¼ cup (50 grams) of sugar until they lighten in color, 2 to 3 minutes. While whisking the egg mixture constantly, drizzle in about half of the hot milk. Add the rest of the hot milk all at once. Cook the custard over medium heat until it is thick enough to coat a silicone spatula (running a finger down the back should leave a clear track) or registers 176°F (80°C) on an instant-read thermometer, about 5 minutes, constantly stirring and

(continued on page 253)

scraping the bottom of the pan with the spatula. Take the pan off the heat, add the sweetened pistachio cream, and whisk until blended.

Scrape the custard through the strainer into the bowl set over ice water. Scrape any custard clinging to the bottom of the strainer into the bowl. Discard the solids in the strainer. Stir the custard frequently to cool to room temperature, about 10 minutes. Remove the bowl from the ice water, cover with plastic wrap, and refrigerate for at least 8 hours or overnight.

Coarsely chop the remaining ⅓ cup (45 grams) of pistachios.

Whisk the chilled custard until smooth, scrape it into the bowl of an ice cream maker, and churn according to the manufacturer's instructions, mixing in the chopped pistachios during the last few minutes.

Scrape the ice cream into a heavy-duty plastic container with a tight-fitting lid and cover with plastic wrap, pressing it directly onto the surface of the ice cream. Cover and freeze for at least 8 hours or overnight before serving.

Storage: The ice cream will keep in the freezer for up to 1 week. Before serving, let the container stand at room temperature until the ice cream is soft enough to scoop, 10 to 15 minutes.

ROASTED STRAWBERRY ICE CREAM

If you've ever tried making strawberry ice cream, you know how challenging it is to give it both a creamy texture and an intense fresh strawberry taste.

They don't show it, but at 92 percent, strawberries contain the highest percentage of water among sweet fruits. To be specific, you'll be adding a cup of water to the ice cream base with every pint of strawberries. The excess water will dilute the flavor and turn into unwanted ice crystals when frozen, ruining both the taste and texture of your ice cream. You can cook them beforehand to evaporate the water, but you'll lose their fresh strawberry flavor. If you like chunks of fruit in your ice cream, the job is even tougher: the watery chunks of fruit added to the custard base will freeze into tiny ice cubes.

I have just the recipe to kill these two birds with one stone. It starts with cooking the fruit, but not in the traditional sense. Macerating the berries with sugar "cooks" them without losing their fresh flavor and drives out the water. I roast a portion of the macerated berries until sweet and sticky, for fruit chunks that remain soft when frozen. I incorporate the drained berry juices into the custard in place of milk, blending the remaining macerated berries into the cooked custard. The result is the creamiest and most intense strawberry ice cream you'll ever taste, with sweet, sticky fruit bits in every spoonful.

Makes about 1¼ quarts (1.25 liters)

5¾ cups (1.52 pounds; 690 grams) fresh strawberries, hulled

¾ cup plus 2 tablespoons (175 grams) granulated sugar

1 cup (240 grams) heavy cream

4 large egg yolks

Pinch of fine sea salt

Cut the larger berries lengthwise (top to bottom) into quarters and the smaller ones lengthwise in half. In a large bowl, gently toss the berries with ¾ cup (150 grams) of the sugar and let stand until the berries release their juices and the sugar dissolves, about 1 hour, gently stirring occasionally with a silicone spatula.

Scrape the berries and their juices into a mesh strainer set over a large bowl and let drain completely, about 20 minutes, shaking the strainer gently to help drain the juices as needed.

Set a rack in the middle of the oven and preheat the oven to 300°F (150°C). Line a baking sheet with parchment paper.

Cut ¾ cup (150 grams) of the drained berries into ¾-inch (2-cm) pieces and arrange them on the prepared sheet in a single layer. Bake until the berries shrink and their edges start to caramelize, 35 to 40 minutes. Set the sheet on a wire rack to cool completely. Peel the berries from the parchment and transfer them to a small bowl. Cover the bowl with plastic wrap and refrigerate until ready to use.

In a large bowl, puree the remaining drained berries with an immersion blender (or in a food processor fitted with a metal blade) until smooth.

Fill a large bowl with ice and cold water. Place the bowl with the strawberry puree over the ice bath with the bottom touching the water. Set a fine-mesh strainer on top.

Pour the drained juices from the strawberries into a medium saucepan. Add the cream, set the pan over medium-high heat, and bring to just below a boil, stirring frequently.

Meanwhile, in a separate medium saucepan, use a narrow wire whisk to mix the yolks, remaining 2 tablespoons (25 grams) of sugar, and salt until the yolks lighten in color, 2 to 3 minutes. While whisking the egg mixture constantly, drizzle in about half of the hot cream mixture. Add the rest of the hot cream mixture all at once.

(continued on page 256)

Cook the custard over medium heat until it is thick enough to coat a silicone spatula (running a finger down the back should leave a clear track) or registers 176°F (80°C) on an instant-read thermometer, about 5 minutes, constantly stirring and scraping the bottom of the pan with the spatula.

Scrape the custard through the strainer into the bowl with the strawberry puree. Scrape any custard clinging to the bottom of the strainer into the bowl and whisk until blended. Stir the custard frequently to cool to room temperature, about 10 minutes. Remove the bowl from the ice water, cover with plastic wrap, and refrigerate for at least 8 hours or overnight.

Whisk the chilled custard until smooth, scrape it into the bowl of an ice cream maker, and churn according to the manufacturer's instructions, mixing in the roasted strawberries during the last few minutes.

Scrape the ice cream into a heavy-duty plastic container with a tight-fitting lid and cover with plastic wrap, pressing it directly onto the surface of the ice cream. Cover and freeze for at least 8 hours or overnight before serving.

Storage: The ice cream will keep in the freezer for up to 1 week. Before serving, let the container stand at room temperature until the ice cream is soft enough to scoop, 10 to 15 minutes.

BLACKBERRY SWIRL FROZEN YOGURT

If you freeze a churned mixture of yogurt and sugar, you inevitably get a stone-hard frozen yogurt crowded with large ice crystals. That I've included a frozen yogurt recipe here is evidence that icy, stone-hard frozen yogurt needn't be your destiny.

This creamy version, scoopable right out of the freezer, owes its texture to sugar—but not just any sugar, *invert sugar*. Without delving into the hygroscopic quality of sugar and the rotation of plane-polarized light, the conversion of sucrose (table sugar) into glucose and fructose gives you invert sugar, which may be prepared at home by simply heating sugar with a small amount of acid until it reaches the soft-ball stage (239°F; 115°C). During that process, sugar splits into glucose and fructose in a syrup that doesn't fully crystallize. It gives baked goods a soft texture and keeps them moist longer, and it makes sauces and confections smooth and shiny. In the case of ice creams, sorbets, and frozen yogurts, it minimizes the size and number of ice crystals, leaving them with a creamy texture and keeping them softer while frozen. As you'll see in the Pomegranate Sorbet (page 264), I like to use invert sugar in sorbets made with fruit juice, too.

The type of yogurt is also key to the outcome. I always use full-fat strained Turkish yogurt; its low water content keeps the frozen yogurt smooth and creamy, and the tanginess balances the sugar's sweetness. Strained Turkish yogurt is thicker and tangier than the Greek-style yogurts available in the United States; for the best result, use the thickest, tangiest Greek yogurt you can find.

Makes about 1 quart (1 liter)

YOGURT BASE

1 cup (200 grams) granulated sugar

½ cup (120 grams) water

¼ teaspoon citric acid or cream of tartar

3¼ cups (748 grams) plain full-fat strained (Greek-style) yogurt

BLACKBERRY SWIRL

½ cup (2.7 ounces; 75 grams) fresh blackberries

⅓ cup (67 grams) granulated sugar

2 teaspoons (10 grams) freshly squeezed lemon juice

To make the yogurt base, put the sugar in a medium heavy-bottomed saucepan and shake the pan to level the sugar. Pour the water around the inside edge of the pan. Stir in the citric acid and set the pan over medium-high heat. After stirring just once to incorporate the citric acid after it dissolves, cook until the sugar syrup registers 239°F (115°C) on an instant-read thermometer or the syrup forms a soft and pliable ball when a bit is dropped into cold water (soft-ball stage), 10 to 12 minutes. Take the pan off the heat, add the yogurt in two batches, and whisk until smooth. Cover the pan with plastic wrap and refrigerate for at least 8 hours or overnight.

To make the blackberry swirl, in a small saucepan, mash together the berries, sugar, and lemon juice with a silicone spatula. Set the pan over medium-high heat and cook until the mixture has the consistency of runny jam, 5 to 7 minutes, stirring occasionally. Scrape the sauce into a fine-mesh strainer set over a medium heatproof bowl and strain, pressing hard with the spatula until only the seeds are left in the strainer. Scrape any sauce clinging to the bottom of the strainer into the bowl. Discard the seeds. Let the sauce cool to room temperature. You will have about ¼ cup (75 grams) of blackberry sauce. Cover the bowl with plastic wrap, pressing it directly onto the surface of the sauce, and refrigerate for at least 1 hour.

Whisk the chilled yogurt base until smooth, scrape it into the bowl of an ice cream maker, and churn according to the manufacturer's instructions.

(continued on page 259)

Scrape one-quarter of the frozen yogurt into a 1-quart (1-liter) heavy-duty plastic container with a tight-fitting lid and spread it evenly. Whisk the blackberry sauce until smooth. Drizzle 1 tablespoon (19 grams) of the sauce lengthwise over the frozen yogurt in separate thin lines. Repeat layering until you run out of the yogurt and sauce, ending with the sauce. Insert a chopstick (or the tip of a small knife) at a 90-degree angle to the container and glide through the layers in a zig-zag motion to create a swirl pattern. Cover the container with plastic wrap, pressing it directly onto the surface of the frozen yogurt. Cover and freeze for at least 8 hours or overnight before serving.

Storage: The frozen yogurt will keep in the freezer for up to 1 week.

ISABELLA GRAPE *&* KEFIR ICE CREAM

For me, the texture of ice cream is as important as its taste. And when it comes to the most desired aspect of texture—creaminess—nothing can beat the emulsifying power of egg yolks. In the case of fruit ice creams, some might favor thickening the base with cornstarch, arguing that yolks obscure the bright flavor of the fruits, but that can easily be solved by intensifying the starring flavor in the ice cream base.

I've come across just one exception: the Isabella grape.* The yolks don't just obscure its unique perfume, they completely change its taste. I've found that milk and cream also don't play well with Isabella grapes, so I use kefir, which adds a mild tanginess. Without the egg yolks, your eyes can feast on this ice cream's unbelievably bright shade of purple.

Makes about 1 quart (1 liter)

2.2 pounds (1 kilogram) fresh Isabella* or Concord grapes, stemmed

¾ cup plus 2 tablespoons (175 grams) granulated sugar

1 cup (240 grams) unflavored milk kefir

2 tablespoons (15 grams) cornstarch

* *With aliases that include Fragola, Framboisier, Raisin De Cassis, and California Concord, the Isabella grape belongs to the species of grapevine that includes the Concord grape, with which it may be substituted.*

In the bowl of a food processor fitted with a metal blade, process the grapes and sugar until pureed, about 30 seconds. (Do not use an immersion blender as it will crush the seeds too finely, making it difficult to strain them out later.)

Scrape the grape puree into a large saucepot, cover, and bring to a boil over high heat. Reduce the heat to medium-high and cook, partially covered, for 5 minutes.

Scrape the puree into a fine-mesh strainer set over a large heatproof bowl, pressing hard with a silicone spatula until only seeds and skins are left in the strainer. Scrape any puree clinging to the bottom of the strainer into the bowl. Discard the seeds and skins. You will have about 3 cups (720 grams) of grape puree.

Scrape the strained puree back into the saucepot and add ½ cup (120 grams) of the kefir. Set the pot over medium-high heat and bring the mixture to just below a boil, stirring occasionally with a whisk.

Meanwhile, in a medium bowl, whisk the remaining ½ cup (120 grams) of kefir and the cornstarch with a fork until the cornstarch dissolves. While whisking the grape mixture constantly, drizzle in the kefir mixture. Cook until slightly thickened, 6 to 8 minutes, whisking constantly. Take the pot off the heat, scrape the ice cream base into the large bowl, and let cool to room temperature. Cover the bowl with plastic wrap and refrigerate for at least 8 hours or overnight.

Whisk the chilled base until smooth, scrape it into the bowl of an ice cream maker, and churn according to the manufacturer's instructions.

Scrape the ice cream into a heavy-duty plastic container with a tight-fitting lid and cover with plastic wrap, pressing it directly onto the surface of the ice cream. Cover and freeze for at least 8 hours or overnight before serving.

Storage: The ice cream will keep in the freezer for up to 1 week. Before serving, let the container stand at room temperature until the ice cream is soft enough to scoop, 10 to 15 minutes.

How to Choose, Cut, Seed & Juice a Pomegranate

My fascination with pomegranates started with the bowls of pomegranate arils I enjoyed as a snack when I was little and grows with each recipe I develop. Over the years, I must have cut, seeded, and juiced almost a quarter ton of pomegranates, half of which were for the recipes I developed for this book—a sorbet recipe that follows (see page 264) and the Pomegranate Jam on page 298. Both recipes call for fresh, hand-squeezed pomegranate juice. Using a juicer might seem like a shortcut, but I strongly advise against it as the tannins in the membranes will make the juice bitter. Juicing pomegranates by hand is easier than you might think, and it's well worth the effort. Theoretically, you could substitute store-bought fresh pomegranate juice, but at least as far as the jam is concerned, I just can't see the point of preserving something that comes in a bottle. If we're thinking alike and pomegranates are bountiful where you live, let's start.

HOW TO CHOOSE

A perfectly ripe pomegranate should feel heavy for its size, have pronounced ridges with flat areas on each side (rather than a perfectly round shape), and a matte, rough, leathery skin without any cracks or soft spots. Pomegranates with yellow, green, light pink, or light orange rinds may be a sweet variety and aren't suitable for the recipes in this book. Look for ones with deep red, burgundy, or reddish-brown rinds, which will encase deep-red arils that are both sweet and tangy.

HOW TO CUT

Holding a paring knife at a 45-degree angle, carve out the crown of the pomegranate by cutting around it in a circle. If the ridges of the fruit aren't pronounced, after removing the crown, score the pomegranate crosswise about ½ inch (1.3 cm) below the crown and peel the rind above to expose the sections divided by the membranes. Score the pomegranate lengthwise (top to bottom) about ⅛ inch (3 mm) deep along the ridges into (typically six) sections, cutting through the red rind and the albedo (pith) underneath but avoiding the arils. Gently pull apart the pomegranate into sections.

HOW TO SEED

Working in the sink over a large bowl, hold a pomegranate section aril side down, slightly suspended in your palm, and tap the rind with a wooden spoon to release the arils into the bowl. Pluck any stubborn arils from the rind, and discard any membranes that have fallen into the bowl. One medium (1 pound; 455 grams) pomegranate will yield about 1⅔ cups (233 grams) of arils; a large one (1.4 pounds; 635 grams) about 2¼ cups (315 grams).

HOW TO JUICE

After pulling apart the pomegranate into sections, without releasing the arils, grasp each section in your hand, aril side down, over a large bowl set in the sink and squeeze as you would a lemon. Strain the juice through a mesh strainer into a separate large bowl, squeezing any arils caught in the strainer with your hands as best you can. Discard the seeds and membranes in the strainer. One medium (1 pound; 455 grams) pomegranate will yield about ½ cup plus 2 tablespoons (150 grams) of juice; a large one (1.4 pounds; 635 grams) about ¾ cup plus 2 tablespoons (210 grams).

POMEGRANATE SORBET

If you've followed my blog from the beginning, you might be familiar with The Mansion. Perched on a hill overlooking the Bosphorus Strait, it is home to two of my friends, their kids, the world's loudest miniature schnauzer, Coco, thirty magnolia trees that isolate it from the outside world, and a pool that doubles as a bathtub for seagulls during the spring and summer. It is where my closest friends gather for almost every occasion, to eat and laugh together and sometimes fight over brutal rounds of the card game Buraco.

Among the occasions we spend together there is the New Year's Eve dinner party, a tradition for almost twenty years now. I've had the pleasure of participating in this feast ever since I moved back from San Francisco and have been largely responsible for the desserts. The menu is almost always the same: A bird twice the size of Coco with mushroom and chestnut stuffing, rice pilaf covered with toasted almonds, thinly sliced carrots cooked in turkey-neck broth and sweetened with maple syrup, a crown roast of lamb filled with Brussels sprouts for those who prefer red meat, two huge trays of *sarma* (vine and cabbage leaves stuffed with a mixture of rice, chestnuts, herbs, and dried currants), at least two salads sprinkled generously with pomegranate arils, and several braised vegetable dishes. And of course, more desserts than you can count on both hands. Over the years, I've baked many intricate desserts for the occasion—The Brioche Tart That Made Julia Child Cry; a layered passion fruit, mango, and chocolate cake; and a chocolate and chestnut Bûche de Noël—but none has been appreciated as much as this pomegranate sorbet, which my friends deem the only dessert that may be enjoyed without the slightest guilt after such an indulgent meal. Amateurs!

When I compare the first pomegranate sorbet I made for the party with the ones I've been making more recently, I don't see much difference in the ingredients, but the method has changed substantially. I used to juice the pomegranates, stir in the sugar, balance it with lemon juice, and churn. The taste would be great, but it would always be too icy to scoop. A deeper look at the properties of sugar helped me to understand the science of sorbet much more clearly, and I've been making the ultimate pomegranate sorbet ever since. It isn't realistic to expect a sorbet to be as creamy as a custard-based ice cream, since the formation of ice crystals is inevitable in such a watery base, but it is possible to reduce their size and number. The solution is *invert sugar*, in this case made by boiling a portion of the juice, lemon juice, and sugar until it reaches soft-ball stage (see page 257). I also get help from vodka, which lowers the freezing point of the sorbet, rendering it scoopable right out of the freezer.

Makes about 1 quart (1 liter)

3½ cups (840 grams) freshly squeezed pomegranate juice (from about 7 pounds; 3.2 kilograms; 5 large pomegranates; see page 263)

1 cup (200 grams) granulated sugar, plus more to taste

2 tablespoons (30 grams) freshly squeezed lemon juice, plus more to taste

2 tablespoons (30 grams) vodka

In a medium saucepan, combine 1 cup (240 grams) of the pomegranate juice, the sugar, and the lemon juice. Set the pan over medium-high heat and cook, stirring occasionally, until the syrup registers 239°F (115°C) on an instant-read thermometer or forms a soft and pliable ball when a bit is dropped into cold water (soft-ball stage), about 18 minutes. Take the pan off the heat and whisk in the remaining 2½ cups (600 grams) of pomegranate juice. Cover the pan with plastic wrap and refrigerate for at least 8 hours or overnight.

Before churning, stir in the vodka and taste the sorbet base. Keeping in mind that freezing will subdue its sweetness, gradually stir in more sugar or lemon juice to adjust the sweetness if needed, aiming for something a bit sweeter than you would prefer to drink as a beverage.

Pour the sorbet base into the bowl of an ice cream maker and churn according to the manufacturer's instructions.

Scrape the sorbet into a heavy-duty plastic container with a tight-fitting lid and cover with plastic wrap, pressing it directly onto the surface of the sorbet. Cover and freeze for at least 8 hours or overnight before serving.

Storage: The sorbet will keep in the freezer for up to 1 week.

ISABELLA GRAPE SORBET

What sets apart a great sorbet from a good one is the balance of sweetness and acid. Lemon juice is a typical acid choice, but at times its flavor can be too prominent. Fruits with high sugar content, such as Isabella grapes,* demand a lot of acid to balance their sweetness, making lemon a poor choice as it will mask the starring fruit's fresh taste. Here, I use citric acid, my preferred seasoning of sweet fruits, for fresh grape taste and a clean finish.

Makes about 1 quart (1 liter)

3.3 pounds (1.5 kilograms) fresh Isabella* or Concord grapes, stemmed

1 cup (200 grams) granulated sugar, plus more to taste

1 teaspoon (4 grams) citric acid, plus more to taste

1 tablespoon (15 grams) vodka

* With aliases that include Fragola, Framboisier, Raisin De Cassis, and California Concord, the Isabella grape belongs to the species of grapevine that includes the Concord grape, with which it may be substituted.

In the bowl of a food processor fitted with a metal blade, process the grapes and sugar until pureed, about 30 seconds. (Do not use an immersion blender as it will crush the seeds too finely, making it difficult to strain them out later.)

Scrape the grape puree into a large saucepot, stir in the citric acid, cover, and bring to a boil over high heat. Reduce the heat to medium-high and cook, partially covered, for 5 minutes.

Scrape the puree into a fine-mesh strainer set over a large heatproof bowl, pressing hard with a silicone spatula until only seeds and skins are left in the strainer. Scrape any puree clinging to the bottom of the strainer into the bowl. Discard the seeds and skins. Cover the bowl with plastic wrap and refrigerate for at least 8 hours or overnight.

Before churning, stir in the vodka and taste the sorbet base. Keeping in mind that freezing will subdue its sweetness, gradually stir in more sugar, or citric acid dissolved in a small amount of boiling water, to adjust the sweetness if needed, aiming for something a bit sweeter than you would prefer to drink as a beverage.

Pour the sorbet base into the bowl of an ice cream maker and churn according to the manufacturer's instructions.

Scrape the sorbet into a heavy-duty plastic container with a tight-fitting lid and cover with plastic wrap, pressing it directly onto the surface of the sorbet. Cover and freeze for at least 8 hours or overnight before serving.

Storage: The sorbet will keep in the freezer for up to 1 week.

CONFECTIONS & DRINKS

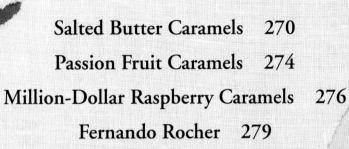

SALTED BUTTER CARAMELS

On the second day of my first trip to Paris, I met David Lebovitz at the Blanche metro station across from the Moulin Rouge, and he took me to the best candy shop on earth: A l'Etoile d'Or.

There is nobody in the world like its owner, Denise Acabo. With her cute schoolgirl uniform complete with plaid skirt, tie, and navy V-neck sweater, blond pigtails, and an endless passion for every item in her shop, Denise is one of the most charming people I've ever met. Add to that Jacques Genin's salted butter caramels; Henri Le Roux's luscious salted butter caramel spread, Le Caramélier; Franck Kestener's Atlantique—my favorite chocolate in the world, a square of dark chocolate confection filled with oozing salted caramel atop a crunchy shortbread layer; Bernachon chocolate bars; and the company of a personal hero. It was an unforgettable day.

The moment I stepped into the shop, the Jacques Genin salted butter caramels, lined up on a white marble counter, caught my eye. In an hour or so, we'll step outside, I'll take a bite of the mango and passion fruit caramel, and the world will never be the same.

As I gathered items on my shopping list, Denise entered through a door at the back, greeted us warmly as she finished braiding her hair, and began to describe every item in the shop. David kindly translated her words, but I was listening with half an ear. With those salted butter caramels beckoning me from across the room, how could I stay focused? As soon as Denise pulled sheets of paper from a drawer and started chatting with David, I ran across the floor and began stacking caramels on a tray.

After we stepped outside, David suggested I start by sampling the mango and passion fruit caramel. I unwrapped it as fast as I could, slipped it into my mouth, and started melting, just like the sweet, acidic, buttery caramel on my tongue, my knees growing weak with the short but glorious finish. Once the euphoria subsided, I felt I'd found a new mission in life: to make salted butter caramels as good as Jacques Genin's.

I'm generally self-deprecating about my own recipes, even more so when they're inspired by the works of great masters, but I could not be more proud of this recipe and of the two caramels that follow.

Makes 24 caramels

¾ cup plus 1 tablespoon (195 grams) heavy cream

2 tablespoons (1 ounce; 30 grams) unsalted butter

1 vanilla bean, split and seeds scraped (see page 32)

¼ teaspoon (2 grams) fine sea salt

1 cup (200 grams) granulated sugar

⅓ cup (107 grams) honey

½ teaspoon (2 grams) fleur de sel or flaky sea salt, such as Maldon

Cut a sheet of parchment paper that is long enough to cover the bottom and sides of an 8½-by-4½-by-2¾-inch (21.5-by-11.5-by-7-cm; 6-cup) loaf pan with 2 inches (5 cm) of overhang on each side. Crumple up the parchment and straighten it out half a dozen times to soften it, so that it will fit into the corners without sharp edges. Line the pan with the parchment paper across the bottom and up the sides, pressing creases at the bottom and top edges. Place a mesh strainer over the pan and set a small glass under the handle to steady it.

In a small saucepan over medium heat, bring the cream, butter, vanilla seeds, and salt to just below a boil, stirring frequently. Take the pan off the heat and cover to keep warm. You may use the leftover vanilla pod halves in Homemade Vanilla Extract (page 323) or Vanilla Sugar (page 326).

Put the sugar in a medium heavy-bottomed saucepan and shake the pan to level the sugar. Pour the honey over the sugar and set the pan over medium heat. Once the sugar begins to liquefy around the edges, push the melted sugar toward the center with a silicone spatula and swirl the pan or stir gently to moisten the dry parts. Once the sugar melts completely, stop stirring, insert a candy thermometer into the pan, and cook until the mixture registers 309°F (154°C) or solidifies into stiff threads that break easily when a bit is dropped into cold water (hard-crack stage), about 10 minutes. Take the pan off the

(continued on page 273)

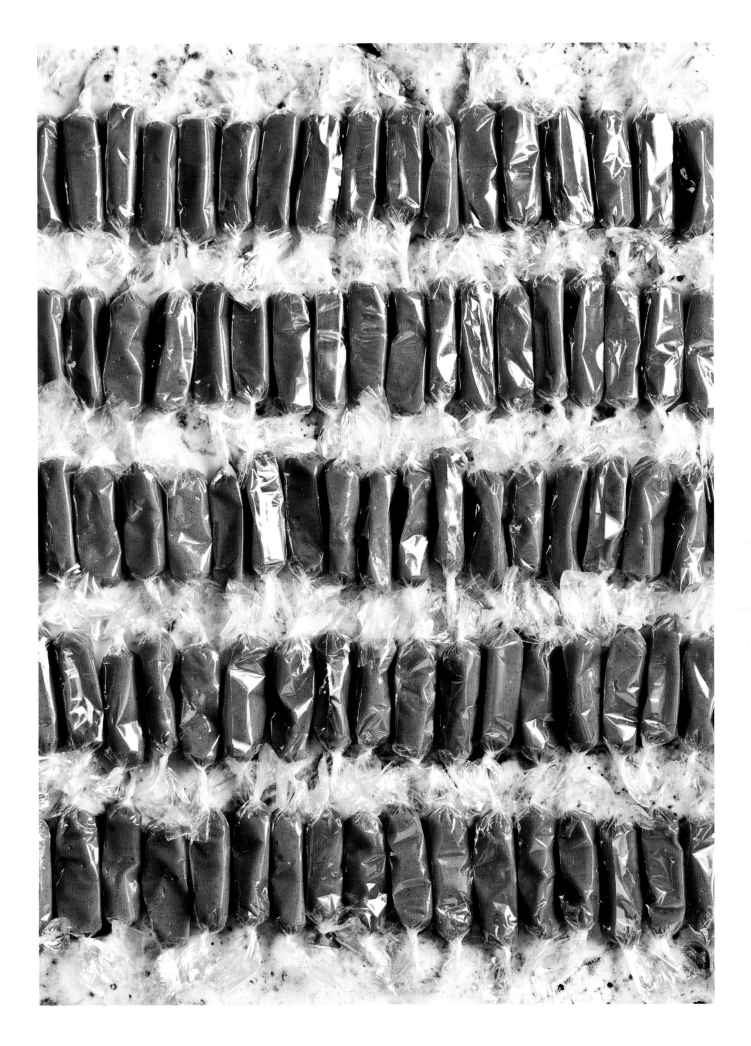

heat and, holding it at arm's length, immediately add the warm cream mixture. Be careful; the caramel will bubble up vigorously and hot steam will rise. Whisk until blended, set the pan over medium-high heat, and cook, occasionally scraping the bottom of the pan with the spatula to prevent scorching, until the mixture registers 257°F (125°C) or forms a hard ball that holds its shape but is still malleable when a bit is dropped into cold water (hard-ball stage), 8 to 10 minutes. Watch the temperature closely as it may suddenly shoot up.

Scrape the caramel through the strainer into the prepared pan. Scrape any caramel clinging to the bottom of the strainer into the pan with a clean silicone spatula. Tap the pan against the counter a few times to eliminate bubbles. Let cool for 15 minutes, then sprinkle the fleur de sel evenly over the top. Let stand undisturbed at room temperature, uncovered, until set, about 6 hours or overnight.

Cut 24 sheets of cellophane or waxed paper, each about 3 by 5 inches (7.5 by 12.5 cm).

Carefully lift the caramel from the pan using the parchment overhang, peel away the parchment, and transfer the caramel to a cutting board. Using a large oiled knife, cut the caramel in half lengthwise, then cut each half crosswise into ⅝-inch-thick (1.6-cm) pieces. You will have 24 caramels, each measuring ⅝ by 2 inches (1.6 by 5 cm).

Individually wrap the caramels in cellophane, twisting the ends closed.

Storage: The wrapped caramels will keep in an airtight container at room temperature for up to 2 weeks.

PASSION FRUIT CARAMELS

If I were a passion fruit, I'd aspire to grow up to be a passion fruit caramel. It is the best thing a passion fruit can be—smooth, rich, sweet, and tangy. Plus, you get to marry butter, sugar, and cream, all at the same time!

These caramels are inspired by the Jacques Genin mango and passion fruit caramels I discovered at A l'Etoile d'Or (see page 270), but they are different from his in both taste and texture. I prefer my caramels on the chewier side, so that they melt slowly in my mouth and prolong their glorious finish. Even though passion fruit and mango are a perfect couple, I prefer to put the passion fruit in the spotlight, so mango came out of the mix. In my research, I noticed that most caramel recipes used corn syrup to prevent crystallization; I prefer mild honey, which contributes to the flavor without dominating the passion fruit.

When I gifted my two friends, just back from vacationing in Provence, with a small box of these caramels, they looked at each other and, eyes wide, simultaneously blurted out, "These are better!" When I asked, "Better than what, exactly?" they replied, "The ones we ate two nights ago at l'Oustau." L'Oustau de Baumanière has two Michelin stars. Just sayin'.

Makes 24 caramels

¾ cup plus 2 tablespoons (175 grams) granulated sugar

¾ cup plus 1 tablespoon (185 grams) fresh or frozen passion fruit pulp (from about 1.5 pounds; 680 grams passion fruit)

⅓ cup (80 grams) heavy cream

¼ cup (80 grams) honey

Pinch of fine sea salt

2 tablespoons (1 ounce; 30 grams) unsalted butter

Cut a sheet of parchment paper that is long enough to cover the bottom and sides of an 8½-by-4½-by-2¾-inch (21.5-by-11.5-by-7-cm; 6-cup) loaf pan with 2 inches (5 cm) of overhang on each side. Crumple up the parchment and straighten it out half a dozen times to soften it, so that it will fit into the corners without sharp edges. Line the pan with the parchment paper across the bottom and up the sides, pressing creases at the bottom and top edges. Place a mesh strainer over the pan and set a small glass under the handle to steady it.

Combine all the ingredients in a medium heavy-bottomed saucepan. Set the pan over medium-high heat and stir with a silicone spatula until the sugar melts completely. Insert a candy thermometer into the pan and continue cooking, occasionally scraping the bottom of the pan with the spatula to prevent scorching, until the mixture registers 253°F (123°C) or forms a hard ball that holds its shape but is still malleable when a bit is dropped into cold water (hard-ball stage), 20 to 25 minutes. Watch the temperature closely as it may suddenly shoot up.

Scrape the caramel through the strainer into the prepared pan. Scrape any caramel clinging to the bottom of the strainer into the pan with a clean silicone spatula. Tap the pan against the counter a few times to eliminate bubbles. Let stand undisturbed at room temperature, uncovered, until set, about 6 hours or overnight.

Cut 24 sheets of cellophane or waxed paper, each about 3 by 5 inches (7.5 by 12.5 cm).

Carefully lift the caramel from the pan using the parchment overhang, peel away the parchment, and transfer the caramel to a cutting board. Using a large oiled knife, cut the caramel in half lengthwise, then cut each half crosswise into ⅝-inch-thick (1.6-cm) pieces. You will have 24 caramels, each measuring ⅝ by 2 inches (1.6 by 5 cm).

Individually wrap the caramels in cellophane, twisting the ends closed.

Storage: The wrapped caramels will keep in an airtight container at room temperature for up to 2 weeks.

MILLION-DOLLAR RASPBERRY CARAMELS

Right after my Turkish cookbook came out, I went through a bit of a caramel-making craze. I was gifting a half dozen Salted Butter Caramels (page 270) to friends and family together with the book and was soon beseeched for more. After a while, I became bored cooking the same caramels over and over again, so I began to experiment with different flavors. I was sad that I hadn't had time to finalize the Passion Fruit Caramels (page 274) before the book went to print, so I started there. Then came this raspberry version, around which time I received serious offers to open a caramel shop. I remember my close friend, Emine, backing me into a corner, imploring me to swear I wouldn't share the recipe with a single soul. She believed it might have been my million-dollar invention.

Who knows? Maybe she's right, but at the end of the day I was born to eat, not feed. So here you have it in your own hands: my recipe for million-dollar raspberry caramels.

Makes 24 caramels

2¼ cups (9.5 ounces; 270 grams) fresh raspberries

1 cup (200 grams) granulated sugar

⅓ cup (80 grams) heavy cream

2 tablespoons (40 grams) honey

2 tablespoons (1 ounce; 30 grams) unsalted butter

2 tablespoons (30 grams) freshly squeezed lemon juice

Cut a sheet of parchment paper that is long enough to cover the bottom and sides of an 8½-by-4½-by-2¾-inch (21.5-by-11.5-by-7-cm; 6-cup) loaf pan with 2 inches (5 cm) of overhang on each side. Crumple up the parchment and straighten it out half a dozen times to soften it, so that it will fit into the corners without sharp edges. Line the pan with the parchment paper across the bottom and up the sides, pressing creases at the bottom and top edges. Place a mesh strainer over the pan and set a small glass under the handle to steady it.

In a medium bowl, mash the berries and 6 tablespoons (75 grams) of the sugar with a silicone spatula and let stand until the berries release their juices and the sugar dissolves, about 15 minutes. Scrape the berries and their juices into a fine-mesh strainer set over a medium saucepan and strain, pressing hard with the spatula until only the seeds are left in the strainer. Scrape any puree clinging to the bottom of the strainer into the pan. Discard the seeds. You will have about 1 cup (240 grams) of sweetened berry puree.

Combine the remaining ½ cup plus 2 tablespoons (125 grams) of sugar, the cream, and the honey in a medium heavy-bottomed saucepan. Set the pan over medium-high heat and stir with a silicone spatula until the sugar melts completely. Insert a candy thermometer into the pan and continue cooking, without stirring, until the mixture registers 245°F (118°C) or forms a firm but malleable ball when a bit is dropped into cold water (firm-ball stage), 8 to 10 minutes.

Add the berry puree, butter, and lemon juice, and stir until blended. Continue cooking, occasionally scraping the bottom of the pan with the spatula to prevent scorching, until the mixture registers 253°F (123°C) or forms a hard ball that holds its shape but is still malleable when a bit is dropped into cold water (hard-ball stage), 10 to 15 minutes. Watch the temperature closely as it may suddenly shoot up.

Scrape the caramel through the strainer into the prepared pan. Scrape any caramel clinging to the bottom of the strainer into the pan with a clean silicone spatula. Tap the pan against the counter a few times to eliminate the bubbles. Let stand undisturbed at room temperature, uncovered, until set, about 6 hours or overnight.

(continued on page 278)

Cut 24 sheets of cellophane or waxed paper, each about 3 by 5 inches (7.5 by 12.5 cm).

Carefully lift the caramel out of the pan using the parchment overhang, peel away the parchment, and transfer the caramel to a cutting board. Using a large oiled knife, cut the caramel in half lengthwise, then cut each half crosswise into ⅝-inch-thick (1.6-cm) pieces. You will have 24 caramels, each measuring ⅝ by 2 inches (1.6 by 5 cm).

Individually wrap the caramels in cellophane, twisting the ends closed.

Storage: The wrapped caramels will keep in an airtight container at room temperature for up to 2 weeks.

FERNANDO ROCHER

When you enrobe a truffle in tempered chocolate and roll it in nuts, you get a spherical confection known as a *rocher*, French for "boulder." When you add drunken sour cherries that are worth their weight in gold, you get *my* kind of rocher, the Fernando Rocher.

I go into great depth about chocolate tempering in the Brownies chapter (see page 76), where I assure you that the tempering gods will be on your side just so long as you use an instant-read thermometer. If you aren't ready to tackle tempering, simply forgo the coating, roll the ganache balls in a bowl of sifted cocoa powder, and call these Sour Cherry Truffles. If, on the other hand, you are brave enough to take the tempering challenge, you'll be rewarded with sour cherry–flecked, melt-in-your-mouth truffles enrobed in an almond-studded bittersweet chocolate shell that shatters irresistibly in your mouth.

It takes at least three months to mature the homemade sour cherry liqueur, and for the cherries to get properly drunk. If you haven't already made it and don't want to wait, substitute a jar of store-bought sour cherries in liqueur, such as Griottines, which are made with Morello cherries, brandy, and kirsch.

If you are making these as the crowning touch on Chocolate Cheesecake (page 133), it's worth doubling the recipe so that you are assured of having enough left for the cheesecake after finally restraining yourself from devouring them all.

Makes 20 rochers

TRUFFLES

5.6 ounces (160 grams) bittersweet chocolate (70% cacao), finely chopped

⅓ cup (80 grams) heavy cream

2 tablespoons (1 ounce; 30 grams) unsalted butter, softened

2 teaspoons (10 grams) strained Esin Giz's Sour Cherry Liqueur (page 288) or store-bought brandy and kirsch liqueur with sour cherries, such as Griottines

¼ cup (45 grams) drained drunken sour cherries from Esin Giz's Sour Cherry Liqueur (page 288) or from a jar of store-bought sour cherries soaked in liqueur, such as Griottines

COATING

1 cup (100 grams) sliced blanched almonds

10 ounces (285 grams) bittersweet chocolate (70% cacao)

To make the truffles, put the chocolate in a medium heatproof bowl.

In a small saucepan over medium heat, bring the cream to just below a boil, stirring frequently. Take the pan off the heat and pour the hot cream over the chocolate. Stir gently with a silicone spatula until the chocolate melts and is completely smooth. If there are unmelted pieces, place the bowl over a warm water bath and stir gently to completely melt the chocolate. Add the butter and liqueur. Blend with an immersion blender until smooth.

Press the drained sour cherries between paper towels to remove excess moisture, cut them into ¼-inch (6-mm) pieces, and stir them into the ganache.

Scrape the ganache into a shallow bowl and level the top with a small offset spatula. Cover the bowl tightly with plastic wrap, pressing it directly onto the surface of the ganache, and let stand at room temperature until the ganache is firm enough to roll, about 1 hour.

Using a melon baller or a dessert spoon, scoop ganache mounds of about 2 teaspoons (0.4 ounces; 11 grams) each and place them on a plate. Quickly roll each mound between your palms into a smooth ball and place it back on the plate. (To make truffles, roll the ganache balls in sifted unsweetened cocoa powder, and you are finished.) Let stand at room temperature, uncovered, until firm, 30 to 40 minutes.

To make the coating, set a rack in the middle of the oven and preheat the oven to 350°F (175°C). Spread out the almonds on an unlined baking sheet in a single layer and bake until golden brown, 8 to 10 minutes. Immediately transfer the toasted nuts to a bowl to cool completely. (Alternatively, toast the nuts in an ungreased nonstick pan over medium heat, shaking the pan frequently to prevent scorching.) Break the cooled almonds into smaller pieces by pressing on them with your fingers. Spread the broken almonds out in a single layer on a baking sheet lined with parchment paper.

(continued on page 281)

Temper the chocolate using one of the techniques on page 82 and transfer it to a small bowl.

To assemble the rochers, use a dipping fork to dip a ganache ball into the tempered chocolate, rolling it in the chocolate to coat it well. Lift out the ball, let the excess chocolate drip back into the bowl, then drop the ball onto the almonds and use another fork to roll and coat it in nuts all around. Repeat to coat the remaining ganache balls.

Let the dipped rochers stand for a few minutes to set the chocolate coating, then individually wrap each rocher in foil, or transfer them all to an airtight container, separating the layers with parchment or waxed paper. Serve at room temperature.

Storage: The rochers will keep at room temperature for 3 days.

ESİN GİZ'S ELDERFLOWER CORDIAL

Esin Giz, or as I call her, Esin *teyze* ("aunt from mother's side"—a term commonly used in Turkey for unrelated elders to denote respect and intimacy), is a master gardener, embroiderer, and doll maker.

In 1954, at the age of twenty-six, she toured half the world on a ship with her doll exhibition to benefit the largest humanitarian organization in Turkey, the Turkish Red Crescent Society, starting from Piraeus in Greece, docking in Barcelona, Casablanca, the Canary Islands, Cuba, Miami, North Carolina, D.C., and Philadelphia, and ending in New York City with a showing at the Waldorf Astoria as part of the Technical Institutes for Girls' exhibition of Turkish garments.

At eighty-nine, she remains equally compassionate, diligent, and productive. She generously opened her entire collection of embroidered tablecloths and napkins for me to use as props. Among them is her masterpiece, a tablecloth she embroidered with colorful butterflies, fragments of which I've used as backgrounds for the chapter openers and the Devil Wears Chocolate Swirls (page 150).

You start getting to know her the moment you step into her apartment's garden. You enter through a small gate whose color changes throughout the year to match or complement the most prominent plants and flowers blooming in her garden at the time. When lilacs and clematises take over in spring, she paints the gate and her wrought-iron table and chairs violet. In the fall, as the Boston ivy turns burgundy red, she paints everything green and removes the colorful decorations to let that brilliant color shine.

The seasons make their way into her home, too. In the summer, after a small walk through the apartment's foyer, accompanied by the sound of birds chirping from the speakers she's hidden behind the plants, you are greeted by beaded and sequined ice cream cone ornaments hanging on an upside-down broom by her entrance. She gifts them one by one, making room for felt mushrooms in the fall, little angels in the winter, and colorful butterflies in the spring—all handmade with scraps from her daily craft projects. She shows you to a chair overlooking the apartment's front garden, which she tends daily. Near the northern coast of the Sea of Marmara, her garden is crowded with centuries-old seaside pine trees and easy-growing ground covers—lily turfs, oxalises, and a variety of ornamental grasses—chosen to tolerate the pine-needle-acidified soil. Sunny areas are covered in jasmine vines and ancient rose shrubs, while full-shade areas are decorated with vibrant blue pinwheels. A fire-orange bird sculpture built for the garden by her friend, Hans Bäurle, stands bright in the middle of it all. As you immerse yourself in her lush jungle, she pops her usual question: "Would you like a glass of elderflower cordial?"

There are two large elderflower trees in her back garden, which she brought from Austria more than half a century ago when they were wee naked saplings. Every year, on a day in early June, she awakens before dawn and picks the flowers when their fragrance is at its peak. She prepares enough elderflower syrup to enjoy and share year-round, drying a bunch of flowers to make tea in the winter, which relieves the symptoms of her recurring bronchitis. She no longer eats fried food, but she used to dip the flowers in a batter made of almond flour, wheat flour, salt, eggs, and beer, then fry them in butter.

The recipes and stories she has shared with me over the years would fill a book of their own, but I had space only for two of them and chose the ones that have become classics in my home. I hope they become so in yours, too.

(recipe on page 287)

Makes 2.8 quarts (2.65 liters)
elderflower syrup, enough for
60 cordials

ELDERFLOWER SYRUP

10 cups (2 kilograms) granulated
  sugar

5¼ cups (1.26 kilograms) water

¼ cup (52 grams) citric acid

5 lemons, cut into 8 wedges each,
  seeds removed

25 (8.8 ounces; 250 grams) fresh
  elderflower heads, stalks trimmed

FOR EACH CORDIAL

3 tablespoons (60 grams) cold
  Elderflower Syrup

1 cup (240 grams) cold water

To make the elderflower syrup, in a 6-quart (6-liter) saucepot, stir together the sugar and water. Set the pot over medium-high heat and bring to a boil, stirring frequently until the sugar dissolves. Raise the heat to high and boil for 3 minutes. Take the pot off the heat, add the citric acid, and stir until it dissolves. Add the lemon wedges and let the syrup cool completely, about 2 hours.

Shake the elderflower heads over a sink to remove any debris or bugs. Add the flowers to the syrup and submerge by gently pressing on them with a spatula. Cover the pan and let steep for 24 hours.

Ladle the syrup into a mesh strainer set over a large bowl and let drain completely. Squeeze the flowers and lemons through the strainer to extract the juices and let drain. Strain the syrup again, this time through a mesh strainer lined with double-thick cheesecloth set over another large bowl. Using a funnel, transfer the syrup to sterilized glass bottles or jars and secure them with stoppers or lids. Refrigerate until cold.

To make an elderflower cordial, pour the syrup into a 12-ounce (355-ml) glass. Add the cold water, stir until blended, and serve.

Storage: The elderflower syrup will keep in the refrigerator for up to 1 year.

ESİN GİZ'S SOUR CHERRY LIQUEUR

This sour cherry liqueur has been a tradition in Esin Giz's (see page 283) family for more than a century. Her grandmother would make it for *Şeker Bayramı* ("Bayram of Sweets")—a religious holiday that marks the end of Ramadan—and serve it with chocolate on the side. Esin Giz has been making it for seventy years, starting each year no later than July so that it is ready for her birthday in October.

When it was produced in Istanbul, her choice of brandy had been Metaxa (5 Stars)—a Greek liqueur based on aged brandy blended with aged Muscat wine and a secret distillate of infused rose petals and Mediterranean herbs. Later, she switched to a Turkish brandy until its production was discontinued; she now uses French Cognac.

We both enjoy it cold, but you can strain the liqueur into a decanter and keep it at room temperature for a few hours before serving.

The sour cherries kept in the liqueur are worth their weight in gold. She adds them to cakes and fruit salads, while I reserve them to make Sour Cherry Brownies (page 88), Sour Cherry and White Chocolate Macarons (page 68), and Fernando Rocher (page 279). Mixing just a handful of them with fresh sour cherries will elevate a cobbler (see page 185) or crumble (see page 190).

It takes three months for the liqueur to fully mature, so plan ahead.

Makes 2 quarts (2 liters);
serves about 35

- 7 ½ cups (2.31 pounds; 1.05 kilograms) pitted fresh sour cherries (from about 2.76 pounds; 1.25 kilograms sour cherries with pits and stems)
- 2 ½ cups (500 grams) granulated sugar
- 4 cinnamon sticks
- 15 whole cloves
- 1 bottle (700 ml) Cognac or brandy

Put 1½ cups of the cherries in a 2 ½-quart (2.5-liter) or larger jar. Add ½ cup of the sugar, 1 of the cinnamon sticks, and 3 of the cloves. Continue layering in the same manner until you have used all of the cherries, sugar, cinnamon, and cloves.

Pour the Cognac over the top and secure the lid.

Let the liqueur age in a cool, dark place for 3 months, shaking the jar occasionally during the first couple of days to help dissolve the sugar.

Serve cold or at room temperature in liqueur or shot glasses, with a drunken cherry in each glass.

Storage: The liqueur will keep in the refrigerator for at least 1 year. The drunken cherries in the liqueur are best used within the first 6 months.

HOT CHOCOLATE

Taking the caramel I make as the base for my Salted Caramel Ice Cream (page 248) to its darkest point before burning made such a big difference in taste that, right after sampling the first spoon, I sat down in front of the computer and went through all my recipes for the book and searched for more opportunities to use it.

I found three candidates and started working. Two of those recipes aren't yet ready to share, but when they are I know they will be spectacular. The third was the earlier version of this hot chocolate recipe. None of the original ingredients or their ratios has changed; the only difference is cooking the sugar until it turns the darkest shade of brown—but what a difference!

Serves 2

¼ cup (50 grams) granulated sugar

½ cup plus 1 tablespoon (135 grams) water

⅔ cup (160 grams) whole milk, plus more if needed

2 teaspoons (4 grams) Dutch-processed unsweetened cocoa powder, plus more if needed

Pinch of fine sea salt, plus more if needed

2.8 ounces (80 grams) bittersweet chocolate (70% cacao), coarsely chopped

Put the sugar in a medium heavy-bottomed saucepan and shake the pan to level the sugar. Pour 1 tablespoon (15 grams) of the water around the inside edge of the pan. Set the pan over medium-high heat and cook without stirring until the caramel turns a very dark brown, just short of black, about 7 minutes. The caramel should register 400°F (204°C) on an instant-read digital thermometer, but the amount of caramel is too small to get an accurate reading, so you'll need to gauge it with your eyes.

Take the pan off the heat and, holding it at arm's length, immediately pour in the remaining ½ cup (120 grams) of the water and the milk. Be careful; the caramel will bubble up vigorously and hot steam will rise. Add the cocoa powder and salt. Set the pan over medium-high heat and whisk constantly until the cocoa powder dissolves and the hardened caramel liquefies, about 3 minutes.

Take the pan off the heat, add the chocolate, and whisk until it melts completely. Taste and make any desired adjustments: more milk to thin it, more cocoa or salt if it is too sweet. Serve immediately.

Storage: The hot chocolate will keep in an airtight container in the refrigerator for up to 2 days. Before serving, reheat in a medium saucepan over low heat until hot, whisking constantly.

RASPBERRY LEMONADE

Waiting for raspberry season is torture. In winter, the imported berries sold in İstanbul in small plastic boxes cost a fortune and never taste as they should, so when the raspberry season hits the farmers' market, I go crazy buying much more than I can use.

If the blueberry bushes on my balcony have been generous and I've been smart enough to buy a box of blackberries as well, I reserve the best-looking raspberries to make Blanche (page 170). If not, a Raspberry, White Chocolate, and Yogurt Tart (page 172) is in order. Some are thrown into my morning Granola (page 236), bruised ones go into the Strawberry and Raspberry Crumble (page 190), and a handful of the berries get buried in the Raspberry and Pistachio Crumb Cake (page 116). With whatever is left, I make batches of raspberry sauce to freeze for buttercream to use on a future Triple Raspberry and Lemon Birthday Cake (page 152), or this raspberry syrup for on-the-spot lemonades.

I like my lemonade quite strong, and the amount of syrup and lemon juice I use per glass reflects that. Keeping in mind that crushed ice will inevitably dilute the flavor, feel free to play around with the ratios to suit your taste.

Makes about 2 cups (560 grams) raspberry syrup, enough for 8 lemonades

RASPBERRY SYRUP

3 cups (12.7 ounces; 360 grams) fresh raspberries

1¾ cups (350 grams) granulated sugar

3 lemons

⅔ cup (160 grams) water

¼ teaspoon citric acid

FOR EACH LEMONADE

Crushed ice

4 to 5 fresh raspberries

⅓ cup (80 grams) freshly squeezed lemon juice

¼ cup (70 grams) cold Raspberry Syrup

¼ cup (60 grams) cold water

To make the raspberry syrup, in a medium saucepan, mash the berries and ¾ cup (150 grams) of the sugar with a silicone spatula until the sugar dissolves.

Using a fine-tooth rasp grater, grate the zest of the lemons (avoiding the bitter white pith) directly into the saucepan.

Set the pan over medium-high heat and bring to a boil, mashing and stirring constantly. Remove the pan from the heat. Scrape the berry puree into a fine-mesh strainer set over a separate medium saucepan and strain, pressing hard with the spatula until only the seeds are left in the strainer. Scrape any puree clinging to the bottom of the strainer into the bowl. Discard the seeds.

Add the remaining 1 cup (200 grams) of sugar, the water, and the citric acid to the puree. Set the pan over medium-high heat and bring to a boil. Reduce the heat to medium and cook for 5 minutes, stirring and scraping the bottom of the pan frequently. Remove the pan from the heat and pour the syrup into a sterilized 1-pint (500-ml) jar. Secure the lid, let cool completely, and refrigerate until cold.

To make a lemonade, fill a pint (500-ml) glass with crushed ice, scattering in the fresh raspberries as you go. Combine the lemon juice, raspberry syrup, and cold water in a shaker and shake well. Pour over the crushed ice and serve immediately.

Storage: The raspberry syrup will keep in the refrigerator for at least 1 month.

JAMS & JELLIES

GREEN APPLE PECTIN STOCK

Green apple pectin stock is an indispensable ingredient in most of my jam and jelly recipes. Cooking the apples until soft, straining their juices, then reducing the juice further adds extra steps, but the resulting jam is well worth the effort. I generally recommended using the stock for fruits that are low in pectin, such as pomegranates and strawberries, but its benefits go so far beyond thickening jams that I also use it with fruits with sufficient natural pectin to gel on their own.

The major advantage of using the stock is that it allows me to cut the granulated sugar in the recipe considerably. The resulting jam will have the same sugar concentration, but most of it will come from the fruit, so you'll taste more fruit and less sugar. The yellow-pink stock doesn't affect the color or taste of the jam except that it adds tartness, which helps to balance the sweetness. It also shortens cooking time, preserving more fresh fruit flavor. You won't need the stock in quince recipes, as the fruit is very rich in pectin, nor in the milk-based Dulce de Leche or Cajeta (page 315).

I'm on the fence as to whether the apple butter made with the leftover solids is worth the time spent by the stove, but in case you are loath to discard them, I've added instructions below.

Makes 1½ cups (360 grams)

2.2 pounds (1 kilogram; 4 to 5 large) Granny Smith apples

5 cups (1.2 kilograms) water

Note: To make apple butter with the leftover solids, transfer the solids in batches to a mesh strainer set over a large heatproof bowl and press hard with a silicone spatula until only seeds and skins are left in the strainer. Discard the solids left in the strainer after each batch. You will have about 2⅔ cups (640 grams) of apple puree. Scrape the puree into a large, high-sided non-stick skillet. Stir in ¾ cup (150 grams) of granulated sugar, 2 tablespoons (30 grams) of fresh lemon juice, and ¾ teaspoon (2 grams) of ground cinnamon. Cook over medium heat until thick, about 1 hour 30 minutes, stirring and scraping the bottom of the skillet frequently to prevent scorching. Transfer to a clean glass jar, secure the lid, let stand until it is barely warm, then refrigerate for up to 2 weeks.

Without peeling and coring them, cut the apples into 1½-inch (4-cm) pieces, put them into a 6-quart (6-liter) saucepot, and add the water. Set the pot over high heat, cover, and bring to a boil. Reduce the heat to medium-high and cook until the apple pieces fall apart when pressed against the side of the pot, about 15 minutes. Take the pot off the heat, uncover, and let cool for 10 minutes.

Set a fine-mesh strainer over a large heatproof bowl. Ladle the stock first and then the apple pieces into the strainer and let drain completely, about 30 minutes, occasionally stirring the solids gently, without pressing down on them, to help drain the juices. Discard the solids or use them to make apple butter (see Note).

To easily determine the amount of stock in the pan as it is reduced, weigh an empty medium saucepan and make a note. Pour the strained stock into the pan and bring to a boil over high heat, then reduce the heat to medium-high and cook, uncovered, until reduced to 1½ cups (12.7 ounces; 360 grams), about 30 minutes. Near the end of the cooking time, weigh the pan with the stock and subtract the weight of the pan. If the stock weighs more than 12.7 ounces (360 grams), continue reducing until you reach the target weight. The stock is now ready to use in recipes.

Don't worry if you reduce it a bit too far; your pectin stock is just stronger. Use the full amount if the recipe calls for 1½ cups of pectin stock, or weigh (or measure) it and use two-thirds of it if the recipe calls for 1 cup.

Storage: The pectin stock will keep in an airtight container in the refrigerator for up to 1 week or in the freezer for up to 2 months.

POMEGRANATE JAM

Several years ago, in yet another fall working with pomegranates, I decided to make pomegranate jam. I was certain I hadn't seen a recipe for it in the cookbooks I owned, so I searched online and couldn't find even a mention. How could it be that, in a world with countless recipes for anything you can imagine, there wasn't a single pomegranate jam recipe? I figured either no one had ever thought to preserve pomegranates, which seemed unlikely, or it wasn't such a good idea. I had to find out for myself. After a few trials, I came up with a recipe I was excited about and shared it on my Turkish blog with the following introduction: *It is sweet. It is sour. It is extraordinary. It is even better than the cherry jam my friend's mom makes, which smells like chocolate. You'll rest your cheek against it and fall asleep.*

I know how ridiculous that last sentence sounds in English, but it is impossible to translate more clearly. In Turkish, the expression glorifies the jam and suggests that whoever makes it will sense an instant connection with it. It portends a sense of comfort and happiness, similar to a relaxed and peaceful face on the brink of sleep. That expression turned into my seal of approval, reserved for extraordinary recipes only, and became so popular with my Turkish readers that I ended up using it as the subtitle of my Turkish book.

There was just one slight problem: The jam was too runny. I had considered that to be an advantage—the better to fill the nooks and crannies of a toasted slice of bread—but I was determined to bring it to a thicker consistency when it came time to update the recipe for my book.

The day I first met with my Turkish publisher and decided to write my first cookbook, I came home with five pounds of pomegranates and got right to work. A few weeks and almost fifty pounds of pomegranates later, I still had not reached my goal. I was in a state of madness—trying the same thing over and over again but expecting different results. When I stopped trying and started reading, I quickly learned that pomegranates were extremely low in pectin.

Pectin is a natural soluble fiber found in many fruits and plants. When pectin-rich fruits like apples and quinces are cooked with sugar and acid, their pectin breaks down and gels. When preserving pectin-poor fruits like pomegranates, no amount of sugar or acid will thicken it beyond a thick syrup; added pectin is needed to reach a spreadable consistency. Delving deeper, I came across a reference to green apple pectin stock, which changed my jam making forever (see page 296).

Now, the recipe deserves the accolade even more; you'll rest your cheek against it and fall asleep.

Makes about 1⅓ pints (650 ml)

2 ½ cups (600 grams) freshly squeezed pomegranate juice (from about 5.5 pounds; 2.5 kilograms; 4 large pomegranates; see page 263)

1 ¾ cups (350 grams) granulated sugar

1½ cups (360 grams) Green Apple Pectin Stock (page 296)

2 tablespoons (30 grams) freshly squeezed lemon juice

⅔ cup (93 grams) pomegranate arils (reserved before juicing the pomegranates; see page 263)

In a 6-quart (6-liter) saucepot, combine the pomegranate juice, sugar, pectin stock, and lemon juice.

Set the pot over high heat and bring to a boil, stirring frequently until the sugar dissolves. Reduce the heat to medium-high, insert a candy thermometer into the pot, and cook until it registers 221°F (105°C), about 30 minutes, occasionally stirring and skimming off the foam. Raise the heat to high, bring the mixture to a rolling boil, and cook until it registers 227°F (108°C), about 5 minutes longer. If you don't have a candy thermometer, you can conduct the wrinkle test (see page 300) to check its consistency.

Remove the pot from the heat and let the jam cool to room temperature.

Stir in the pomegranate arils.

Leaving ¼ inch (6 mm) of head space, divide the jam between one 1-pint and one 6-ounce (or one 500-ml and one 150-ml) sterilized jars and secure the lids.

Storage: The jam will keep in the refrigerator for up to 6 months.

THE WRINKLE TEST

The most accurate way to gauge whether a jam will properly set is by temperature. If you don't have a candy thermometer, you can get a good idea using the wrinkle test.

Here's how: Before making the jam, place a couple of saucers in the freezer. When you think the jam is about ready, take the pan off the heat, place a teaspoon of jam on one of the chilled saucers, and freeze for 2 minutes. Test the chilled jam by nudging it with your fingertip—if it wrinkles it has set. If it does not, return the jam to a rolling boil and retest every 2 minutes until it is ready.

VANILLA BEAN *&* APRICOT JAM

I make jam in order to enjoy my favorite fruits long after they disappear from the market stalls, doing everything in my power to capture the fresh fruit's essence. I pick the fruits at their peak, add the minimum sugar needed for a perfect set, and minimize cooking time. Combining fruits or adding flavorings defeats my purpose of remaining true to the fruit, but this jam is an exception, and I have my reasons for it.

First, even though vanilla is a strong flavor it is gentle with fruits, enhancing the honey-like flavor of my favorite apricot variety in Turkey, the *şekerpare*—a small, oval fruit with pale orange flesh and yellow-orange skin featuring prominent red cheeks. It is juicy and sweet, extremely flavorful, and is a freestone variety. Its firm flesh makes it ideal for this recipe, as the pieces retain their shape after cooking. If you can find Royal Blenheim apricots (also known as Royals or Blenheims) while they are firm-ripe, Robadas, or the Autumn Royal that ripens later in the season, they would be perfect for this recipe, but any variety should work so long as it's sweet, juicy, flavorful, and reasonably firm when ripe.

My second reason for adding the vanilla is to dot the golden jam with a thousand vanilla seeds, allowing it to double as a pretty glaze for cakes and fruit tarts. The glaze adds an attractive shimmer, enhances the fruit's sweetness, preserves its freshness, and revives the fruit after its time in the oven.

Makes 1½ pints (750 ml)

1.76 pounds (800 grams) firm-ripe fresh apricots

2 cups (400 grams) granulated sugar

1½ cups (360 grams) Green Apple Pectin Stock (page 296)

⅓ cup (80 grams) freshly squeezed lemon juice

1 vanilla bean, split and seeds scraped (see page 32)

Cut the apricots in half lengthwise (top to bottom), remove and discard the pits, and cut the halves into ¾-inch (2-cm) pieces.

In a 6-quart (6-liter) saucepot, toss together the apricot pieces and sugar and let stand until the apricots release their juices and the sugar dissolves, about 45 minutes, stirring gently with a silicone spatula occasionally.

Add the pectin stock and lemon juice, set the pot over high heat, and bring to a boil, stirring frequently. Reduce the heat to medium-high and cook until the mixture stops foaming, about 15 minutes, occasionally stirring and skimming off the foam. Add the vanilla seeds, insert a candy thermometer into the pot, and cook until it registers 221°F (105°C), about 15 minutes. If you don't have a candy thermometer, use the wrinkle test (see page 300) to check its consistency. You may use the leftover vanilla pod halves in Homemade Vanilla Extract (page 323) or Vanilla Sugar (page 326).

Leaving ¼ inch (6 mm) of head space, divide the jam between one 1-pint (500-ml) and one ½-pint (250-ml) sterilized jars. Secure the lids and let cool to room temperature.

Storage: The jam will keep in the refrigerator for up to 6 months.

RASPBERRY JEWEL PLUOT JAM

If I were to make a list of 10 Things to Smell Before You Die, this jam bubbling on the stove would undoubtedly be among the top three. I hope my other jam recipes aren't saddened when I say that this is the best jam I've ever made.

As you might have learned reading about the Raspberry Jewel Pluot Galette (page 192), pluots are very rich in pectin. Adding the pectin stock may seem like overkill, but it helps to hold down the sugar, shortens the cooking time, and adds tanginess, all of which make the bright flavor of this wondrous fruit shine.

Makes 1 quart (1 liter)

2.65 pounds (1.2 kilograms; about 12 large) firm-ripe fresh Raspberry Jewel pluots

2¼ cups (450 grams) granulated sugar

1 cup (240 grams) Green Apple Pectin Stock (page 296)

2 tablespoons (30 grams) freshly squeezed lemon juice

Cut the pluots in half lengthwise (top to bottom), remove and discard the pits, and cut the halves lengthwise into ¼-inch-thick (6-mm) slices.

In a 6-quart (6-liter) saucepot, toss together the pluot slices and sugar and let stand until the pluots release their juices and the sugar dissolves, about 1 hour, occasionally stirring gently with a silicone spatula.

Add the pectin stock and lemon juice, set the pot over high heat, and bring to a boil, stirring frequently. Reduce the heat to medium-high, insert a candy thermometer into the pot, and cook until it registers 221°F (105°C), about 25 minutes, occasionally stirring and skimming off the foam. If you don't have a candy thermometer, use the wrinkle test (see page 300) to check its consistency.

Leaving ¼ inch (6 mm) of head space, ladle the jam into a sterilized 1-quart (1-liter) jar. Secure the lid and let cool to room temperature.

Storage: The jam will keep in the refrigerator for up to 6 months.

ISABELLA GRAPE JELLY

There are few things that I look forward to more than Isabella grape season. In Turkey, most refer to this grape as *kokulu Karadeniz üzümü* ("aromatic Black Sea grape"), referring to the region where it grows wild and abundantly. The grape is from the same species of grapevines as the Concord grape and has more than fifty aliases.* Its season is quite short, just six to eight weeks, so I buy them every week when I can, consuming most of them raw by squeezing the aromatic yellow-green flesh into my mouth and sucking the last remnant of juice from the skin until my lips turn purple, and reserving as many as I can to make ice cream and sorbet.

Knowing how much I love them, Emine, who sells her garden's bounty at the farmers' market, warns me the week prior to season's end. The following week, I bring two large plastic crates to the market, as I know she will be stashing away whatever is left in her garden for me. I carry them home, wash them in large basins, stem them, and divide them into freezer bags. I freeze most of them for making Isabella Grape and Kefir Ice Cream (page 260) and Isabella Grape Sorbet (page 266), but considering that each batch will last me only a day or two, I always reserve some for a few batches of this jelly so that I may enjoy them longer.

Makes 1 pint (500 ml)

2.76 pounds (1.25 kilograms) fresh Isabella* or Concord grapes, stemmed

1¾ cups (350 grams) granulated sugar, or as needed

2 tablespoons (30 grams) freshly squeezed lemon juice

1 cup (240 grams) Green Apple Pectin Stock (page 296)

* With aliases that include Fragola, Framboisier, Raisin De Cassis, and California Concord, the Isabella grape belongs to the species of grapevine that includes the Concord grape, with which it may be substituted.

In the bowl of a food processor fitted with a metal blade, process the grapes and ½ cup (100 grams) of the sugar until pureed, about 30 seconds. (Do not use an immersion blender as it will crush the seeds too finely, making it difficult to strain them out later.)

Scrape the grape puree into a large saucepot, cover, and bring to a boil over high heat. Reduce the heat to medium-high and cook, partially covered, for 10 minutes. Take the pot off the heat, uncover, and let cool for 10 minutes. Stir in the lemon juice.

Scrape the puree into a fine-mesh strainer set over a 1-quart (1-liter) glass measuring cup and strain, gently stirring the solids without pressing down on them to drain the juices. Discard the solids. Measure and note the volume (or weight) of the juice, which should be about 2½ cups (630 grams).

Transfer the juice to a 6-quart (6-liter) saucepot and add ½ cup (100 grams) of sugar for every 1 cup (250 grams) of juice. (For 2½ cups [630 grams] of juice this will be the remaining 1¼ cups [250 grams] of sugar.) Add the pectin stock.

Set the pot over high heat and bring to a boil, stirring frequently until the sugar dissolves. Reduce the heat to medium-high, insert a candy thermometer into the pot, and cook until it registers 221°F (105°C), about 25 minutes, occasionally stirring and skimming off the foam. Raise the heat to high, bring the mixture to a rolling boil, and cook until it registers 227°F (108°C), about 5 minutes longer. If you don't have a candy thermometer, use the wrinkle test (see page 300) to check its consistency.

Leaving ¼ inch (6 mm) of head space, ladle the jelly into a sterilized 1-pint (500-ml) jar. Secure the lid and let cool to room temperature.

Storage: The jelly will keep in the refrigerator for up to 6 months.

QUINCE JELLY

Did you know that the prophet Nostradamus had a bestselling cookbook? His two-volume medical cookbook, *Le Traité des Fardements et des Confitures*, was published around 1557. The first volume of his treatise deals with cosmetics and includes recipes that explain how to turn your hair blond, how to prepare a love potion, and even how to cure the plague. The entire second volume is dedicated to preserves, in which he included several recipes using quinces.

Here's how he describes his quince jelly: Of "superb beauty, goodness, flavor, and excellence, fit to set before a king. . . . For the color will be as diaphanous as an oriental ruby. So excellent will the color be—and the taste even more so—that it may be given to sick and healthy alike."

He instructs you to remove the seeds and claims that the fruit will turn into jelly without them, but I see no harm in including them and choose to take the wisdom of Turkish grandmothers over his. Aside from that small detail, the only difference between our recipes are the spices I like to add.

I don't know about you, but I'm making this jelly every year. This guy knows what he's talking about.

If you don't want to let the quince solids go to waste, you can make quince butter using the same method I describe for turning the apple solids left from making Green Apple Pectin Stock into apple butter (page 296). Thinking I could kill two birds with one stone, I tried making Membrillo (page 312) with the leftover solids but found that the resulting paste lacked flavor, so I can't recommend that.

Makes 1½ pints (750 ml)

2.76 pounds (1.25 kilograms; 3 to 4 large) fresh quinces

8 cups (1.92 kilograms) water

8 whole cloves

4 cardamom pods

2 whole star anise

2 tablespoons (30 grams) freshly squeezed lemon juice

3 cups (600 grams) granulated sugar, or as needed

Without peeling and coring them, cut the quinces into 1½-inch (4-cm) pieces and put them into a 6-quart (6-liter) saucepot. Add the water, cloves, cardamom, and star anise. Set the pot over high heat, cover, and bring to a boil. Reduce the heat to medium-high and cook until the quince pieces fall apart when pressed against the side of the pot, about 45 minutes. Take the pot off the heat, uncover, and let cool for 10 minutes. Stir in the lemon juice.

Set a mesh strainer lined with a double layer of cheesecloth over a large heatproof bowl. Ladle the liquid and then the quince pieces into the strainer and let drain completely, about 30 minutes. Gather up the ends of the cheesecloth, twist tightly, and tie a knot to make a bag. Squeeze the bag to extract the jelled juices. Scrape the jelled juices clinging to the bottom of the bag into the bowl. Discard the solids or use to make quince butter (see headnote). Measure and note the volume (or weight) of the juice, which should be about 5⅔ cups (1.35 kilograms).

Return the quince juice to the saucepot and add ½ cup plus 1½ teaspoons (106 grams) of sugar for every 1 cup (240 grams) of juice. (For 5⅔ cups [1.35 kilograms] of juice this will be 3 cups [600 grams] of sugar.)

Set the pot over high heat and bring to a boil, stirring frequently until the sugar dissolves. Reduce the heat to medium-high, insert a candy thermometer into the pot, and cook until it registers 221°F (105°C), about 45 minutes, occasionally stirring and skimming off the foam. Raise the heat to high, bring the mixture to a rolling boil, and cook until it registers 227°F (108°C), about 8 minutes longer. If you don't have a candy thermometer, use the wrinkle test (see page 300) to check its consistency.

(continued on page 311)

Leaving ¼ inch (6 mm) of head space, divide the jelly between one 1-pint (500-ml) and one ½-pint (250-ml) sterilized jars. Secure the lids and let cool to room temperature.

Storage: The jelly will keep in the refrigerator for up to 6 months.

MEMBRILLO

Cotognata in Italy, *pâte de coing* in France, *marmelada* in Portugal, *membrillo* in Spain, and *ayva pestili* in Turkey; great minds think alike. Quince paste has the most intense quince flavor you'll ever taste.

You can use any kind of pan to shape the paste, and a decorative one can render it an edible sculpture. I prefer an 8-inch square pan as it gives me slices close in size to the cheeses I'll be serving alongside. Once set, I cut it into four equal squares serving six to eight guests each, and individually wrap them for future cheese boards. Manchego is the classic pairing, but I also love it with sharp, nutty, and tangy cheeses. Layering the slices with fresh bay leaves prevents them from sticking together and makes it easier for guests to snare them.

Don't forget to stash away one square to make Pistachio, Quince, and Kaymak Macarons (page 62) when quinces go out of season.

Makes four 4-inch (10-cm) squares, about 2.2 pounds (1 kilogram) total

2.2 pounds (1 kilogram; 2 to 3 large) fresh quinces

4 cups (960 grams) water

10 whole cloves

3 cups (600 grams) granulated sugar, or as needed

Fresh bay leaves, for serving

Without peeling and coring them, cut the quinces into 1½-inch (4-cm) pieces and put them into a 6-quart (6-liter) saucepot. Add the water and cloves. Set the pot over high heat, cover, and bring to a boil. Reduce the heat to medium-high and cook until the quince pieces fall apart when pressed against the side of the pot and only 1 inch (2.5 cm) of liquid is left in the pot, 45 to 50 minutes. Take the pot off the heat, uncover, and let cool for 10 minutes.

Puree the mixture with an immersion blender (or in a food processor fitted with a metal blade) until smooth. Ladle the puree into a fine-mesh strainer set over a large heatproof bowl in four equal parts and strain, pressing hard with a silicone spatula until there is only pulp left in the strainer. Discard the pulp after straining each batch. Scrape any puree clinging to the bottom of the strainer into the bowl. Measure and note the volume (or weight) of the puree, which should be about 3½ cups (860 grams).

Return the quince puree to the saucepot and add ¾ cup plus 5 teaspoons (171 grams) of sugar for every 1 cup (245 grams) of puree. (For 3½ cups [860 grams] of puree this will be 3 cups [600 grams] of sugar.)

Set the pot over medium-high heat and bring to a boil, stirring frequently until the sugar dissolves. Reduce the heat to medium-low and cook until the puree thickens and is a deep orange, about 1 hour, stirring and scraping the bottom of the pot every 20 minutes with a silicone spatula to prevent scorching. Reduce the heat to low and cook until it is thick enough to slightly mound and briefly hold its shape when dropped from the spatula and is dark reddish-orange, about 1 hour 30 minutes longer, stirring and scraping the bottom of the pan pot every 15 minutes to prevent scorching. If the bottom layer scorches at any point, stop stirring and tilt the paste into a clean pot without scraping.

When it is ready, take the pot off the heat, spoon a teaspoon of paste onto a saucer, and freeze for 3 minutes. If the paste peels off in one piece it has set. If it does not, set the pot over low heat and continue to cook, testing in 10-minute increments until it is ready.

(continued on page 314)

Grease the bottom and sides of an 8-inch (20.5-cm) square pan. Line the pan with two overlapping strips of parchment paper that are the width of the pan bottom and long enough to cover the bottom and sides with 2 inches (5 cm) of overhang on each side. Grease the lower parchment to secure the top sheet.

Scrape the quince paste into the prepared pan, spread it evenly with an oiled small offset spatula, and let cool to room temperature. Cover the pan tightly with plastic wrap and refrigerate for at least 4 hours or overnight.

Using the parchment overhang as handles, lift the membrillo out of the pan and transfer it to a cutting board. Using a large oiled knife, cut it into 4 equal squares and wrap each square with plastic wrap.

To serve, cut one square into thin slices. Arrange the slices on a serving plate, layering fresh bay leaves between the slices to prevent them from sticking together, and serve at room temperature or cold.

Storage: The membrillo will keep in the refrigerator for up to 6 months.

DULCE DE LECHE

When I broke the news to my family that I was going to write a baking book and gave them a summary of the contents, my sister-in-law's first question was which recipes I would include in the jam chapter. When she heard there would be one for "milk jam" she thought she had misheard me. Despite being a jam lover, she had never heard of such a thing. This was about eight years ago. Nowadays, even the most remote farmers' markets in İstanbul have stands selling dulce de leche, the caramelized milk sweet enjoyed in Latin countries around the world. I'm not surprised. Something so milky, sweet, sticky, and gooey should know no boundaries.

I can't say I treat dulce de leche as jam, spreading it on toasted bread, but I can't stop drizzling it over almost everything I bake. It is especially good with recipes packing a bittersweet chocolate punch. Take a look at what happens when you bury dollops of it in a brownie batter on page 88.

I must say I like its Mexican sister even better. Also known as Mexican caramel, cajeta is made with goat's milk and my version packs a strong punch of vanilla and cinnamon. Check the end of the recipe for instructions.

Makes 1 pint (500 ml)

7 cups (1.68 kilograms) whole milk

2 cups (400 grams) granulated sugar

1 teaspoon (5 grams) pure vanilla extract

¼ teaspoon (2 grams) baking soda

Warning: When heating a homogenous liquid such as milk, it may go past its boiling point with no bubbles or other visible sign of boiling, and then explode on contact. To prevent superheating, keep a wooden spoon in the pot at all times while reducing the milk.

To easily determine the amount of milk in the pot as it is reduced, weigh an empty 6-quart (6-liter) saucepot and make a note. Pour the milk into the pot and bring to just below a boil over high heat, keeping a wooden spoon in the pot at all times and watching it carefully. Reduce the heat to medium and simmer until the milk is reduced to 3⅓ cups (1.76 pounds; 800 grams), about 1 hour 30 minutes, occasionally stirring and skimming off the skin. Near the end of the cooking time, weigh the pot with the milk and subtract the weight of the pot. If the milk weighs more than 1.76 pounds (800 grams), continue reducing until you reach the target weight.

Pour the reduced milk through a mesh strainer into a clean 6-quart (6-liter) saucepot. Add the sugar, vanilla, and baking soda. Set the pot over medium-high heat and stir constantly with a silicone spatula until the sugar melts. When the mixture starts to rise in the pot, reduce the heat to medium (if it threatens to boil over, briefly remove from the heat) and simmer until it turns a caramel color and starts to bubble up from the sides, about 45 to 60 minutes. Raise the heat to medium-high, insert a candy thermometer into the pot, and cook until it registers 223°F (106°C), 5 to 10 minutes, stirring and scraping the bottom of the pot constantly. If you don't have a candy thermometer, use the wrinkle test (see page 300) to check its consistency.

Leaving ¼ inch (6 mm) of head space, transfer the Dulce de Leche through a fine-mesh strainer into a sterilized 1-pint (500-ml) jar. Secure the lid and let cool to room temperature.

Storage: The Dulce de Leche will keep in the refrigerator for up to 2 weeks. Before serving, put the jar in a small saucepan with 2 inches (5 cm) of simmering water until the contents are runny.

(variation on page 317)

CAJETA

Follow the recipe for Dulce de Leche on page 315, making the following changes: Substitute goat's milk for the cow's milk. After reducing and straining the milk, add the seeds and pod of 1 vanilla bean (split and seeds scraped; see page 32) and 1 cinnamon stick in place of the vanilla extract. As soon as the mixture comes to a boil and starts to bubble up from the sides, remove the vanilla pod and cinnamon stick, then continue to follow the remaining recipe instructions. After rinsing the leftover vanilla pod thoroughly with cold water and letting it dry out completely, you may use it to make Vanilla Sugar (page 326).

BASE RECIPES

VANILLA PASTRY CREAM

Crème pâtissière, or pastry cream, should be in every home baker's arsenal. Thickened with egg yolks and starch and enriched with butter, it may be flavored with vanilla, chocolate, coffee, liqueurs, fruits, or other flavorings. It is essential to many fruit tarts (including my favorite, Blanche, page 170), cream pies, and *pâte à choux*–based pastries, such as Profiteroles (page 231) and Éclairs (see page 234).

When made with vanilla extract, this may be considered a master pastry cream that welcomes almost infinite variation. I'll share two of my favorites—mocha and chocolate—but feel free to play with it by steeping the finely grated zest of a citrus fruit or aromatic tea leaves in the milk, or by adding extracts or liqueurs.

Makes 2½ cups (about 650 grams)

2 cups (480 grams) whole milk

1 vanilla bean, split and seeds scraped (see page 32) or 2 teaspoons (10 grams) pure vanilla extract

5 large egg yolks

⅔ cup (133 grams) granulated sugar

⅓ cup (40 grams) cornstarch

Pinch of fine sea salt

3½ tablespoons (1.7 ounces; 50 grams) cold unsalted butter, cut into small pieces

If using a vanilla bean, in a medium saucepan over medium-high heat, bring the milk and the vanilla seeds and pod to a simmer. Take the pan off the heat, cover, and let steep for 30 minutes. Retrieve the vanilla pod from the milk, rinse thoroughly with cold water, and let dry out completely before using it to make Vanilla Sugar (page 326), if desired. Set the pan with the vanilla milk over medium heat and bring to just below a boil. **If using vanilla extract,** simply bring the milk and vanilla extract to just below a boil. Take the pan off the heat and cover to keep the vanilla milk hot.

Fill a medium bowl with ice and cold water. Place a medium bowl over the ice bath with the bottom touching the water. Set a mesh strainer on top.

In a separate medium saucepan, whisk the yolks, sugar, cornstarch, and salt with a narrow wire whisk until the yolks lighten in color, 2 to 3 minutes. While whisking the egg mixture constantly, drizzle in about half the hot vanilla milk. Add the rest of the hot vanilla milk all at once, then set the pan over medium heat. Cook until the mixture comes to a full boil and is thick enough to mound when dropped from the whisk, constantly whisking and scraping the bottom of the pan with the whisk, about 8 minutes.

Scrape the thickened pastry cream into the strainer over the ice bath and strain, pressing with a silicone spatula. Scrape any pastry cream clinging to the bottom of the strainer into the bowl. Add the butter pieces, whisking until blended. Stir the pastry cream frequently until it reaches room temperature, about 5 minutes. Remove the bowl from the ice water and cover with plastic wrap, pressing it directly onto the surface of the pastry cream to prevent a skin from forming. Refrigerate for at least 4 hours or overnight.

The pastry cream is now ready to use in recipes.

Storage: The pastry cream will keep in the refrigerator for up to 3 days. Whisk until smooth before using.

(variations on page 322)

MOCHA PASTRY CREAM

Makes about 3 cups (800 grams)

Prepare the Vanilla Pastry Cream on page 320 using vanilla extract; cover and refrigerate until cold. Put 3.5 ounces (100 grams) coarsely chopped bittersweet chocolate (70% cacao) into a medium saucepan and pour ¼ cup (60 grams) very strong brewed hot coffee or espresso over the top. Stir with a silicone spatula over low heat until the chocolate melts completely. Scrape the chocolate mixture into the chilled pastry cream, whisking until blended. Cover the bowl with plastic wrap, pressing it directly onto the surface of the pastry cream to prevent a skin from forming. Refrigerate for at least 1 hour before using.

CHOCOLATE PASTRY CREAM

Makes about 3 cups (770 grams)

Prepare the Vanilla Pastry Cream on page 320 using vanilla extract. Immediately after adding the butter, add 4.2 ounces (120 grams) finely chopped bittersweet chocolate (70% cacao), whisking until it melts completely and is thoroughly blended into the pastry cream. Continue as instructed in the recipe.

HOMEMADE VANILLA EXTRACT

This year, my homemade vanilla extract turns seven!

I started with just three vanilla beans and have been feeding my extract with leftover beans ever since. It has turned into a monster. The smell is so intense, I could make a fortune selling tickets to take a whiff.

When I use only the seeds of a vanilla pod in a recipe, the leftover pod halves go directly into the bottle. If you use a lot of vanilla beans, I'd recommend tripling the recipe and using a 1-quart (1-liter) bottle so that you have enough space for the pods and to add vodka as needed to balance the strength later on. My rule of thumb is to add ¼ cup (60 grams) of vodka for every ten used vanilla pods, keeping in mind that the pods will not intensify the extract as much as an unused vanilla bean and that the vodka dilutes the extract in the short run—I recommend waiting a month or so for the used pods to strengthen the extract before adding more vodka. If you don't use more than ten vanilla beans per year, omit extra vodka—stronger extract is always a plus.

Use vanilla pods that have been steeped in milk, cream, or other perishable liquids to make Vanilla Sugar (page 326) rather than risk spoiling your extract.

Makes 1 cup (240 grams)

3 vanilla beans, split (see page 32)

**1 cup (240 grams) vodka, plus
more as needed**

**Additional used vanilla bean pods,
as desired**

Put the vanilla beans in a ½-pint (250-ml) clear glass bottle with an airtight lid (or a swing stopper). If the bottle isn't as tall as the beans, cut them in half crosswise to fit them into the bottle. Pour the vodka over the beans to cover the beans completely. Secure the lid and store in a cool, dark place for at least 2 months before using, shaking the bottle once a week to encourage extraction.

Add used vanilla pods as they become available and vodka as needed, following the guidelines above.

Storage: The extract will keep in a cool, dark place at room temperature for several years.

VANILLA SUGAR

I use leftover vanilla pods that have been steeped in milk or cream to delicately scent sugar with vanilla, first rinsing them thoroughly in cold water, pressing them between paper towels, and leaving them to dry completely at room temperature before burying them in a jar of sugar. This "poor man's vanilla sugar" isn't intense enough to add vanilla flavor to recipes, but it adds an aromatic touch to cocktails, coffee, and tea.

For the rich man's version, intense enough to replace vanilla extract when substituted for plain granulated sugar in recipes, follow the recipe below.

Makes 5 cups (1 kilogram)

5 cups (1 kilogram) granulated sugar

2 vanilla beans, split and seeds scraped (see page 32)

Additional used vanilla bean pods, as desired

Put the sugar in a large bowl and add the vanilla seeds. Use your palms to rub the seeds into the sugar.

Transfer half of the vanilla sugar to a 1.5-quart (1.5-liter) jar, burying the pods halfway into the sugar. Add the remaining vanilla sugar.

Secure the lid and let the vanilla seeds infuse in the sugar for at least 1 week before using. The sugar will absorb moisture from the beans and will become damp and clumped over time. Shake the jar well before using.

Feed the sugar with additional leftover vanilla pods as they become available. If they have been steeped in milk, cream, or other liquids, thoroughly rinse them with cold water, press them between paper towels to remove excess moisture, and let dry completely at room temperature before burying them in the jar.

Storage: The vanilla sugar will keep at room temperature for several years.

FLAKY PIE DOUGH

Were it not for the tender, flaky crust beneath, would the glistening pluot slices on page 193 be as enticing? Without the contrast of the savory crust shattering with each bite, would we notice how creamy the blue cheese filling is in the Fig, Thyme, and Blue Cheese Galette (page 196)? And would the thyme honey taste as sweet? In a galette, pie, or quiche, the crust is everything.

Flaky pie dough is considered one of the most difficult pastries to master, but I beg to differ. I'll go so far to say that it is as easy as pressing a button. I have but one essential rule: keep the butter cool throughout the process, never letting it soften, or worse, melt. To ensure this, chill the butter and liquid ingredients thoroughly before beginning, and work fast. A food processor is ideal, making the recipe foolproof, but you can also put the dough together with your reliably cold, fast hands.

All that's left after mixing is to roll it out. A surefire way to execute this rapidly—again keeping the butter pieces firm—is to start by pounding the chilled dough with a heavy rolling pin, flattening the pastry without overworking it. Once you've pounded it into a rough disk, a few rolls of the pin complete the job.

Makes 17 ounces (480 grams), enough for one 13-inch (33-cm) galette dough or one 10¼-inch (26-cm) round quiche crust (for a 10¼-inch [26-cm] double-crust pie, double the recipe)

10 tablespoons plus 2 teaspoons (5.3 ounces; 150 grams) cold unsalted butter

⅓ cup (80 grams) ice water

1 teaspoon (5 grams) cider vinegar

1⅔ cups (233 grams) all-purpose flour

1 tablespoon (13 grams) granulated sugar

½ teaspoon (4 grams) fine sea salt

Cut the butter into 1-inch (2.5-cm) pieces and freeze for 20 minutes.

In a small pitcher, stir together the water and vinegar and refrigerate until needed.

In the bowl of a food processor fitted with a metal blade, process the flour, sugar, and salt until blended. Add the butter pieces, pulsing until they are the size of hazelnuts. While pulsing, gradually drizzle in all but 2 tablespoons (30 grams) of the cold water–vinegar mixture through the feed tube until the dough resembles coarse meal.

To test it, squeeze a small piece of the dough in the palm of your hand. If it mostly sticks together (photo 1), you have added enough liquid. If not, gradually pulse in the remaining 2 tablespoons (30 grams) of water-vinegar until the dough holds together when squeezed.

Empty the dough into a medium bowl and gently press it into a ball with your hands. For a double recipe, divide the dough into two balls (17 ounces; 480 grams each) and follow the steps below for each of the balls.

Wrap the dough with plastic wrap, flatten it into a 6-inch (15-cm) disk (photo 2), and refrigerate for at least 4 hours. (The dough will keep, double-wrapped with plastic wrap, in the refrigerator for up to 3 days or in the freezer for up to 2 months. Thaw overnight in the refrigerator before using.)

Flatten the dough between two large sheets of parchment paper into a rough disk about 9½ inches (24 cm) in diameter by pounding it with a rolling pin (photo 3). Roll out the dough into a round about 13⅜ inches (34 cm) in diameter, occasionally flipping the dough with the parchment, then lifting and smoothing the parchment to avoid creases. If the dough becomes soft and sticky as you roll, transfer the dough and parchment to a baking sheet and freeze for 5 to 10 minutes before continuing.

For a 13-inch (33-cm) galette, peel off the top parchment and trim the edges with a pizza cutter or paring knife to form a neat 13-inch (33-cm) round (photo 4). Transfer the dough and parchment to a baking sheet, cover with the top parchment sheet, and refrigerate

(continued on page 330)

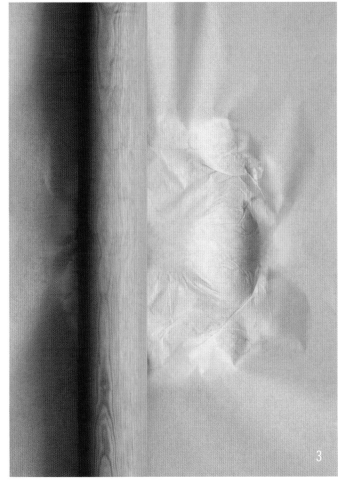

for 30 minutes. Gather the scraps into a small ball, wrap with plastic wrap, and refrigerate for patching the crust later if needed. The chilled galette dough is now ready to use in recipes.

For a 10¼-inch (26-cm) double-crust pie, peel off the top parchment sheets and trim the edges with a pizza cutter or paring knife to form two neat 13-inch (33-cm) rounds. Cover with the top parchment sheets, stack the covered doughs on a baking sheet, and refrigerate for 30 minutes. Gather the scraps into a small ball, wrap with plastic wrap, and refrigerate for patching the crusts later if needed. The chilled dough rounds are now ready to use in recipes.

For a partially baked 10¼-inch (26-cm) quiche crust, peel off the top parchment and trim the edges with a pizza cutter or paring knife to form a neat 13-inch (33-cm) round. Cover with the top parchment sheet and flip the whole thing over. Peel away the top parchment sheet. Drape the dough over the rolling pin and center it over a 10¼-inch (26-cm) round tart pan; unroll the dough over the pan. Use your hands to ease the dough across the bottom and up the sides of the pan, taking care not to stretch it. Fold the excess dough over into the pan to make double-thick walls that are about ¼ inch (6 mm) higher than the sides of the pan (photo 5). While pressing the dough along the seam and fluted sides of the pan with the index finger of one hand, push down on the rim of the pan with the thumb of the opposite hand to make a level edge all around that is about ⅛ inch (3 mm) higher than the sides of the pan (photo 6). Don't worry if the edge is thicker in some areas. Transfer the pan to a baking sheet and freeze for 15 minutes.

Holding a sharp paring knife with the tip pointing downward, run the knife along the sides of the crust, trimming away any thick areas of dough to even the sides. Release the trimmings by cutting crosswise where they meet the bottom crust. Run a finger along the seam where the sides meet the bottom to seal any breaks in the crust (photo 7). Gather the scraps and trimmings into a small ball, wrap in plastic wrap, and refrigerate for patching the crust later if needed. Transfer the pan to a baking sheet and freeze for 20 minutes.

Set a rack in the middle of the oven and preheat the oven to 400°F (200°C).

Crumple up a sheet of parchment paper and straighten it out half a dozen times to soften it, so that it will fit into the corners of the dough without sharp edges (photo 8). Line the dough with the parchment paper across the bottom and up the sides, pressing creases at the bottom and top edges. Fill the pan with pie weights or dried beans.

Bake the crust for 20 minutes. Remove the pie weights and parchment and continue baking until the edges and bottom of the crust are light golden, about 10 minutes longer. Set the baking sheet on a wire rack. Patch any cracks or holes in the crust with small scraps of the reserved dough. The partially baked crust is now ready to use in Tomato Confit and Pesto Quiche (page 202).

(continued on page 332)

NOTES (FLAKY PIE DOUGH)

*The quiche recipe on page 202 calls for a partially baked crust. For a **fully baked quiche crust,** after removing the weights and parchment, continue baking until the edges and bottom are golden, 20 to 25 minutes.*

Use the following guidelines for other pan sizes:

- For *eight 4¼-inch (11-cm) small round tart pans,* divide the dough into 8 equal parts (2.1 ounces; 60 grams each). Roll each into a 6¼-inch (16-cm) round and trim them into neat 6-inch (15-cm) rounds before fitting them into the pans. Baking time will vary depending on the recipe used but will be shorter than for a full-size crust.

- For a *9-inch (23-cm) square tart pan,* roll out the dough into a 12¼-inch (31-cm) square and cut it into a neat 11¾-inch (30-cm) square before fitting it into the pan.

- For a *9½-inch (24-cm) round tart pan,* measure out 14.1 ounces (400 grams) of the dough; reserve the rest for another use. Roll out the dough into a 12½-inch (32-cm) round and cut it into a neat 12¼-inch (31-cm) round before fitting it into the pan.

- For a *13¾-by-4¼-inch (35-by-11-cm) rectangular tart pan,* measure out 12.7 ounces (360 grams) of the dough; reserve the rest for another use. Roll out the dough into a 7½-by-17-inch (19-by-43-cm) rectangle and cut it into a neat 7-by-16½-inch (18-by-42-cm) rectangle before fitting it into the pan.

VANILLA BEAN SHORT TART DOUGH

This short tart dough, also known as *pâte sablée*, is sweet, tender, and rich. It is also too fragile to roll; instead, you simply press it into the pan.

I use a combination of vanilla bean seeds and vanilla extract for flavor. With half a vanilla bean plenty for a single batch, I always double the recipe to use the whole bean and freeze half for an impromptu tart. The dough also makes great cookies (see page 178).

Makes 17 ounces (480 grams), enough for one 9-inch (23-cm) square tart crust, one 10¼-inch (26-cm) round tart crust, one 13¾-by-4¼-inch (35-by-11-cm) rectangular tart crust, or eight 4¼-inch (11-cm) round tart crusts

9 tablespoons (4.5 ounces; 125 grams) unsalted butter, softened

½ cup (80 grams) confectioners' sugar

½ vanilla bean, split and seeds scraped (see page 32)

2 large egg yolks, at room temperature

1 tablespoon (15 grams) heavy cream or whole milk

1 teaspoon (5 grams) pure vanilla extract

¼ teaspoon (2 grams) fine sea salt

1⅔ cups (233 grams) all-purpose flour

In the bowl of a stand mixer fitted with the paddle attachment, beat the butter, sugar, and vanilla seeds at the lowest speed until the sugar is incorporated. Raise the speed to medium-high and beat until creamy, about 2 minutes. Add the yolks, cream, vanilla extract, and salt. Beat until blended, about 2 minutes, scraping down the sides of the bowl as needed. Add the flour and beat at the lowest speed just until incorporated. Remove the bowl from the mixer and press the dough into a ball with your hands. Pinch off a teaspoon-size piece of dough, wrap, and refrigerate for patching the baked crust later if needed. (The dough will keep, wrapped airtight, in the refrigerator for up to 3 days or in the freezer for up to 2 months. Thaw overnight in the refrigerator, then let stand at room temperature until soft enough to press into the pan.) You may use the leftover half vanilla pod in Homemade Vanilla Extract (page 323) or Vanilla Sugar (page 326).

To make a **9-inch (23-cm) square tart crust or a 10¼-inch (26-cm) round tart crust,** use all of the dough. To make a **13¾-by-4¼-inch (35-by-11-cm) rectangular tart crust,** measure out 12.7 ounces (360 grams) of the dough; reserve the rest for another use, such as cookies (page 178). To make **eight 4¼-inch (11-cm) round tart crusts,** divide the dough into 8 equal pieces (2.1 ounces; 60 grams each). In all cases, use two-piece tart pans with removable bottoms.

For each crust, place the dough into the center of a tart pan. Using the heel of your hand, press the dough across the bottom of the pan as smoothly and evenly as possible, accumulating excess dough along the seam of the pan. While pressing the excess dough along the seam and fluted sides of the pan with the index finger of one hand, push down on the rim of the pan with the thumb of the opposite hand to make an even and evenly thick edge, making sure it's not too thick at the seam where the bottom meets the sides of the pan.

Transfer the pan to a baking sheet and freeze until firm, 30 to 40 minutes.

Meanwhile, set a rack in the middle of the oven and preheat the oven to 340°F (170°C).

Crumple up a sheet of parchment paper and straighten it out half a dozen times to soften it, so that it will fit into the corners of the dough without sharp edges. Line the chilled dough with the parchment paper across the bottom and up the sides, pressing creases at the bottom and top edges. Fill the pan with pie weights or dried beans.

(continued on page 335)

For a partially baked crust, bake for 25 minutes, remove the pie weights and parchment, and continue baking until the edges and bottom are light golden, about 6 minutes longer (about 4 minutes longer for 4¼-inch [11-cm] round tart crusts). Patch any cracks or holes in the crust with small scraps of the reserved raw dough.

For a fully baked crust, bake for 25 minutes, remove the pie weights and parchment, and patch any cracks or holes in the crust with small scraps of the reserved raw dough. Continue baking until the edges are golden brown and the bottom is golden, 15 to 17 minutes longer (about 11 to 13 minutes longer for 4¼-inch [11-cm] round tart crusts).

Set the baking sheet on a wire rack to cool completely. The tart crust is now ready to use in recipes.

ALMOND SHORT TART DOUGH

Omit the vanilla bean. Replace all the flour with 1⅓ cups (187 grams) all-purpose flour plus ½ cup (50 grams) blanched almond flour.

COCOA SHORT TART DOUGH

Omit the vanilla bean. Replace all the flour with 1½ cups (210 grams) all-purpose flour sifted with ¼ cup (25 grams) Dutch-processed unsweetened cocoa powder. Color is not a reliable gauge of doneness for a dark crust. When baked, it should look dry and the edges should be firm to the touch.

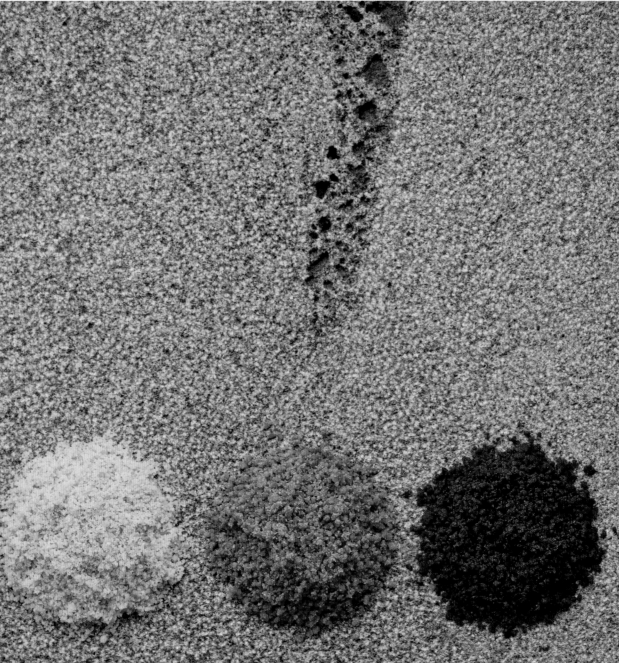

VANILLA WAFER CRUMBS

Would I peel, seed, and cut a 6.6-pound pumpkin into pieces, bake them, puree them, blot the puree to remove excess moisture, and use the drained puree to make the smoothest, creamiest, and most pumpkin-y pumpkin cheesecake ever (page 136), then bake it on a crust made with store-bought wafers? I don't think so. Some may say life is too short to make homemade wafer crumbs. I say, life is too short to eat a cheesecake that is anything short of spectacular.

If you think like I do, you will be pleased to find here my go-to wafer crumbs, along with two variations. It takes two minutes to prepare the dough, maybe a minute to roll it out, and fifteen minutes to bake it. Cleanup takes about as long as it does to make them, so as long as I'm making one batch I make all three kinds: first the vanilla crumbs, then the cocoa, and finally the cinnamon and ginger crumbs. In that order, I can make all three without stopping to wash the processor bowl or clean up between batches. Follow the same order when you pulse the baked wafers into crumbs and again, the flavors will stay separate.

Three batches of wafer crumbs in ten minutes not including baking time. Making wafer crumbs at home is actually faster than running out to the store for wafers and pulsing them at home.

Makes 1¾ cups (210 grams)

- ¾ cup (105 grams) all-purpose flour
- ¼ cup plus 2 tablespoons (60 grams) confectioners' sugar
- Pinch of fine sea salt
- 4 tablespoons plus 1 teaspoon (2.2 ounces; 60 grams) cold unsalted butter, cut into small pieces
- 2 teaspoons (10 grams) cold whole milk
- 1 teaspoon (5 grams) pure vanilla extract

Set a rack in the middle of the oven and preheat the oven to 350°F (175°C).

In the bowl of a food processor fitted with a metal blade, process the flour, sugar, and salt until blended. Add the butter pieces and pulse until coarse crumbs form. Add the milk and vanilla and process until the dough gathers around the blade, about 1 minute.

Scrape the dough onto a large sheet of parchment paper. Cover with another sheet of parchment and roll out the dough to an even thickness of ⅛ inch (3 mm). Transfer the dough and parchment to a baking sheet and peel off the top parchment.

Bake until golden on top and light brown on the edges, 14 to 16 minutes. Remove the baking sheet from the oven and transfer the wafer with its parchment onto a wire rack to cool completely.

Break up the wafer into large pieces and transfer them to the food processor. Pulse until crumbs form, about 1 minute. The crumbs are now ready to use in recipes.

Storage: The wafer crumbs will keep in an airtight container at room temperature for up to 3 days, in the refrigerator for up to 1 week, or in the freezer for up to 2 months.

COCOA WAFER CRUMBS

Replace the flour with ⅔ cup (93 grams) all-purpose flour and 2 tablespoons (13 grams) Dutch-processed unsweetened cocoa powder. Color is not a reliable gauge of doneness for a dark wafer. When baked, it should look dry and be firm to the touch.

CINNAMON & GINGER WAFER CRUMBS

Decrease the confectioners' sugar to ¼ cup (40 grams), add ½ teaspoon (2 grams) each ground cinnamon and ground ginger with the flour, and replace the milk and vanilla with 1 tablespoon (20 grams) of maple syrup.

CRÈME FRAÎCHE

When researching whether I could rightfully call the tangy cream I'd been making at home crème fraiche, I learned that the utmost authority in the matter was the *Institut national de l'origine et de la qualité*, a French organization that regulates the country's agricultural products and grants a seal of approval called the *Appellation d'Origine Contrôlée* (AOC), or controlled designation of origin, attesting to the product's origin and quality following set standards. This was when I learned that the only crème fraîche worthy of AOC status comes from Isigny-sur-Mer, a seaside commune in the Normandy area of northwest France. Since I don't have access to Isigny's highly regarded dairy products, I have no choice but to accept the fact that my homemade crème fraîche will not be blessed by the French. But I think it still deserves a medal, and so can yours, so long as you use cream that is good enough to drink straight from the bottle.

Commercial buttermilk isn't easy to find in İstanbul, so I make my crème fraîche with strained yogurt, which introduces a different type of bacteria. The difference in taste and texture is undetectable, however, so use whichever you have on hand.

Makes 1 cup (240 grams)

1 cup (240 grams) heavy cream (not ultra-pasteurized), at room temperature

1 tablespoon (14 grams) plain full-fat strained (Greek-style) yogurt or buttermilk, at room temperature

In a 1-pint (500-ml) jar, whisk the cream and yogurt with a fork until blended. Secure the lid and keep the jar in a warm spot in your kitchen until it is thick and moves in one piece when gently shaken, 18 to 24 hours.

The crème fraîche is now ready to use in Tomato Confit and Pesto Quiche (page 202). For other uses, whisk with a fork until smooth, then secure the lid and refrigerate for at least 8 hours before using. The cream will become firmer and tangier over time.

Storage: The crème fraîche will keep in the refrigerator for 1 week.

TOMATO CONFIT

Confit sounds like a fancy chef's technique, but it's actually one of the oldest methods of preserving. Derived from the French word *confire*, which means "to preserve," confit refers to the process of slowly cooking food in a liquid that both flavors and preserves it. For fruits, the preserving liquid is either sugar syrup or honey; for vegetables, it is olive oil; and for meats, it is usually their own fat.

I can't claim that this is the best way to preserve tomatoes, but this technique has the power to turn even off-season supermarket tomatoes into something succulent and meltingly tender. Roasting the tomatoes slowly in a pool of extra-virgin olive oil brings out their sweetness and deepens their flavor. While that's happening, the juices they release perfume the oil and give it a golden hue.

The recipe makes twelve confit tomato halves, seven of which I urge you to use for making Tomato Confit and Pesto Quiche (page 202). Serve the rest alongside a cheese board, or use them to elevate a classic BLT sandwich. You'll also get half a cup of tomato-infused olive oil, into which you must dunk slices of Rosemary and Sea Salt Focaccia (page 209). It also makes a great salad dressing. Now that I think about it, a panzanella is in order.

Makes 12 tomato confit halves and ½ cup (108 grams) tomato-infused olive oil

6 large (about 3 pounds; 1.35 kilograms) firm-ripe heirloom tomatoes

¾ cup (162 grams) extra-virgin olive oil

15 sprigs fresh thyme

½ teaspoon (4 grams) fine sea salt

Set a rack in the middle of the oven and preheat the oven to 270°F (130°C).

Hull the tomatoes with the tip of a paring knife and cut them crosswise in half. Hold each half over a bowl, cut side down, and gently squeeze to drain the juices. Using your fingers or a small spoon, scoop out the seeds. Reserve the juices and seeds for another use, such as a soup or pasta sauce.

Spread ¼ cup (54 grams) of the olive oil on an unlined 15-by-10-inch (38-by-25.5-cm) jelly-roll pan or roasting pan. Scatter the thyme sprigs and sprinkle ¼ teaspoon (2 grams) of the salt evenly over the oil. Evenly space the tomato halves, cut side down, on the pan.

Bake until the tomato skins loosen, about 30 minutes. Remove the pan from the oven and carefully pinch off and discard the skins. Drizzle the remaining ½ cup (108 grams) of olive oil over the tomatoes and sprinkle them evenly with the remaining ¼ teaspoon (2 grams) of salt. Continue to bake until the tomatoes are falling apart and the olive oil is an orange-gold color, about 1 hour 30 minutes, basting the tomatoes with the oil in the pan every 30 minutes.

Transfer the pan to a wire rack to cool completely. The confit tomato halves are now ready to use in Tomato Confit and Pesto Quiche (page 202). To serve them on their own, use a fork to transfer the tomatoes to a shallow bowl, pour the infused oil over them, and serve with Rosemary and Sea Salt Focaccia (page 209) or other bread. If you're not going to use the confit tomatoes right away, transfer them to a 1-quart (1-liter) jar, discarding the thyme sprigs. Pour the infused oil over them and secure the lid.

Storage: The confit tomatoes will keep in the refrigerator for up to 1 week. Before using, bring to room temperature by submerging the jar up to its brim in hot water.

PESTO

In summer, when farmers' markets are overflowing with bunches of basil, I start planning for winter. I buy as much as I dare, wash and dry it, and make pesto, stacking it in ½-cup portions in the freezer. Come winter, those freezer bags save the day when I have energy only to toss things together into a meal.

For the amount of pesto below, I use a mortar and pestle and firmly believe you should, too. It helps to emulsify the pesto, making it coat pasta and other foods more evenly. Making countless batches for winter is another story. I might have once baked cream puff swans, but grinding twenty cups of pesto by hand is beyond my patience, especially on a sticky summer day. You'll find both methods below. Either way, don't forget to save half a cup of pesto to make Tomato Confit and Pesto Quiche (page 202).

Makes about 1 cup (240 grams)

1 large garlic clove, peeled

¼ teaspoon (2 grams) fine sea salt

4 cups (60 grams) tightly packed basil leaves

¼ cup (35 grams) pine nuts, toasted if desired

1.8 ounces (50 grams) Parmigiano-Reggiano, finely grated

⅓ cup plus 1 tablespoon (86 grams) extra-virgin olive oil, plus more for storing

To make the pesto in a mortar and pestle, put the garlic and salt into the mortar and pound them with the pestle into a paste. Add the basil leaves in batches, grinding them against the sides of the mortar into a paste. Add the pine nuts and cheese and pound until mashed. Add the olive oil in a thin stream, stirring it in with a wooden spoon.

To make the pesto in a food processor, using a fine-tooth rasp grater, grate the garlic directly into the bowl of a food processor fitted with a metal blade. Add the salt, basil, and pine nuts, and pulse until the leaves and nuts are coarsely chopped. Add the cheese and olive oil and process until creamy, scraping down the sides of the bowl as needed.

The pesto is now ready to use in Tomato Confit and Pesto Quiche (page 202). To use the pesto later, transfer it to a ½-pint (250-ml) jar, add olive oil to cover the top, and secure the lid.

Storage: The pesto will keep in the refrigerator for up to 1 week or in a resealable freezer bag in the freezer for up to 3 months. Before using, bring to room temperature by submerging the jar or freezer bag in hot water.

PÂTE À CHOUX

Pâte à choux, or cream puff pastry, is a classic French dough used to make cream puffs, profiteroles, and éclairs, as well as showstoppers like Gâteau Saint-Honoré, *croquembouche*, and Paris-Brest. You can transform it into savory *gougères* by adding grated cheese and herbs.

Most of the sweet pastries made with pâte à choux are filled with a sweetened cream filling, which inevitably softens the dough over time. To prolong their crispness, I make the dough with water rather than milk or a mixture of the two, and bake them much longer than you are likely to see recommended in other baking books. They should be golden brown on the outside and, once cooled, should sound hollow when tapped on the bottom.

Makes 45 cream puff shells or 16 éclair shells

1 cup (240 grams) water

7 tablespoons (3.5 ounces; 100 grams) unsalted butter

2 tablespoons (25 grams) granulated sugar

½ teaspoon (4 grams) fine sea salt

1¼ cups (175 grams) all-purpose flour

4 large eggs, at room temperature, plus more if needed

Set two racks just above and below the middle of the oven and preheat the oven to 375°F (190°C).

For cream puff shells, draw forty-five 1¼-inch (3-cm) circles on two sheets of parchment paper, leaving about 1½ inches (4 cm) all around them. ***For éclair shells,*** draw eight ¾-by-6¾-inch (2-by-17-cm) rectangles on each of two sheets of parchment paper, leaving about 1½ inches (4 cm) all around them. Line two baking sheets with the parchment, writing side down.

For cream puff shells, fit a large pastry bag with a ⅝-inch (1.6-cm) plain round tip (Ateco #808). ***For éclair shells,*** fit the pastry bag with a ⁹⁄₁₆-inch (1.4-cm) open star tip (Ateco #827). Twist the tip of the bag, place it in a tall glass, and fold the top of the bag down over the edge of the glass.

In a medium heavy-bottomed saucepan over medium-high heat, bring the water, butter, sugar, and salt to a boil. Remove the pan from the heat, add the flour, and stir vigorously with a wooden spoon until the dough comes together in a mass. Set the pan over medium heat and cook until a thin crust forms on the bottom of the pan, about 3 minutes, constantly stirring and slapping the dough against the sides of the pan.

Scrape the dough into the bowl of a stand mixer fitted with the paddle attachment and beat at medium speed for 2 minutes to cool the dough. Add the eggs, one at a time, beating until well blended after each addition. After the last addition, beat until the dough is shiny, thick, and elastic, about 3 minutes. To test the consistency, pinch off a piece of dough with your thumb and index finger and pull your fingers apart. If the dough stretches without breaking, it is ready. If it breaks, beat an extra egg in a small bowl with a fork until frothy and beat it into the dough, 1 tablespoon (15 grams) at a time, until the dough is stretchy, checking the consistency after each addition.

Scrape the dough into the prepared pastry bag, unfold the cuff, and twist to enclose the dough.

Dab small amounts of dough under the four corners of each parchment to secure them in place. Holding the pastry bag at a 90-degree angle to the parchment, pipe out the dough following the templates you drew on the back, finishing each by lifting the tip upward with a quick twist of your wrist. For an even rise, gently smooth the pointed peaks with a damp fingertip.

(continued on page 347)

Bake for 25 minutes, then rotate the sheets top to bottom and side to side. Slip the handle of a wooden spoon between the oven and the door to prop it slightly ajar and continue baking until the shells are golden brown on top, 20 to 30 minutes.

Set the sheets on wire racks to cool for 10 minutes. Tap on the bottom of one of the shells. If you hear a hollow sound, they are well dried out; let them cool completely. If they do not sound hollow, they may still be slightly moist inside; return the sheets to the still hot (but no longer on) oven, prop the door ajar with the handle of a wooden spoon, and let them continue to dry out and cool completely in the oven.

The shells are now ready to be filled and glazed.

Storage: The shells are best used shortly after they are made, but they will keep in an airtight container at room temperature for several hours.

INGREDIENTS

The recipes you make can only be as delicious as the ingredients you use. A good grasp of technique and attention to detail are paramount, too, but baking starts long before you step into the kitchen.

Here are the defining characteristics of the most common ingredients used in the book, along with suggestions about substitutions and storage.

CHEMICAL LEAVENERS

Baking soda, also called bicarbonate of soda or sodium bicarbonate, is an alkaline chemical agent that combines with acidic ingredients—such as natural cocoa powder, yogurt, or honey—to produce carbon dioxide gas. The gas enlarges the air bubbles you've created when agitating the batter during mixing, making baked goods rise. Baking soda has a long shelf life. Always sift baking soda before using.

Baking powder is a mixture of baking soda, an acid, and a small amount of starch to prevent its activation before using. The most common type of baking powder in the United States is double-acting, reacting first upon mixing with liquids and then a second time when exposed to heat during the baking process. Baking powder loses its potency over time; if it bubbles vigorously when mixed with hot water, it is good to use.

CHOCOLATE, COCOA POWDER & CACAO NIBS

See page 78.

CITRIC ACID

Citric acid is a weak organic acid that occurs naturally in citrus fruits. It adds an acidic taste to foods and drinks and is also a natural preservative. I use it to make invert sugar (see page 257) and as seasoning for sorbets and drinks.

COFFEE

The recipes for Double Chocolate Bundt Cake (page 102) and Mocha Éclairs (page 234) call for very strong brewed coffee. To be precise, I use ¼ cup (24 grams) of medium-fine ground coffee to 1 cup (240 grams) of water, for about ¾ cup (180 grams) of very strong brewed coffee. You can substitute an equal amount of espresso.

DAIRY

All recipes in this book call for **unsalted butter**, which allows me to control the amount of salt in my recipes. The brands I use contain 82 percent butterfat. Always make sure that your butter is fresh before using it. Shave a thin layer with the tip of a knife and check the color; if the outside layer is darker than the inside and there is an off smell, it is no longer fresh and may impart a stale flavor in recipes. Wrapped airtight and placed in a resealable freezer bag, butter will remain fresh in the freezer for several months.

I use only whole **milk**, which contains around 3.5 percent fat.

Heavy cream has 36 to 40 percent milk fat. For the best result, stay away from ultra-pasteurized versions, and buy only cream that is good enough to drink straight from the bottle.

For **yogurt**, I prefer full-fat strained Turkish yogurt. At about 8 percent fat, it is thicker and tangier than most strained (Greek-style) yogurts in the United States. For the best result in recipes, use the thickest, tangiest strained yogurt you can find.

The **cream cheese** I use has a lower fat content (around 27 percent) than the full-fat cream cheeses in the States, which are at least 33 percent fat. All of the recipes have also been tested with full-fat Philadelphia brand cream cheese and work equally as well.

Kefir is a tangy fermented drink made by inoculating milk with kefir grains. I use whole-milk kefir, which I call for in Isabella Grape and Kefir Ice Cream (page 260) and the Whole-Wheat and Kefir Pullman Loaf (page 217).

EGGS

I use large eggs weighing 2.2 to 2.5 ounces (62 to 71 grams) in the shell, or about 1.9 ounces (54 grams) without the shell. A large egg yolk measures about 1 tablespoon (0.7 ounces; 20 grams) and a large egg white measures about 2 tablespoons (1.23 ounces; 35 grams). Unless weight is specified in a recipe, you can use large eggs without weighing them. Quickly bring eggs to room temperature by submerging them in a bowl of warm water for 10 minutes.

FLOURS

I use three types of flour in the recipes.

All-purpose flour is made from a blend of hard and soft wheats that have been stripped of their germ and bran. It has a protein content of 9.5 to 11.5 percent and is available bleached or unbleached. I prefer unbleached all-purpose flour, but you may use either.

Bread flour has a higher protein content of about 12 to 14 percent, making it ideal for bread-making due to the higher gluten content, which provides better structure.

Whole-wheat flour retains the wheat's bran and germ.

I use the scoop-and-sweep method to measure flour by volume: use a spoon to fluff up the flour in the bin, dip the measuring cup into the flour and scoop it up, then sweep across the top of the cup with the back of a knife to level it. This method should give you approximately 140 grams of flour per cup, which is the figure I have used to convert flour weights to volume. For the most reliable outcome, more than for any other ingredient, it is essential to measure flour by weight.

FOOD COLORING

I use Wilton brand gel food coloring, which is called for in scant amounts in two of the macaron shell recipes. You can also use the powdered variety. Always start with a small amount of coloring, mixing it in thoroughly before deciding whether to add more, and taking into account that the color will become lighter when baked.

FRUITS & VEGETABLES

The recipes in the book were tested with fresh fruits and vegetables. If you have only frozen produce available, thaw it overnight in the refrigerator before using, unless you will be cooking or baking it straight from the freezer. I've specified weights for both whole and prepared quantities (e.g., stones and stems removed, peeled) so that you may easily substitute frozen fruits and vegetables in their equivalent state.

NUTS & SEEDS

The fats in nuts and seeds oxidize over time and cause them to go rancid. For the freshest nuts, buy only as much as you'll use and taste them before using. For longer storage, keep them in an airtight container in the refrigerator or in a resealable freezer bag in the freezer and let them come to room temperature before using in recipes.

To save time, purchase the nuts in the form called for in the recipes, such as whole, blanched, sliced, or ground. When processing whole nuts in a food processor to make nut flour, make sure to include a portion of the recipe's dry ingredients, such as flour and confectioners' sugar, to prevent them from turning to a paste as they release their oils.

Stir tahini vigorously to mix in the oil that has separated out before using.

OATS

I prefer old-fashioned rolled oats for baking because they absorb liquids more quickly, bake faster, and provide a lighter, crispier texture than those labeled thick or extra-thick. Using a different type of oat will affect baking and cooking times, as well as the finished texture.

OIL

Extra-virgin olive oil is the only oil I use in baking. For the recipes in this book, I don't recommend substituting other oils.

SALTS

I use **fine sea salt** for baking and **fleur de sel** (preferably from Guérande) and **Maldon sea salt** (big flat crystals) as finishing salts.

SPICES

Purchase spices in small quantities (enough to last three to six months) from a source with high turnover to ensure freshness and store them in a cool, dark place.

SUGARS & SWEETENERS

Granulated sugar in my recipes may be either cane or beet sugar.

Confectioners' sugar (also called powdered sugar) is finely ground cane sugar with a small amount (about 3 percent) of starch added.

Brown sugar is cane sugar with added molasses; categorized as light or dark depending on the amount added.

You can find all sorts of **molasses** in Turkey, and my favorite is grape molasses, the mildest among them. You can buy Turkish grape molasses (Koska brand) on Amazon.com, or use light molasses in its place. Made by reducing pomegranate juice, pomegranate molasses is quite tart (the authentic version contains no added sugar) and is not a good substitute for molasses in the recipes.

Keeping in mind that a highly aromatic **honey** may overshadow other ingredients, use any type of honey you like.

VANILLA POD & VANILLA EXTRACT

See page 32.

YEAST

The recipes in this book call for **instant yeast**, which has smaller granules and contains more live cells than **active dry yeast**, and doesn't need to be activated before using. For every teaspoon of instant yeast, you can substitute 1¼ teaspoons of active dry yeast, activating it by soaking it in warm water before using.

MEASUREMENTS & CONVERSIONS

VOLUME

I have provided most measurements in the recipes in both volume and weight. Imperial volume measures of both liquid and solid ingredients are converted to metric as follows:

U.S.	Metric
1 cup	240 ml
¾ cup	180 ml
⅔ cup	160 ml
½ cup	120 ml
⅓ cup	80 ml
¼ cup	60 ml
1 tablespoon	15 ml
1 teaspoon	5 ml

TEMPERATURE

Fahrenheit	Celcius	Gas Mark
250°F	120°C	gas mark ½
275°F	135°C	gas mark 1
300°F	150°C	gas mark 2
325°F	160°C	gas mark 3
350°F	175°C	gas mark 4
375°F	190°C	gas mark 5
400°F	200°C	gas mark 6
425°F	220°C	gas mark 7
450°F	230°C	gas mark 8
475°F	245°C	gas mark 9
500°F	260°C	gas mark 10

WEIGHT

Weights can vary considerably depending on the method used to measure them. For flour, I provided weight equivalents using the scoop-and-sweep method (see page 351). For other ingredients where the measuring method affects the weight—such as cocoa powder, confectioners' sugar, cornstarch, nut flours, matcha, baking powder, and spices—I have provided weight equivalents using the spoon-and-sweep method, where the ingredient is spooned into a measuring cup or spoon, then swept across the top with the back of a knife to level it.

Where a volume measurement isn't useful (e.g., for chocolate or some of the fresh produce), weight measurements are provided in both ounces and grams. In converting Imperial to metric weights, I have rounded to the nearest 5 grams above 1 ounce and to the nearest 50 grams above 1 kilogram.

When converting butter volume to weight, ounces are rounded to the nearest 0.1 ounce and grams to the nearest 5 grams.

U.S.	Metric
1 ounce	28.35 grams
1 pound (16 ounces)	453.6 grams

LINEAR

Centimeters are rounded to the nearest 0.1 centimeter below ¾ inch and to the nearest 0.5 centimeter above ¾ inch.

Inch	Metric
1 inch	2.54 cm

EQUIPMENT

When it comes to equipment, I believe in buying once and buying right. I made some bad purchasing decisions when I began baking, but as the years have passed I've learned what to look for in each tool. Despite an abusive six years of recipe testing for this book, everything I own looks as good as the day I bought it. It seems I've learned my lesson well.

The equipment described below will make your life in the kitchen easier and the time you spend there more enjoyable. That doesn't mean you need to have everything I've mentioned. Beyond the basics—cake pans, knives, baking sheets, and the like—the three most essential tools for any serious home baker are a kitchen scale, an instant-read thermometer, and an oven thermometer.

ALUMINUM FOIL

For cakes and tarts with sticky fillings or soft toppings that might suffer under plastic wrap, I cover them with a tent made from heavy-duty aluminum foil, poking holes in the foil with a fork when necessary to prevent condensation. The tent also comes in handy for cakes too large for a cake dome, such as Devil Wears Chocolate (page 144) and Monte Bianco (page 158). For 8-inch (20.5-cm) or larger cheesecakes baked in a water bath, I use 18-inch (45.5-cm) wide foil to cover the bottom and sides with a single sheet to prevent water from seeping in.

BAKING PANS

I prefer heavy-gauge, nonstick aluminized steel cake pans that are sturdy and light in color. For the best results, always choose the shape and size called for in recipes. My favorite brands are Chicago Metallic, Cuisinart, Matfer Bourgeat, Nordic Ware, Williams-Sonoma Goldtouch series, and USA Pan. The measurements below are measured from the inside.

For layered cakes, you'll need two **8-inch (20.5-cm) round pans** that are at least 2 inches (5 cm) deep, each having a 6½-cup (1.56-liter) capacity.

For brownies, I prefer an **8-inch (20.5-cm) square pan**, 2¼ inches (5.7 cm) deep with a 9-cup (2.16-liter) capacity. For cakes, I use a **9-inch (23-cm) square pan**, 2 inches (5 cm) deep, with a 10-cup (2.4-liter) capacity.

The **loaf pan** called for in my recipes measures 8½ by 4½ inches (21.5 by 11.5 cm) on top and 7½ by 3½ inches (19 by 9 cm) on the bottom, is 2¾ inches (7 cm) deep, and has a 6-cup (1.44-liter) capacity.

The **Pullman loaf pan** used in the Whole-Wheat and Kefir Pullman Loaf (page 217) is a lidded pan measuring 13 by 4 by 4 inches (33 by 10 by 10 cm).

I use two springform pan sizes: For the Chocolate Cheesecake (page 133), a **9-inch (23-cm) springform pan** that is 3 inches (7.5 cm) deep with a 10-cup (2.4-liter) capacity, and for the Matcha and Pistachio No-Bake Cheesecake (page 140), a **6½-inch (16.5-cm) springform pan** that is 2½ inches (6.5 cm) deep with a 5⅔-cup (1.36-liter) capacity.

I use a selection of **Bundt pans** with a variety of patterns, all having a 10-cup (2.4-liter) capacity.

BAKING SHEETS

My favorite baking sheets are the rimmed sheets with thick rolled edges made by Cuisinart. They are made from heavy-gauge aluminized steel and are the sturdiest sheet pans I've ever used. I have them in two sizes. The large one is 17 by 12 by 1 inch (43 by 30.5 by 2.5 cm), which is the largest size that will fit into my oven. You can use a half-sheet pan (18 by 13 by 1 inch; 45.4 by 33 by 2.5 cm) in its place. The smaller one is 15 by 10 by 1 inch (38 by 25.5 by 2.5 cm), which is a standard-size jelly-roll pan. You can use a 15½-by-10½-by-1-inch (39.5-by-26.5-by-2.5-cm) jelly-roll pan in its place.

I use the larger pan for baking cookies and the smaller one for toasting nuts and baking focaccia and granola. Unless a recipe calls for a specific size, you can substitute a rimmed or unrimmed baking sheet of another size, as appropriate. You'll need at least two (and preferably four) identical rimmed baking sheets for baking macaron shells.

CAKE LIFTER

I use a 10-inch (25.5-cm) cake lifter made by Nordic Ware, which is large enough to transfer most cakes and sturdy enough to lift most three-layered cakes.

CAKE STRIPS

When baking layered cakes, I wrap dampened cake strips around the pans to prevent domed tops. The damp cloth strip keeps the sides of the pan cool, allowing the sides and center of the cake to rise at the same speed, resulting in a level top. Silicone cake strips needn't be moistened before using.

COOKIE CUTTERS

I own one set of plain and one of fluted round cookie cutters made from professional-gauge 18/8 stainless steel, each with 11 graduated sizes ranging from ⅞ to 3 ⅝ inches (2.2 to 9.2 cm). These sets are convenient to have on hand, though for the recipes in this book the only ones you'll need are a 2-inch (5-cm) and 1 ⅜-inch (3.5-cm) plain round cookie cutter, and a 1 ½-inch (4-cm) fluted round cookie cutter.

DIGITAL SCALE

If you like to bake, do yourself a favor and get a digital scale. You'll rewarded with more consistent results, less cleanup, and a streamlined process. Look for a model that easily toggles between ounces and grams, preferably in decimals or both decimals and fractions, in 1-gram or smaller increments. Most won't go below 1 gram; to accurately weigh rather than use measuring spoons for very small quantities, look for a model featuring 0.1- or at least 0.5-gram increments. Make sure the scale includes a tare function (most will), a button that resets the scale to zero so that you may weigh additional ingredients sequentially in the same bowl, or can zero out the bowl or pan weight to determine the weight of its contents.

FINE-MESH SHAKER

A fine-mesh shaker is ideal for dusting cookies and cakes with confectioners' sugar and cocoa powder, allowing you to evenly cover surfaces with the thinnest possible layer and prevent clumps. Look for one with an airtight plastic cover to prevent moisture from seeping in for storage.

FOOD PROCESSOR

My food processor is one of the most frequently used appliances in my kitchen. I use a Magimix Compact 3200 XL, which comes with three bowls in different sizes, multiple blades, and slicing and grating discs. I typically use the largest bowl, which has a 2.75-quart (2.6-liter) capacity, just enough for a double-batch of pie dough. I also use the food processor for grinding nuts, pureeing fruit, preparing cookie dough, and mixing cake batters (see page 113).

ICE CREAM MAKER

There are two basic types of ice cream maker. The most common type includes a bowl that must be placed in the freezer for several hours before churning a batch of ice cream. The second has a built-in compressor, eliminating the need (and freezer space required) to pre-freeze the bowl. This latter type is more expensive and takes up more counter space, but it allows you to churn multiple batches back to back.

I don't own either. I have yet to find an ice cream maker that I like in Turkey, so I use the ice cream bowl attachment of my KitchenAid mixer. Like the less expensive ice cream makers, the attachment must be frozen for several hours before using it to churn ice cream. Since I never wish to spend a day without homemade ice cream, I keep the bowl in the freezer at all times. One major advantage of this attachment is that it allows you to churn the custard more quickly, trapping more air for a lighter texture.

ICE CREAM SCOOP

I am obsessed with vintage ice cream scoops and have a nice collection in different sizes. The only scoop you'll need for the recipes in the book is one with a 2-tablespoon (30-ml) capacity and preferably a release mechanism.

IMMERSION BLENDER

An immersion blender has many advantages over a standard blender or food processor. You can use it to puree the mixtures directly in the saucepan, saving time and cleanup. Its small blade makes it easier to puree thick mixtures, especially in small amounts, while moving it around the edges of the pan. A stainless steel wand is preferable for working with hot ingredients.

KITCHEN TORCH

A kitchen torch comes to mind when it's time to caramelize the sugar atop a crème brûlée, but it has many other uses. It will come in handy for toasting meringue layers, warming the outside of springform pans to release cheesecakes, and heating knives to easily and cleanly cut chocolate-covered brownies or cakes layered with dense fillings.

KNIVES

I prefer a 10-inch (25.5-cm) **chef's knife** for chopping, with a full tang running the length of the handle for proper balance. A long (12- to 14-inch; 30.5- to 35.5-cm) serrated **bread knife** is useful for cutting cake layers and trimming domed tops and high edges. For slicing fruit, I use a 4-inch (10-cm) **paring knife**. A **chestnut knife** has a very short, curved blade that is ideal for cutting through the tough outer shell of a chestnut and the thin skin underneath while avoiding the meat. If you don't have one, a bird's beak knife will do the job.

MADELEINE PAN

I use a nonstick 12-shell madeleine pan, each shell measuring about 3⅛ by 2⅛ by ¾ inch (8 by 5.5 by 2 cm) at the widest and deepest points, and having a 2-tablespoon (30-ml) capacity.

MEASURING CUPS & SPOONS

Dry measuring cups and spoons come in sets that include the following standard sizes: 1 cup (240 ml), ½ cup (120 ml), ⅓ cup (80 ml), ¼ cup (60 ml), 1 tablespoon (15 ml), 1 teaspoon (5 ml), ½ teaspoon (2.5 ml), and ¼ teaspoon (1.2 ml).

Liquid measuring cups have pouring spouts and are marked on the side with volume measurements for cups, fluid ounces, and milliliters. One with a 2-cup (500-ml) capacity is sufficient for most recipes.

MESH STRAINERS

I refer to two types of mesh strainers in the book. I use a regular mesh strainer, with a mesh size of 1/16 inch (1.6 mm), for draining liquids from solids and straining custards. I reach for a fine-mesh strainer, with its smaller 1/32-inch (0.8-mm) mesh, for sifting dry ingredients or when aiming for a silky texture or a perfectly clear liquid. You can mimic a fine-mesh strainer by layering a regular mesh one with a double thickness of cheesecloth. Look for a stainless-steel strainer with heatproof handles and a curved hook on the side opposite the handle that will allow it to rest securely over bowls and pans.

MIXERS

I own a KitchenAid 5-quart **stand mixer**, the ideal size for a home baker. It comes with three attachments: a flat beater I refer to as the paddle attachment in recipes, a wire whisk, and a dough hook. I highly recommend buying extra paddle and whisk attachments and an extra mixing bowl for making multiple batters back to back, or for separately beating the egg whites in a recipe.

The speeds I refer to in the recipes are (KitchenAid 5-quart mixers only): lowest speed (setting 1), low (2), medium-low (3), medium (5), medium-high (7), and high (10).

A **hand mixer** may not work for stiff bread doughs and is less convenient for two-handed operations, like drizzling in a hot syrup or gradually adding sugar, but it will take care of most other mixing jobs. A model that works at multiple speed levels and comes with multiple attachments will provide results closest to a stand mixer.

MIXING BOWLS

My recipes call for large, medium, and small mixing bowls, which refer to 5-quart (5-liter), 2-quart (2-liter), and 1-quart (1-liter) capacities, respectively. It is useful to have at least two of each size. I recommend stainless steel bowls, but you can also use glass. For meringue-based desserts, you may want to invest in a copper mixing bowl, which helps to stabilize meringue, or use stainless steel.

MUFFIN PAN

For muffins, I use a nonstick standard 12-cup muffin pan, each cup measuring 2¾ inches (7 cm) at the top, about 1⅜-inch (3.5-cm) deep, and having a ½-cup (120-ml) capacity.

OVEN THERMOMETER

An oven thermometer is useful for checking your oven's accuracy. Once a year, I conduct tests at the temperatures I most frequently use by placing the thermometer in the center of an oven rack set in the middle of the oven and running the oven at each temperature for at least 30 minutes. (Hanging the thermometer toward the back of the oven may produce misleading results, as that area tends to run hotter than the center.) If the results don't match your oven settings, make a note and, if you aren't able to have it calibrated, set your oven accordingly.

PARCHMENT PAPER

I can't imagine my life in the kitchen without parchment paper, and I wonder how bakers managed before its invention. In addition to the rolls and sheets, I am a fan of the parchment rounds precut for lining round cake pans and keep a large supply of 8- and 9-inch (20.5- and 23-cm) rounds on hand.

In some recipes, I instruct you to crumple the parchment into a ball and straighten it out again half a dozen times to soften it, a trick I learned from Heston Blumenthal. The softened parchment is more easily shaped, doesn't require pleating, and fits into the corners of cake and tart pans without sharp edges.

PASTRY BAGS & TIPS

It's a pain to wash reusable pastry bags (especially after piping buttercream), so I use disposable plastic ones. You'll need pastry tips in several sizes for piping macaron, éclair, and cream puff shells, madeleine batter, fillings, and decorative garnishes. I use Ateco stainless steel pastry tips, including the following, which are used in the recipes: #10, #34, #261, #804, #808, #827, and #846.

PASTRY BRUSH

A pastry brush is indispensable for glazing cakes and fruit fillings, applying egg wash on pastries, buttering cake pans (especially so that you can reach all the nooks and crannies of Bundt pans with intricate designs), and brushing excess flour from the surface of doughs. I prefer natural brushes with soft bristles and always check to see that the bristles are firmly held in place before buying.

PEELER

I am partial to my Victorinox serrated peeler. Its micro-serrated edges are ideal for peeling fruits and vegetables, especially those with thin, slippery skins.

PIE PAN

My pie pan of choice is an Emile Henry deep-dish ceramic pie pan with a ruffled edge, measuring 7 inches (18 cm) on the bottom and 10¼ inches (26 cm) at its widest point on top, and is 2⅜ inches (6 cm) deep.

RASP GRATER

When it comes to removing the zest from citrus fruits, no grater does a better job than a fine-tooth rasp grater. Grate the zest directly into the mixing bowl to incorporate its precious aromatic oils into the dough or batter.

ROLLING PIN

I prefer a wooden French rolling pin (without handles), which allows me better control when applying pressure.

SAUCEPANS & SAUCEPOTS

When I refer to a **small saucepan**, I mean a pan with a 1-quart (1-liter) capacity. A **medium saucepan** has a 2-quart (2-liter) capacity and a **saucepot** refers to a large pot holding at least 6 quarts (6 liters). I prefer heavy-duty stainless steel and enameled cast-iron pots and pans (with handles). For making caramel, especially if you are not using a thermometer and will gauge the color by eye, use a pan with a light-colored interior, such as stainless steel or enamel.

SPATULAS

I could never have too many **silicone spatulas**, which I use for stirring, scraping, and folding. I especially like Le Creuset's spoonulas, with their slightly cupped blades. You will want to have at least one large silicone spatula for folding and a couple of standard-size ones with straight blades for stirring and scraping saucepan bottoms. Mini silicone spatulas are invaluable for scraping every last bit of batter from stand mixer attachments and food processor blades; it's worth keeping a few on hand.

I use a **small metal offset spatula** with a 4½-inch (11.5-cm) blade for spreading batters and fillings, and a **large metal offset spatula** with a 9¾-inch (25-cm) blade for tempering chocolate and leveling buttercreams and frostings.

TART PANS

I call for fluted tart pans with removable bottoms in the following sizes: **10¼-inch (26-cm) round tart pan**, **9-inch (23-cm) square tart pan**, and **13¾-by-4¼-inch (35-by-11-cm) rectangular tart pan**, all about 1 inch (2.5 cm) deep. The individual **4¼-inch (11-cm) round tart pans** are ¾ inch (2 cm) deep. My favorite tart pans are from Gobel.

THERMOMETERS

An **instant-read digital thermometer** is an essential tool for the home baker, allowing you to instantly identify when you have reached a desired temperature. You'll use it when cooking caramel, glazes, syrups, curds, Swiss meringue, and custards for ice cream bases, as well as to measure the internal temperature of baked breads. While I provide visual clues, a thermometer will always be most precise.

For jams, jellies, and candy—especially those brought to a rolling boil—I prefer a **candy thermometer** for accuracy, practicality, and safety.

WHISKS

My favorite whisk is a 10-inch (25.5-cm) stainless-steel French whisk that allows me to reach into the corners of the saucepan with its elongated, narrow shape. I use my 8-inch (20.5-cm) French whisk when working with small amounts of batter. For whipping air into cream and egg whites, and for folding dry ingredients into airy batters, I reach for a 12-inch (30.5-cm) balloon whisk.

WIRE RACKS

Wire racks with raised feet allow for air circulation to more quickly cool just-baked cookies and cakes. I suggest having at least two of them on hand to accommodate large batches of cookies and multiple cake layers.

SOURCES

Amazon
www.amazon.com
Leblebi (double-roasted chickpeas), roasted chickpea
flour, pistachio flour, blanched whole hazelnuts,
sliced blanched almonds, glutinous rice flour, sour
cherries soaked in liqueur, citric acid, grape molasses,
matcha, dried lemon verbena

Bob's Red Mill
www.bobsredmill.com
800-349-2173
Blanched almond flour, blanched hazelnut flour,
unsweetened shredded dried coconut, brown sesame
seeds, old-fashioned rolled oats

Chicago Metallic
www.chicagometallicbakeware.com
Cake pans

Cuisinart
www.cuisinart.com
800-726-0190
Ice cream makers, baking sheets, cake pans

Guittard
www.guittard.com
800-468-2462
Bittersweet chocolate, cacao nibs

Kalustyan's
www.kalustyans.com
800-352-3451
Pistachios, pistachio flour, hazelnuts, blanched
hazelnut flour, grape molasses, tahini

King Arthur Flour
www.kingarthurflour.com
800-827-6836
Bread flour, blanched almond flour, blanched
hazelnut flour, instant yeast, fresh sourdough starter,
citric acid

KitchenAid
www.kitchenaid.com
800-541-6390
Heavy-duty stand mixer

Nordic Ware
www.nordicware.com
877-466-7342
Bundt pans, springform pans

Scharffen Berger
www.scharffenberger.com
855-972-0511
Bittersweet chocolate, cacao nibs

Sur La Table
www.surlatable.com
800-243-0852
Cake pans, baking sheets, cookie cutters, cutlery, baking tools, cake decorating supplies, spatulas

Trader Joe's
www.traderjoes.com
Freeze-dried raspberries, nuts, dairy products

Ucuzcular Baharat
www.ucuzcularspices.com
+90-212-528-2895
Spice Bazaar No. 51, Eminönü, İstanbul, Turkey
Pure salep

USA Pan
www.usapan.com
724-457-4220
Pullman loaf pan

Valrhona
www.valrhona-chocolate.com
718-522-7001
Bittersweet chocolate, white chocolate, blond chocolate, Dutch-processed unsweetened cocoa powder, cacao nibs

Vanilla Saffron Imports
www.saffron.com
415-648-8990
Vanilla beans

Williams-Sonoma
www.williams-sonoma.com
877-812-6235
Cake pans, baking sheets, cookie cutters, cutlery, food processor, baking tools, cake decorating supplies, spatulas

Wilton
www.wilton.com
888-373-4588
Cake decorating supplies, including pastry bags, pastry tips, cookie cutters, and food coloring

ACKNOWLEDGMENTS

First and foremost, a big thank you to the readers of my blog, who have kept me going all these years and have encouraged and cheered me every step of the way. I hope you're holding my book in your hands and I hope it was worth the wait.

To my mom, for instilling in me the importance of doing the best I can no matter how small the task is and feeding me so well. You are my everything.

To my dad, who always showed his love and appreciation in his unexpected ways. You are greatly missed.

To my brother, for buying me my first camera, your support, and sage advice.

To my agent and dear friend Carole Bidnick, for believing in me, your guidance, support, and constant cheer. I couldn't have done this without you.

To everyone at Abrams for making this possible. Special thanks to Michael Sand for believing in my book, to my editor Camaren Subhiyah for your flawless guidance, to John Gall for your artistic eye, and to Erin Slonaker for your eagle eyes.

To Ayşe Durukan and Murat Pilevneli, for being my pillars of strength, sharing your prop collections that made my stories complete, and comforting advice.

To Esin Giz, for being so generous with your knowledge, contributing your treasured recipes, and gracing the pages of my book with your inimitable embroideries.

To Jennie Schacht, for sharing your wealth of knowledge, teaching me so much about writing, your expert advice, encouragement, and friendship.

To Rachel Boller Berman, for tirelessly testing the recipes, your invaluable feedback, and friendship. I'll be forever grateful. Also thanks to Maryann Boller, Ryan Berman, and sweet Olive Berman for helping out Rachel with the herculean task.

To my dearest friend Özlem Özdener, for inspiring me to become a food blogger and believing in me before anyone else did.

To Keiko Oikawa, for being a constant source of inspiration.

To Dianne Jacob, for your encouragement and my treasured San Francisco sourdough starter.

To Janet Fletcher, Çağatay Kandaz, Işıl Karahanoğlu, Emine Gülçelik, Selim Gülçelik, Zeynep Man Rek, Ayçe Yücel, Ayşem Çelikiz, Mustafa Pilevneli, Begüm Koçum, Yelda Benezra, Katie Parla, Toni Tajima, Aylin Öney Tan, Hande Kutlar Leimer, Çağdaş Aydın, Erhan Ay, Vera Scialom, Mahir Ketboğa, Sandy Leonard, Tulya Madra, İmran Fins, Azra Kertmelioğlu, Banu Bingör, Feridun Bingör, Mustafa Emin Büyükcoşkun, and Cem Mumcu for your contributions, advice, encouragement, and for keeping me sane.

To my baking heroes and heroines Nick Malgieri, Dorie Greenspan, David Lebovitz, Rose Levy Beranbaum, and Pierre Hermé, for teaching me most of what I know, for the inspiration, and for being so generous and kind.

To my Okuyan Us family, publisher of my Turkish cookbook, for letting me be me, your enthusiasm, patience, and support.

INDEX

ABOUT THE AUTHOR

Cenk Sönmezsoy (pronounced jenk sun-mass-soy) is an author, blogger, photographer, and food stylist based in İstanbul. After graduating from college, he moved to San Francisco, where he earned an MBA from the University of San Francisco and worked at a high-tech PR firm. On realizing that he'd rather eat glass than sit through another client conference call discussing another "groundbreaking" product, he returned to İstanbul. There, in 2006, he started a food blog that grew bigger and faster than he ever could have imagined. Published both in English and Turkish, *Cafe Fernando* has been cited as one of the "World's 50 Best Food Blogs" by *The Times of London*. *Saveur* named it "Best Culinary Travel Blog" in 2010, and the following year awarded the brownies he designed for Dolce & Gabbana "Best Original Baking and Desserts Recipe." In 2012, *Saveur* called the piece Cenk wrote about his dining experience at Chez Panisse the year's "Best Piece of Culinary Writing."

He ditched the corporate world in 2010, became a full-time food blogger, and began work on his first cookbook. His Turkish cookbook, *Cafe Fernando–Bir pasta yaptım, yanağını dayar uyursun*, published in June 2014 by Okuyan Us Publishing, became an instant bestseller. The book was awarded "Best in the World—First Place" in the Blogger category at the 2015 Gourmand World Cookbook Awards and first place at Gourmand's "Best of the Best."

blog: cafefernando.com
portfolio: cenksonmezsoy.com
book: theartfulbakercookbook.com
twitter & instagram: @cafefernando
#theartfulbakercookbook #cafefernando

Recipes, text, photographs, food styling, and design
by Cenk Sönmezsoy

Editor: Camaren Subhiyah
Designer: Cenk Sönmezsoy
Production Manager: Katie Gaffney

Library of Congress Control Number: 2016960264

ISBN: 978-1-4197-2649-1

Printed and bound in China
10 9 8 7 6 5 4 3 2 1

Abrams books are available at special discounts when purchased
in quantity for premiums and promotions as well as fundraising
or educational use. Special editions can also be created to
specification. For details, contact specialsales@abramsbooks.com
or the address below.

ABRAMS
The Art of Books

115 West 18th Street
New York, NY 10011
abramsbooks.com